DEVON AND CORNWALL RECORD SOCIETY

New Series, Vol. 36

General Editor: Professor N. I. Orme

DEVON AND CORNWALL RECORD SOCIETY

New Series, Vol. 36

THE LOCAL CUSTOMS ACCOUNTS OF THE PORT OF EXETER 1266-1321

Edited and translated with an Introduction by

MARYANNE KOWALESKI

M.A., M.S.L., Ph.D.
Associate Professor
Fordham University, New York

1993

ISBN 0 901853 36 4

Typeset for the Society by
BPCC Techset Ltd,
and printed for the Society by
BPCC Wheatons Ltd
Hennock Road, Marsh Barton, Exeter EX2 8RP
United Kingdom

CONTENTS

LIST OF TABLES AND MAP

FRONTISPIECE
Exeter City Archives, Customs Roll 1, temp. Edward I, m 24d

LIST OF TABLES

MAP

ACKNOWLEDGEMENTS

The author and publishers are grateful to the Reverend D. O'L.
Markham, vicar of East Budleigh, for permission to reproduce the
illustration on the cover, which was photographed by Sean Goddard
of the Department of History and Archaeology, University of Exeter,
and to Exeter City Council for the reproduction of the frontispiece.
The map was kindly drawn by Sean Goddard and Nigel Code.

LIST OF ABBREVIATIONS

BL	British Library, London
C 1	PRO, Early Chancery Proceedings
C 135	PRO, Chancery Inquisitions Post Mortem
CChR	*Calendar of Charter Rolls*
CCR	*Calendar of Close Rolls*
CP 40	PRO, Court of Common Pleas Rolls
CPR	*Calendar of Patent Rolls*
CR	DRO, Court Rolls
CRA	ECA, Exeter City Receivers' Accounts
DCRS	Devon and Cornwall Record Society
D&C	ECL, Dean and Chapter Archives
DRO	Devon Record Office
ECA	Exeter City Archives, Devon Record Office
ECL	Exeter Cathedral Library
ED\	ECA, Exeter Deeds
E 101	PRO, Exchequer K.R. Accounts Various
E 122	PRO, Exchequer K.R. Customs Accounts
JUST 1	PRO, Assize and Eyre Rolls
KB 26	PRO, Curia Regis Rolls
KB 27	PRO, Coram Rege Rolls
MCR	ECA, Exeter Mayor's Court Rolls
Misc. Roll	ECA, Miscellaneous Rolls
OED	*Oxford English Dictionary*
PCA	ECA, Exeter Port Customs Accounts
PRO	Public Record Office, Chancery Lane, London
SC 6	PRO, Ministers Accounts
SC 8	PRO, Ancient Petitions

PREFACE

This edition of the local customs accounts of Exeter represents the second of two volumes devoted to the early financial records of the city. The first volume included translations of the city's annual receivers' accounts from 1304 to 1353, along with an early rental, murage account, and the oldest account of the wardens of Exe Bridge.[1] The present volume contains a translation of the city's port customs accounts, including those entered on the mayor's court rolls (1266-1320) and those recorded separately on Customs Roll 1 (1302-21). Few local port customs accounts are extant for medieval England, but those that survive offer valuable details about the ships, merchants, and commodities involved in maritime trade. In contrast to the national port customs accounts which focused exclusively on overseas trade, local accounts enumerated coastal as well as overseas traffic. The Exeter customs accounts are particularly noteworthy because they, unlike other local accounts, recorded all importers, whether liable to custom or not. Among the earliest extant accounts, they survive in a fuller series than the accounts of any other English port in the middle ages.

The work involved in editing these accounts was made much easier by the help and advice I received from archivists and other scholars. My greatest debt is to Margery Rowe and the staff of the Devon Record Office for their cheerful and skilful help in the fifteen years that I have been using the archives of medieval Devon. Without their generous and speedy response to my many requests for photocopies and other assistance, this book would never have been completed. Margery Rowe in particular furnished considerable help and support. I would also like to thank Professor Nicholas Orme, general editor of the Devon and Cornwall Record Society, for his patient and kind guidance in compiling this volume. Thanks are also due to Judith Bennett for her comments on the Introduction, and to Wendy Childs and Richard Unger for taking the time to respond to particular queries. I am particularly grateful to Derek Keene for his help in identifying many of the home ports recorded in these accounts. For financial assistance that allowed me to spend time in Exeter working on this project, I extend thanks to Fordham University and the National Endowment for the Humanities. Finally, I owe special thanks to Professor Joyce Youings who, from the time I first arrived in Exeter as a post-graduate embarking on archival work, offered me practical advice as well as scholarly inspiration.

Maryanne Kowaleski
Fordham University
New York
August 1993

---

[1] *The Receivers' Accounts of the City of Exeter 1304-1353*, ed. Margery M. Rowe and John M. Draisey, DCRS, new series, xxxii (1989).

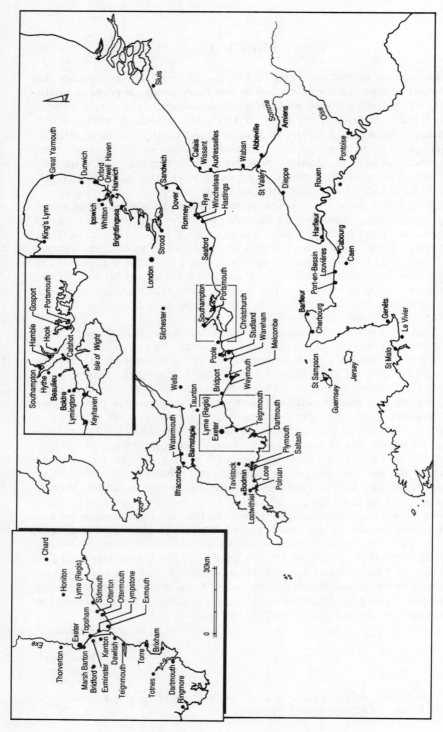

Some places mentioned in the local customs accounts of the port of Exeter, 1266–1321

INTRODUCTION

THE MEDIEVAL PORT OF EXETER

Exeter in the middle ages was the head port of a royal customs jurisdiction that encompassed most of Devon and Cornwall, despite the
fact that the city actually lies up the Exe river over ten miles from the
open sea. With the construction of weirs on the Exe river in the mid-
thirteenth century, access by ship to Exeter proper (which had never
been easy) became virtually impossible. This obstruction meant that
the village of Topsham, located about four miles south of Exeter at
the head of the estuary, had to serve as Exeter's outport. Topsham,
however, probably filled this role even in the Roman period; despite
the claims of later Exonians to the contrary, it is doubtful whether
any but the smallest vessels had ever sailed up the river to unload
goods at Exeter.[1] From at least 1178/9 the lords of Topsham, the
powerful earls of Devon, enjoyed the privilege of collecting wine custom at the port, and from at least 1225/6 they owned permanent
market stalls in the village;[2] both rights suggest that Topsham had
long served as the outport for Exeter, particularly for the larger
ocean-going ships that transported wine from the continent. Indeed,
even before the weirs were built in the mid-thirteenth century, the
number of ships docking at Topsham was very close to the number
that unloaded cargo there after the weirs were constructed.[3]

The earls' rights to collect Exeter town customs at Topsham probably originated as a payment by Exeter citizens for the use of the
earls' manor of Topsham as a landing place.[4] These customs rights,
like those enjoyed by the city, centred on the import trade; local
export duties were never collected at the port by either the earl or

[1] For the finds of Roman coins, pottery, and buildings at Topsham cited in support
of this view, see Chris Henderson, 'Exeter (Isca Dumnoniorum)', in *Fortress into City*,
ed. Graham Webster, London, 1988, pp 92–3.
[2] *The Pipe Roll for the Twenty-Fifth Year of the Reign of King Henry the Second, A.D.
1178–1179*, Pipe Roll Society, xxviii (1907), p 15. For the earl's wine custom and stalls
in 1225/6, see K. Ugawa, 'The Economic Development of Some Devon Manors in the
Thirteenth Century', *TDA*, xciv (1962), pp 661–2. The presence of such stalls (some
later designated specifically for wine) at a small village that did not have a chartered
market until 1300 *(CChR 1257–1300*, p 448) must have resulted from the ships unloading there.
[3] The minimum number of ships arriving can be calculated from keelage (a 2d toll
charged on each ship docking) collected at Topsham; the 5s collected in 1225/6
(Ugawa, 'Economic Development', pp 661–2) and 4s 6½d collected in 1286/7 (PRO SC
6/827/39) after the weirs were built show that at least 30 ships moored at Topsham in
1225/6 and 27 in 1286/7. Given the widespread exemptions to which such tolls were
subject, the actual number of ships docking was probably higher and not far from the
average number (47) docking there in the first decade of the fourteenth century.
[4] See also Andrew Jackson, 'Medieval Exeter, the Exe and the Earldom of Devon,'
TDA, civ (1972), pp 61–2 on this and the following point.

1

the city of Exeter, in part because exports were of such low value compared to imports.[5] From the first mention of these customs rights in the late 1170s, the earls' share was restricted to tolls on wine, a limitation that most likely reflected the necessity for heavily-burdened wine ships, unable to navigate the shallow four-mile stretch of river to Exeter, to unload at Topsham even before the weirs closed off the river to all vessels.[6] The earls' claim to wine custom was also limited to one-third of the amount collected by the city.[7] This division of profits may derive from the "earl's penny," the customary payment of every third penny to the earl, since Topsham was owned by a succession of earls, including Earl Harold before the Norman Conquest.[8] The earls' rights to Exeter town customs may also have been responsible for the unusual fullness of the customs accounts kept by the city, as well as the eventual division of the accounts into two parts, one dealing with wine and the other with general merchandise.[9] Indeed, the often strained relationship between the city and the earl was particularly tense around the time that the city began keeping track of ship entries, an action perhaps taken to assure the earl that he was getting his fair share of the wine custom.

Conflict began when the earl of Devon, Baldwin de Redvers, built a weir (probably between 1239 and his death in 1245) on the Exe river between Topsham and Exeter. The weir allowed him to take greater profits from his salmon fisheries on the Exe, but also effectively blocked any boats at all from reaching Exeter.[10] To make matters worse, his son Baldwin (1235–1262) also established a fair at Topsham in 1257 that was timed to precede Exeter's own Lammas

---

[5] For a longer discussion of Exeter's export trade, see Maryanne Kowaleski, *Local Markets and Regional Trade in Medieval Exeter,* Cambridge, forthcoming, chapter 6.

[6] For the hazards of navigating the Exe estuary, particularly around Topsham, see E.A.G. Clark, *The Ports of the Exe Estuary 1660–1860,* Exeter, 1960, pp 4–10. For explicit statements by shipmasters that their heavily-loaded wine ships could not make it up the treacherous and shallow estuarine channel to Topsham, see DRO, ECA MCR 1360/1, m. 15d; 1364/5, m. 14; 1365/6, m. 6d; 1422/3, m. 7d; DRO, ECA CRA 1433/4, 1440/1; *CPR 1364–7,* p 167.

[7] The earliest statement regarding the one-third share of the earl is in a document dated about 1250 (J. R. Brooking Rowe, *A History of Plympton Erle,* Exeter, 1906, pp 11–12) but the division had clearly been practiced for some time.

[8] O.J. Reichel, 'The Domesday Hundred of Wenford or Wonford', *TDA,* xliv (1912), pp 316–17. Earl Godwin (Harold) had similar rights to one-third of the monies collected from "the waterway where ships moored" in Southwark (*Domesday Book, Surrey,* ed. John Morris, Chichester, 1975, no. 5,28). The "earl's penny" was owed on wide variety of payments, including fines and tolls.

[9] Totals of the sums collected for wine custom and the share delivered to the earl are noted in the earliest accounts (below, pp 85, 99, 113, 118, 134, 158), but no such totals appear for customs collected on other merchandise until 1353/4.

[10] He was noted as the builder in PRO KB 26/167, mm. 1d, 12d. Copies of most of the original documents concerning the on-going disputes with the earls of Devon may be found in DRO, ECA Book 51, ff. 43–48v; DRO, ECA Misc. Roll 3; and John Vowell alias Hoker, *The Description of the Citie of Excester,* ed. Walter J. Harte, J. W. Schopp, H. Tapley-Soper, DCRS, xii (1919), pp 32–4, 626–57. These are discussed and expanded with additional citations by Jackson, 'Medieval Exeter, the Exe and the Earldom', pp 57–79.

fair by only a week or so.[11] The citizens of Exeter complained bitterly
to the king about both initiatives but received no satisfaction; their
frustration boiled over in July 1263 when a group of the most prominent citizens tore down the weir.[12] A heavy fine was exacted by the
crown for this unauthorized destruction, but the people of Exeter
were undeterred. A few months later, many of the same citizens
marched to Topsham and forcibly prevented merchants from landing
and selling their goods there.[13] The citizens lost this dispute as well
since the crown jury impanelled to hear the case both ordered them
to pay another fine for this action and sanctioned the rights of merchants to land and sell cargoes in Topsham without having to come to
Exeter. But the city also received some legal redress; the same jury
confirmed Exeter's claim to exact port customs at Topsham, provided
always that one-third of the sum collected on wine imports was delivered to the lord of Topsham.[14]

This settlement did not lead to a lasting peace. Further problems
erupted with the construction of new weirs in the 1280s and the earls'
acquisition of new market and port facilities at Topsham in the early
fourteenth century. Much of this latter activity was led by Earl Hugh
Courtenay who, after inheriting the earldom in 1293, initiated a long
period of particularly strained relations with the citizens of Exeter.
He vigorously promoted the commercial fortunes of Topsham by
raising a new market, fair, wharf, and a crane for unloading goods
there, fostering the use of Topsham properties for storage and the
hire of his tenants as carters, interfering with the city's legal jurisdiction over ships in the estuary, and extorting extra tolls from ships
and merchants unloading at Topsham.[15] Earl Hugh also caused the
city great distress by enforcing his prerogatives in Exe Island, a sub-
urban manor that lay outside the city's west gate beside the Exe

[11] For the fair charter he acquired, see *CChR 1257–1300*, p 2. For the city's complaints, see *CCR 1259–61*, p 218; and PRO KB 26/167, mm. 1d, 12d. See *CCR 1242–7*,
p 340, however, for a reference to an earlier fair at Topsham (or possibly Exeter) that
his mother enjoyed as part of her dower. For the complicated history of Exeter's fairs,
see Kowaleski, *Local Markets and Regional Trade*, chapter 2.

[12] PRO JUST 1/178, m. 8d; Jackson, 'Medieval Exeter, the Exe and the Earldom', pp
59–60. This Baldwin died in 1262 so the remaining disputes were with his mother, the
Countess Amicia (who held Topsham in dower), and with his sister and heir, Isabella
de Fortibus (countess of Albemarle), who held Topsham from 1284 to her death in
1293.

[13] PRO KB 27/11, m. 12d; PRO KB 27/12, m. 16d; a translation appears in DRO,
ECA Law Papers on Town Customs, Mayor of Exeter v. Lawrence, Box 8, pp 197–200.

[14] The judgment recorded in PRO KB 27/12, m. 16d, does not specify the wine custom, noting only that Countess Amicia had rights to one-third of toll taken by Exeter at
Topsham. Wine custom must have been intended, however, as indicated in the earlier
references to the earl's share (above, n. 2) and the right to wine custom noted in her
inquisition post mortem; (*Calendar of Inquisitions Post Mortem*, London, ii, pp 327–8).
Jackson ('Medieval Exeter, the Exe and the Earldom', p 61) suggests that the judgment
was a mistake or biased in her favour by the jurors.

[15] DRO Misc. Roll 3, no. 5 (printed in Jackson, 'Medieval Exeter, the Exe and the
Earldom', pp 72–5); see also Hooker, *Citie of Excester*, pp 636–45, 652–6.

river.[16] Local animosity against Hugh ran so high that later Exeter writers often portrayed him as the instigator of an all-out trade war against the city, although many of their accusations about his construction of new weirs and a host of other offences were probably not true.[17] The citizens' hostility towards the earl undoubtedly reflected their frustration over the city's lack of succcess in legal actions against him.[18]

This list of injuries visited upon Exeter by the earls of Devon should not, however, obscure the extent to which the city itself acted as an aggressor in maintaining and extending its domain over the Exe estuary. In the 1260s, for example, the city was involved in a dispute with the abbot and convent of Sherborne (Dorset) over their claim to control the ferry and sale of fish at *Checkstone* (a settlement now part of Exmouth) and to collect toll from merchandise landed at there and other places in the abbey's manor of Littleham (where *Checkstone* was located).[19] Exeter seems to have triumphed since the abbot and convent agreed to grant the city their ferry across the mouth of the estuary, in return for which the city allowed the abbey's monks and tenants free passage, as well as the right to buy and sell fish in the estuary without paying custom.[20] But vigorous objections were soon made by estuarine residents to the higher fares that the new owners charged for ferry trips and to the city's claim to a monopoly on all ferry crossings.[21] On several occasions in the fourteenth and fifteenth centuries, Exeter had to mount further defences in court of its claims to the quay, ferry and toll at Exmouth.[22] One victory came as late as 1411 when the city acquired the right to collect tolls on fish sales at Exmouth.[23]

Legal actions and negotiated settlements were not the only tactics employed by the city to enforce its rights in the estuary. As the citizens' raids on the Topsham weirs and port testify, they were not reluctant to resort to more strong-arm methods as well. In 1264–5 men of Exeter conducted a night raid at Littleham, breaking up chests and carrying off goods which presumably had been landed

[16] DRO, ECA Book 60h, ff 21v–32v; Hooker, *Citie of Excester*, 389–95, 407–10; see also MCR 1304/5, mm. 27, 27d; 1318/19, m. 21; 1323/4, m. 7d for the ongoing disputes with the earl.

[17] The sixteenth-century city chamberlain, John Hooker (who wrote DRO Book 60h and *Citie of Excester*) and Richard Izacke (*Remarkable Antiquities of the City of Exeter*, 2nd edn, London, 1724, pp 36–44) clearly exaggerated the wickedness of his deeds.

[18] PRO SC 8/264/13160; Hooker, *Citie of Excester*, 636–56; Jackson, 'Medieval Exeter, the Exe and the Earldom', pp 68–9.

[19] DRO, ECA Misc. Roll 2, no. 34; Hooker, *Citie of Excester*, pp 499–503.

[20] In 1266 (MCR Roll 1, m. 17) the city received 7s 2d from the "passage at *Cheekstone*", but not long afterwards moved the ferry to *Pratteshide* (Peter J. Weddell, 'The Excavation of Medieval and Later Houses and St Margaret's Chapel at Exmouth, 1982–1984', *Proceedings of the Devon Archaeological Society*, xliv (1986), pp 120, 124; and CRA 1339/40 et seq.).

[21] PRO JUST 1/181, m. 36d.

[22] CRA 1410/11; Izacke, *Remarkable Antiquities*, pp 52, 69, 88.

[23] The profits were first enrolled in CRA 1411/12. See also MCR 1460/1, m. 13 for the city's continuing efforts to make fishers carry their catch to Exeter for sale.

there without the city's permission.[24] In the 1270s another group of citizens, this time led by the mayor of Exeter, descended upon Littleham to compel a Devon coroner to recognize their claim to wreck in the estuary, going so far as to steal away a grounded ship upon which the coroner was trying to hold an inquest.[25]

The city pursued its claims over the fish trade in the estuary with similar vigor. In the mid-thirteenth century, the lord of the estuarine manor of Bradham (north of Littleham) charged a city bailiff with forcibly preventing two of his fishermen from selling their fish at Exmouth; the bailiff asserted that they were regrating the city's market (that is, reselling fish they had purchased from others and thereby raising its price).[26] Similar complaints surfaced in the king's eyre court of 1280/1 when the men of East Budleigh hundred (which encompassed all of the eastern bank of the estuary) accused Exeter officals of hindering them from purchasing fish and other cargoes at Exmouth as they once had been able to do.[27] Control over the fish trade throughout the estuary was of vital importance to the Exeter authorities, as seen in the many fines and distraints they levied on fish dealers for custom evasion at Exmouth, Kennford, and Topsham.[28] Control over the valuable woad trade was also strenuously enforced; the city made merchants bring all shipments of woad only to Exeter for sale, under the pretext that this valuable dyestuff had to be examined by the city's woad assayers.[29] The city emphasized its rights over this lucrative trade in the wording of the headings of the merchandise sections of the customs accounts; by the 1310s they were usually titled "accounts of woad and other merchandise".

In 1290 the city managed to get both a jury from Wonford hundred (in which Topsham and Exeter were located) and a city jury to affirm that the entire ten-mile length of the estuary from the mouth of the Exe to Exe Bridge outside the city gates lay within Exeter's jurisdiction.[30] The earls' bailiffs did not always recognize the city's claims, however, as is evident from the tussle that took place shortly afterwards when several Exeter bailiffs tried to arrest a ship at Topsham for evading custom.[31] But the city persevered and continued to punish those who challenged what it perceived to be its jurisdictional rights in the estuary. Even the leading citizens of Exeter

[24] PRO JUST 1/181, m. 42d; the raid was probably linked to the dispute with Sherborne abbey.

[25] PRO JUST 1/186, mm. 37d, 38; Jackson, 'Medieval Exeter, the Exe and the Earldom', p 63. For similar claims by Exeter that sent the city's own coroner to places within the estuary, see JUST 1/181, mm. 35, 37.

[26] PRO JUST 1/181, m. 36d; Misc. Roll 2, no. 52; DRO, ECA Misc. Roll 55, no. 1 (complaints of the Prior of St Nicholas).

[27] PRO JUST 1/181, m. 36d.

[28] For example, MCR Roll 1, mm. 1 (1264), 7 (1265), 1287/8, m. 14; 1288/9, m. 39; see also Kowaleski, *Local Markets and Regional Trade*, chapter 7.

[29] MCR Roll 1, mm. 2 (1264), 9 (1286), 18d (1266).

[30] Hooker, *Citie of Excester*, pp 630–2; PRO SC 8/264/13160.

[31] Below, p 67. See also Jackson, 'Medieval Exeter, the Exe and the Earldom', p 67 for the events surrounding this dispute, and MCR 1304/5, m. 27 for one of the countersuits by the earl.

could be subject to censure, as was Stephen de Smalecombe who dared to use the court of Topsham rather than that of Exeter to pursue an attachment against a shipmaster who owed him money.[32]

By the middle of the fourteenth century, this turbulence had calmed considerably, and the relationship between the earls and the city remained relatively stable throughout the later middle ages.[33] The earls' efforts on behalf of Topsham had effectively reduced Exeter's near monopoly on the sale of maritime cargoes, but Exeter's commercial well-being was not really threatened. Few Topsham traders ever successfully competed with Exeter merchants in the port trade. Perhaps more damaging was the earls' active promotion of transport services and storage facilities at Topsham; its tenants were well-placed to monopolize the carriage of goods by land to Exeter or elsewhere in the hinterland.[34] The earls also profited from the tolls of keelage and cranage at Topsham, as well as their one-third share of wine custom. But keelage (a 2d charge on every vessel that anchored there) rarely amounted to much and was, moreover, not one of the earls' recent innovations as it had been associated with their share of wine custom since at least 1225.[35] Cranage (charged to unload heavy goods with the help of the crane installed by Earl Hugh) brought in more substantial sums, ranging annually from £5 to almost £10.[36] Yet these encroachments on the trading revenues of Exeter were probably less costly to the city than either the loss of the valuable Exe fisheries or the earls' assertion of their rights of lordship in the city's western suburb of Exe Island.[37]

Although the citizens' grievances against the earls tended to focus above all upon the loss of trade and shipping occasioned by the construction of weirs on the Exe, Exeter never lost its right to collect town customs on all goods unloaded at estuarine ports, keeping for itself not only a two-thirds share of the wine custom, but also the whole custom on other merchandise. The city also maintained its

[32] MCR 1310/11, mm. 27, 28.

[33] One exception was the construction of two more weirs by Earl Edward Courtenay in the 1390s which occasioned renewed complaints about flooding and the loss of the fish trade (PRO CP 40/509, m. 150d; BL Additional Charter 64322; Hooker, *Citie of Excester*, pp 649–51, 657; Jackson, 'Medieval Exeter, the Exe and the Earldom', pp 70–1).

[34] For Earl Hugh's attempts to monopolize the land transport of maritime cargoes, see Misc. Roll 3, no. 5 and Jackson, 'Medieval Exeter, the Exe and the Earldom', p 69. For storage at Topsham, see MCR 1332/3, m. 38d; PRO E 101/78/18; Hooker, *Citie of Excester*, pp 633–4. There were very few carters in Exeter, suggesting that these services were more often provided by men of other villages or towns.

[35] Above, n. 3. By the mid-fifteenth century, the earl was also collecting bushellage and plankage while cranage brought in almost £6 and keelage 6s (DRO W1258M/G6/50).

[36] PRO C 135/260/15; BL Additional Charters 64318–19. In 1431/2 (DRO, CR 501) the Courtenays spent over 25s to repair the *machine* at Topsham; see also DRO W1258M/G6/50 for similar expenditures in 1452/3.

[37] After the construction of the weirs, the Topsham fisheries were more valuable than the earl's other fisheries (PRO SC 6/827/39; PRO C 135/260/15; Ugawa, 'Economic Development', pp 1962: 652–3; Jackson, 'Medieval Exeter, the Exe and the Earldom', p 66).

jurisdictional rights to distraint and attachment throughout the estuary if there was a suspicion of customs evasion.[38] The Exeter authorities, moreover, made the earls' promotion of the port facilities at Topsham work to their advantage. By the end of the thirteenth century, Exeter officials were insisting that all ships unload their saleable cargoes only at Topsham, and in the following two centuries, they collected considerable monies from those seeking licences to do so at other estuarine ports.[39] The jurisdictional unity of the estuarine ports was also reflected in the interchangeable nature of such terms as the "port of Exeter", "port of Topsham" or "port of Exmouth" in the local and national port customs accounts.[40] As early as 1250 one description of the port noted "there is at Topsham a sea port called Exmouth because the River Exe empties iteself into the sea, where the ships and boats come".[41] Exeter's jurisdictional control of the estuary was evident too in the royal writs for naval levies or customs collection which, even if directed to the bailiffs of the port of Topsham or Exmouth, were put into effect by Exeter officials, not the bailiffs of Topsham or the other estuarine manors.[42]

CUSTOMS COLLECTION, RATES, AND EXEMPTIONS

In the early fourteenth century, port customs accounted for roughly 8–9 per cent of the total annual revenues of Exeter.[43] The amounts collected each year could vary widely, however, because of fluctuations in trade and because of the exemptions from customs enjoyed by many importers. Wine custom in this period normally averaged annually about £3–5 after the earl of Devon received his one-third share. Custom from other merchandise was generally higher, averaging about £6 each year, but could fall to under £4 (in 1317/18) or rise to almost £12 (in 1320/1). The sums collected for wine custom were often enrolled on the accounts themselves (because of the care taken to assure the earl he was getting his fair share), but totals for the mercantile portions of the account were never listed in this period

[38] MCR 1290/1, m. 15; 1302/3, m. 3d; 1334/5, m. 37d; 1409/10, m.3; DRO, ECA PCA 1398/9.

[39] The licences were usually enrolled in the MCR (below pp 47–69); many have been collected and noted in DRO, ECA Transcript 108. *Colepole* (probably in Exmouth; see below, n. 49) was the landing place most often mentioned; others were *Checkstone*, *Pratteshide* (both in Exmouth; see above, n. 20), *La Clyve* (a small manor in Topsham), and Powderham (sometimes at a place termed *Powderhampole*). In the later middle ages, *le Turffe* (near the border of Exminster and Powderham parishes), *Shilpole* and *Crowdounesworth* (neither identified) were also noted.

[40] Thus, the appearance of these terms in the headings to the customs accounts (below, p 15 especially) and in the formulas used to record ship moorings (below, p 33) were not meant to be taken literally as the exact place where ships docked.

[41] Rowe, *History of Plympton Erle*, p 12.

[42] Jackson, 'Medieval Exeter, the Exe, and the Earldom,' p 62.

[43] Figure derived by comparing customs totals with total receipts minus arrears in the seven surviving city accounts before 1349, as listed in *The Receivers' Accounts of the City of Exeter, 1304–1353*, ed. Margery M. Rowe and John M. Draisey, DCRS, new series, xxxii (1989), p xxiv.

(although they can be calculated by adding up the individual customs noted after each entry).[44] The monies actually collected by the city were enrolled in the annual city accounts (called the receivers' accounts) which, unfortunately, survive for only two of the years covered by the accounts printed here. Comparisons of the sums noted in the port customs accounts and those recorded in the receivers' accounts show that the payments actually received by the city were often less than those anticipated in the port customs accounts.[45] Such disparities occcurred frequently, but only occasionally amounted to more than five shillings.[46]

Not much is known about the procedures involved in the collection of local customs at the port of Exeter. It is clear, however, that importers were obliged to unload their saleable cargoes only at Topsham and to pay custom before unloading or selling their goods. Those caught doing otherwise were subject to fines or forfeiture of their cargoes.[47] Cargoes could be unloaded elsewhere in the estuary only if the shipmaster or importers purchased a licence from the Exeter authorities.[48] *Colepole* (probably located near present-day Exmouth where the estuarine channel is deeper than at Topsham) was the most frequently named alternative landing place in the estuary.[49] *Pratteshide*, site of the Exeter-owned ferry, was another popular landing place, although it was more often mentioned in connection with importers seeking to avoid city custom than those paying for licences to unload there. Among those whom the Exeter authorities successfully prosecuted for landing goods illegally at *Pratteshide* was David Uppehulle, who claimed he was free of custom because he unloaded his wares at land he owned there.[50] Actual concealment of imports to avoid custom seems to have been uncommon and involved

[44] For customs totals for wine, see above, n. 9.

[45] The sums collected for wine custom in 1304–6 (CRA 1304/5 and 1305/6, printed in *Receivers' Accounts*), were about 14s less each than the totals noted in the customs accounts (below, pp 99, 113).

[46] CRA passim; Henri Touchard, 'Les douanes municipales d'Exeter (Devon). Publication des rôles de 1381 à 1433,' Thèse complémentaire pour le Doctorat ès Lettres, Université de Paris, 1967, pp lvii, 365–66.

[47] For example, below, pp 42, 49, 67; and MCR 1304/5, m. 3d; 1306/7, m. 17; 1334/5, m. 37d; 1390/1, m. 42d; 1429/30, m. 27d; PCA 1339/40 (merc. account); Hooker, *Citie of Excester*, pp 939–40. One of the clearest statements of these rights is in MCR 1410/11, m. 3d.

[48] For example, below, pp 47–8, 51, 113.

[49] The exact location of *Colepole* cannot be determined, but court cases suggest it was located in East Budleigh hundred (PRO JUST 1/186, m. 37d) between Lympstone and Littleham parish and lay "three leagues" by water from Topsham (PRO E 101/555/14, m. 1). The reference to a ship from *Colepole* mastered by a man from Kenton, along with a taxpayer with the surname *de Colepole* in Kenton might suggest, however, that the place was located on the other side of the estuary near Kenton (MCR 1291/2, m. 23d; *The Devonshire Lay Subsidy of 1332*, ed. Audrey M. Erskine, DCRS, new series, xiv (1969), p 123). It was especially favoured as a landing place for heavily-laden wine ships (below, pp 47, 49; and MCR 1351/2, mm. 13, 15; 1360/1, mm. 2d, 15d; 1365/6, m. 6d; 1368/9, m. 7d; CRA 1341/2, 1349/50, 1350/1). For other landing places, see above, n. 39.

[50] MCR 1289/90, mm. 12, 14, 15, 20, 21, 22, 25, 30, 32. See also MCR 1301/2, m. 9, and Weddell, 'The Excavation of Medieval and Later Houses,' pp 120, 124.

relatively small cargoes, such as one or two tuns of wine owned by a shipmaster.[51]

Shipmasters and importers probably made their own customs declaration rather than waiting for a municipal representative to inspect and then custom the cargo.[52] The customing process itself seems to have taken place in Exeter, rather than in Topsham where the vessels unloaded. Annotations in the accounts regarding the actual receipt of custom never mention Topsham while those regarding the placement of custom monies in the town pyx (cash box) kept in the Guildhall indicate that at least this part of the customing process transpired at Exeter. The assessment of customs for one large wine ship in the presence of the mayor and bailiffs (i.e., the stewards) also points to the process occurring at a session of the mayor's court.[53] The involvement of important civic officials (such as the mayor, stewards, receiver, or city clerk) in the collection of customs or the purchase of licences to unload elsewhere, also implies that customing took place at Exeter, not at Topsham.[54] The absence of references in the annual receivers' rolls to the expenses these officials may have incurred at Topsham or other estuarine ports provides further (albeit silent) evidence that the customing process occurred at Exeter.[55]

Importers well known to the Exeter authorities were allowed to delay paying custom if they found suitable pledges to guarantee future payment. Some of these importers paid their custom in instalments, as indicated by the later annotations made in the accounts regarding the receipt of sums owed. Most seem to have paid within one or two weeks, the period normally stated in those entries specifying due dates.[56] Pledges came largely from the city's ruling elite (many of whom imported cargoes on the same ship as the merchants who required sureties), although other Exeter merchants, officials, and even some foreign merchants also filled this role.[57] Non-Exeter pledges were rare, however, and those foreigners who served in this capacity, such as John Moset and Bartholomew Bygge of Amiens, were probably accepted as pledges because they had joined the freedom or frequently did business in Exeter.[58] Trustworthy local pledges

---

[51] For example, MCR 1306/7, m. 17; Touchard, 'Les douanes municipales', pp xvi–xvii. For other reasons why customs evasion was probably not rampant, see below, pp 40–3.

[52] For a similar process in Ipswich, see *The Black Book of the Admiralty*, ed. Travers Twiss, 4 vols., London, 1871–6, ii, p 207.

[53] Below, p 69.

[54] See below, Appendix 2, for a more extended discussion of the involvement of these officials in custom collection.

[55] CRA passim. In contrast, small expenses incurred for travel to estuarine ports for other purposes were often noted in the CRA.

[56] Below, pp 120–1, 130, 138, 166.

[57] Compare the names of pledges with those of the ruling elite (listed in Appendix 2, below), and with the names of other importers.

[58] Below, pp 107, 112, 120, 127–8; MCR 1305/6, m. 16d. Moset paid £6 13s 4d to enter the freedom in 1311, the highest entry fee on record (*Exeter Freemen 1266–1967*, ed. Margery M. Rowe and Andrew M. Jackson, DCRS, extra series i (1973), p 11).

were favoured because of the difficulties of ensuring prompt payment of customs; pledges who resided in Exeter could more easily be prosecuted in the local courts if they or the merchants they pledged did not pay in full. The difficulties involved in collecting customs can be seen in the various strategies pursued by the authorities to ensure timely payments.[59] In the thirteenth century, civic officials occasionally held back part of the cargo as security until importers or their pledges paid the sums owed.[60] Not all pledges fullfilled their obligations, however, as indicated by the disparities between the custom assessed in the port accounts and the amounts finally noted in the annual receivers' accounts. In the early fifteenth century, the city tried to tighten the pledging process by forbidding receivers to take sureties for custom unless the receivers were themselves willing to satisfy the city for unpaid balances.[61]

Customs at Exeter were assessed according to the type and amounts of goods unloaded, but not on their value. Those responsible for assessing custom probably consulted a table of rates such as the partial one that survives in the city's custumal (compiled around 1240).[62] Such tables did not, however, cover all contingencies. The complex weights and measures of medieval commerce caused considerable problems; the struggle of customs assessors to deal with this problem can be seen in annotations in the accounts regarding the equivalents of such measures as the bale, hundredweight (abbreviated as C in the text), charge, and seam.[63] Clerical negligence, rounding, and errors in addition generated further inconsistencies in the rates charged. After assessment of their cargoes, importers generally rendered their customs payments in cash, although some remnant of payments in kind was visible in two entries of 1295/6 when the bailiff claimed one hundredweight of the herring cargo.[64] This provision echoed clauses in the city's custumal which dictated that those landing red herring at the port pay one hundredweight of the cargo to the bailiff and one thousandweight to the castle on top of the other customs owed.[65] No trace of the payment to the castle can be found, however, and the customary payment to the city bailiff was never mentioned again after 1295/6.

Except for the fragment extant in the city's custumal, no table of Exeter's local customs rates survives for the middle ages. A list of imports subject to such tolls and the rates charged for each can be compiled, however, from the custom sums noted in the local port

---

[59] Both the receiver and sureties waiting to be repaid by the merchants they pledged were sometimes forced to sue for payments in the borough courts (Kowaleski, *Local Markets and Regional Trade*, chapter 5, esp. table 5.1).

[60] Below, p 52.

[61] Misc. Roll 2, no. 22.

[62] *The Anglo-Norman Custumal of Exeter*, ed. J. W. Schopp, Oxford, 1925, p 24. The custumal's list notes only six commodities and their rates before being cut off.

[63] See Appendix 3, below.

[64] Below, p 50.

[65] *Anglo-Norman Custumal*, p 37; note also the provision (p 31) that sellers of eels from boats owed toll in the form of one out of every seven sticks sold.

accounts. Thus wine was assessed at 4d per tun, woad (a blue dye) at 1s per tun, iron at ½d per quintal, garlic at 1d per seam, herring at 1d per thousandweight and 4d per last, and saffron at 1d per pound.[66] Other goods liable to custom included almonds, anise, archil, canvas, cumin, figs, iron spurs, linen cloth, onions, oxen, pepper, and yarn. Goods that appear not to have been subject to local port customs in this period include all grains, potash (a mordant), weld (a yellow dye) and, surprisingly, salt. By the late fourteenth century, however, the scope of items customed at Exeter had grown to include at least grains and salt.[67] Perhaps Exeter authorities reacted to the declining level of trade in the late fourteenth century (occasioned by the Anglo-French conflicts of the Hundred Years War and the demographic devastations of the Black Death) by widening the purview of customable wares in order to continue collecting similar sums from port customs.[68]

The actual custom rates assessed at Exeter were relatively light compared to both the national rates and the local customs at ports such as Southampton and Yarmouth.[69] The 4d charged on each tun of wine at Exeter was considerably lower than the 2s per tun the royal customs collectors charged aliens from 1303 or the 2–3s per tun subsidy assessed later in the century on all overseas importers.[70] Southampton charged 8d for each tun of wine coming from overseas, while each tun arriving via coastal craft owed 4d, and tuns re-exported by coast paid another 4d.[71] In general, the custom rates at Southampton were greater than at Exeter because they charged slightly higher rates on some goods, covered more commodities, applied an *ad valorem* tax on several items, and were assessed on exports as well as imports. In only a few instances were the Exeter customs heavier. The levy on the expensive dye woad was particularly high (1s per tun) at Exeter compared to the 6d per tun at Southampton and most other ports; iron at

[66] The wine and woad rates are obvious from the many tolls importers of these goods paid. For iron, see below, pp 134, 143; for garlic, pp 107, 178; for herring, pp 92, 179–80; for saffron, p 144.

[67] Salt and wheat were assessed at ½d per quarter from at least the 1360s on (PCA passim); potash may also have been customed (see PCA 1357/8 under the *St Marie cok* of Exmouth) but the decline of potash and weld imports offer too few examples to determine whether these goods were then being customed. See also Touchard, 'Les douanes municipales', pp xix–xxvii for the rates charged on other goods.

[68] For the port trade decline, see Kowaleski, *Local Markets and Regional Trade*, table 3.2, and chapter 6. The sums collected from customs in the late fourteenth century, however, were similar to what they had been in the early part of the century (CRA passim). For the further enlargement of the scope of customs at Exeter in the sixteenth century, see Hooker, *Citie of Excester*, pp 554–66, 662–3. It is also possible rates on some goods may have been raised; for such an occurrence at Southampton, see Henry S. Cobb, 'Introduction', *The Local Port Book of Southampton 1439–40*, Southampton Records Series, v (1961), p xvii.

[69] Cobb, 'Introduction', *Local Port Book of Southampton*, pp xvi–xvii; see also below, n. 73.

[70] N.S.B. Gras, *The Early English Customs System*, Cambridge Mass., 1918, pp 83–4.

[71] *The Oak Book of Southampton*, ii, ed. P. Studer, Southampton Record Society, xi (1911), pp 2–3, and 4–27 for other goods; the rates date from the early fourteenth century.

Exeter ($\frac{1}{2}$d per quintal) was also assessed more heavily than at Southampton ($\frac{1}{4}$d per quintal). Rates at Exeter were also more substantial than at the smaller Devon port of Dartmouth where each wine tun paid only 2d and each thousandweight of herring owed but $\frac{1}{2}$d compared to the 1d charged at Exeter.[72] Although other ports also occasionally charged lower rates than Exeter for important commodities like wine, the scope of their customs was usually wider in that they also collected export duties, which Exeter did not.[73]

Aside from the regular local customs, the city also sometimes charged pavage and murage tolls at the port. The privilege of exacting these tolls was granted by the king, and their profits were to be applied to the repair or construction of city pavements and walls. Although Exeter enjoyed murage grants almost continuously from 1224 to 1310, and again from 1338 to 1377, collection efforts concentrated on the traffic coming through the city gates; murage was assessed at the port in fewer than twenty years between 1338 and 1374.[74] Pavage was exacted at the port even less frequently, in 1320–22 and 1329–32.[75] When charged, however, murage and pavage tolls could be particularly profitable because they touched more commodities than local customs and usually included a 3d tax on each ship liable to toll.[76] In the merchandise account of 1320/1, for example, the city collected almost £14 from pavage but only some £11 7s from local customs.[77] Like local customs, however, pavage and

---

[72] *Rotuli Hundredorum temporibus Henrici III et Edwardi I in Turri Londinensi et in Curia Receptae Scaccarii Westmonasterii Asservati*, 2 vols, ed. W. Illingworth, London, Record Commission, 1812–18, i, p 90.

[73] Sandwich's customs were very similar to those of Exeter: 4d per tun of wine or woad, $\frac{1}{4}$d per quintal of iron, 4d per hundredweight of canvas, and 4d per last of herring (Gras, *Early English Customs*, pp 167–72). Winchelsea's customs were particularly low: only 1d per tun of wine, 2d per bale of almonds, and $\frac{1}{4}$d per last of herring (*ibid.*, pp 177–91, mistakenly labelled as from Sandwich by Gras). Only wine owed local customs at Chester in the fourteenth century although both incoming and outgoing tuns owed 4d each (*Chester Customs Accounts, 1301–1566*, ed. K. P. Wilson, Record Society of Lancashire and Cheshire, cxi (1969), pp 11–12, 143). Rates at Ipswich were also generally lower than at Exeter but the export tolls charged there, along with special dues that varied according to the size of the ship, found no parallel at Exeter (*Black Book of the Admiralty*, ii, pp 185–97).

[74] Most Exeter murage grants are listed in Hilary Turner, *Town Defences in England and Wales*, London, 1971, pp 194–5, 238–40. For years when murage was collected at the port, see PCA 1338/9–1342/3, 1360/1, 1361/2, 1368/9–1372/3; DRO, ECA Misc. Roll 6, mm. 22 (1341–2), 16 (1363–5), 14 (1372/3); CRA 1372/3, 1373/4.

[75] *CPR 1317–21*, p 526; *CPR 1327–30*, p 369; PCA Roll 1, mm. 10 (1322/3 wine account), 11 (1320/1 merc. account, printed below, pp 199–200); PCA 1329/30, 1331/2 (no account survives for 1330/1). Pavage was part of the grant made for five years in 1360 (*CPR 1358–61*, p 357) but only murage was collected at the port.

[76] For a list of the tolls assessed for pavage in 1329/30, see Hooker, *Citie of Excester*, pp 540–3; goods such as grain, potash and weld were charged pavage but were not liable to local town customs.

[77] PCA Roll 1, m. 11 (below, pp 190–201). Murage tolls at the port brought in £6 in 1341/2 (Misc. Roll 6, m. 22) and only £1 1s–£2 8s in the 1360s and 1370s (Misc. Roll 6, mm. 14, 16; CRA 1370/1–1373/4) when the port trade was going through a period of decline and was visited by fewer foreign merchants, who bore the brunt of pavage and murage tolls.

murage were both subject to exemptions so the amounts collected could vary widely from year to year.

Importers could escape paying town customs in basically four ways. Those who imported goods for their own use were normally not liable to customs since they did not intend to sell their imports.[78] Only a few importers fell into this category, however, and most were of gentry or clerical status. References to wine brought in "for drink" by the archdeacon of Wells, the treasurer of Exeter cathedral (Thomas de Henton), or the shipmaster Ralph le Sanger also probably allude to this privilege.[79] Many more importers avoided customs because none were due on the particular items they were importing; coal, grains, salt, and some dyestuffs were among the uncustomed imports at Exeter in this period. A third category of exemption was enjoyed by shipmasters and mariners who claimed portage: the right to freight some cargo free of charge in lieu of wages.[80] At Exeter, shipmasters were usually allowed to bring in two tuns of wine and mariners one tun custom-free by way of portage. Other goods imported in this fashion included alum, canvas, herring, iron, and especially garlic and onions. On occasion, mariners also seem to have sold their rights of portage to merchants freighting goods on their ship.[81]

The fourth and surest way to avoid customs was to enjoy complete exemption by virtue of one's status or residence in a privileged town. For example, those who belonged to the Exeter town freedom—a privileged organization that conferred specific political, legal, and economic rights on its members—were free of all customs in Exeter and elsewhere in England.[82] Franchised residents of other exempt towns, such as the Cinque Ports, London, and Southampton, were also free of port customs, although if unknown to the Exeter authorities they had to come equipped with proof of their status. Some brought copies of charters showing their exemptions while others had to find pledges to back up their assertion or wait until their claim could be proved before having their customs respited.[83] Exeter, like other towns, also kept a list of towns whose citizens enjoyed customs

---

[78] Iron imported to repair the ship was also allowed in custom-free under the condition it not be sold (PCA 1336/7 wine account).

[79] Below, pp 131, 155, 165

[80] *Black Book of the Admiralty*, ii, p 305; F. R. Sanborn, *Origins of the Early English Maritime and Commercial Law*, New York, 1930, pp 72, 402. For the customs of the sea that allowed mariners such freightage (often called *mareage*) in lieu of wages, see *Black Book of the Admiralty*, i, pp 112–3, 122–5, 134–5, 138–43; ii, pp 191, 232–5 (although note the dispute about the interpretation of one of the relevant clauses in Dorothy Burwash, *English Merchant Shipping 1460–1540*, Toronto, 1947, pp 171–6).

[81] Below, p 92; see also *Black Book of the Admiralty*, ii, pp 234–5, 451.

[82] For the freedom, see Rowe and Jackson, 'Introduction', *Exeter Freemen*.

[83] These claims were often registered in the margins of the port customs accounts (for example, below, pp 60, 76, 161). For importers who showed charters or other documents backing up their claims, see MCR 1378/9, m. 3d; 1390/1, rider by m. 18; for importers whose custom was respited after some time had elapsed to prove their claims, see CRA 1396/7, 1410/11; for an importer (from Winchelsea) whose claim was backed by local pledges, see MCR 1296/7, m. 19d.

exemptions, although the list was by no means complete since it omitted many port towns outside Devon.[84] The town's preoccupation with custom status is visible in the many annotations made in the accounts regarding the free or customed status of individual merchants and in the disputes that arose when importers claimed exemptions the city hesitated to recognize.[85] The same preoccupation with custom liability is reflected in the unusually careful listing of each importer's name and cargo in the Exeter accounts.

SHIPS AND MARINERS

The accounts printed here record the entry of 641 ships, almost half of which had home ports in Devon (see Table 1). Not surprisingly, the single largest contingent of ships (22 per cent) was associated with ports in the Exe estuary. The medieval agricultural region of east Devon (which stretched from the Somerset border to the Teign estuary),[86] led by the many vessels from Teignmouth, came next, followed by contributions from south Devon, especially the port of Dartmouth. By the second half of the fourteenth century, this proportion had changed, largely because of the Hundred Years War. A disastrous French raid at Teignmouth in 1340 (from which the port only slowly recovered) caused ship contributions from east Devon to decline to about 8 per cent. In contrast, south Devon ships at Exeter increased because of royal patronage bestowed on Dartmouth and Plymouth during the War. Owned by the newly established duchy of Cornwall, these two ports and their shipping stock expanded greatly during the later middle ages, as did their port facilities, recruitment of mariners, borough privileges, and trade.[87] This south Devon expansion, however, had a more muted effect on the carrying trade of ships from the Exe estuary which declined only slightly in the second half of the century.

About one quarter of the ships at Exeter in this period were attached to home ports elsewhere in England, while another one quarter originated in continental or Channel Island locations. Dorset

---

[84] *Anglo-Norman Custumal*, pp 24–6 includes a fragment of a list that also served as the basis of the copy in DRO, ECA Book 51, ff 223–4 (Hooker's Commonplace Book) although the latter, like the list in Hooker, *Citie of Excester*, pp 302–7, has some later additions. The medieval portion of the list names about 61 places, 80% of which are in Devon and only 9 of which are ports (including the Cinque Ports which are counted as one place); this distribution reflects the overland emphasis of Exeter's medieval trade.

[85] Note the disputes about Taunton importers (below, pp 38–9), the custom status of Newton Abbot and Topsham importers (below, p 38), and other claims questioned by the Exeter authorities (below, pp 60, 76).

[86] The regions noted here are the medieval agricultural regions (for a map, see Maryanne Kowaleski, 'The Port Towns of Fourteenth-Century Devon', *The New Maritime History of Devon*, i, ed. Michael Duffy et al., London, 1992, p 65), not the modern administrative regions.

[87] Kowaleski, 'Port Towns,' pp 62–72. In PCA 1350–99, south Devon ships comprised almost 36% of vessels visiting Exeter while about 21% were associated with ports in the Exe estuary; see also Kowaleski, *Local Markets and Regional Trade*, table 6.3.

TABLE 1: HOME PORTS OF SHIPS AT EXETER, 1266–1321

Home Port	No. of Ship Arrivals	Area Total	% of Total
EAST DEVON		119	18.6
Sidmouth	27		
Ottermouth	9		
Dawlish	1		
Teignmouth	82		
EXE ESTUARY[1]		142	22.1
SOUTH DEVON		48	7.5
Dartmouth	35		
Totnes	2		
Plymouth	8		
Others	3		
NORTH DEVON		2	.3
CORNWALL		7	1.1
DORSET		37	5.8
Lyme	15		
Poole	10		
Weymouth	9		
Others	3		
HAMPSHIRE		53	8.3
Hamble and Hook	22		
Lymington	11 ·		
Southampton	7		
Others	13		
ENGLAND		56	8.7
Yarmouth	21		
Winchelsea	5		
Others	30		
CHANNEL ISLANDS		37	5.8
PICARDY & ARTOIS[2]		47	7.3
NORMANDY		16	2.5
BRITTANY		33	5.1
SOUTH FRANCE		10	1.6
SPAIN		3	.5
UNIDENTIFIED		31	4.8
TOTAL		641	100.0

Source and Notes: PCA 1266–1320/1. The identified ships include twenty whose home ports, while not stated in the accounts, could be identified from other information given in the entries; 2 of these ships were from Teignmouth, 6 from Exmouth, 1 from Weymouth, 5 from Le Vivier (Brittany), and 6 from the Channel Islands.

[1] The jurisdictional unity of the Exe estuary meant that scribes did not carefully distinguish the actual home ports of estuarine ships.

[2] Includes one ship from Sluis in Flanders.

and Hampshire ships were especially frequent visitors, as were Yarmouth herring ships. Most of these vessels engaged in coastal trade between Exeter and other English ports, either transshipping foreign goods from larger ports like Southampton, or carrying local products from ports in southern and eastern England.[88] Some also sailed on overseas routes, with Bordeaux (for wine) or northern France being favourite destinations. Foreign ships at Exeter came largely from Picardy and Artois, followed by the Channel Islands, Brittany, and Normandy. Again, by the second half of the fourteenth century, this pattern had changed. The Hundred Years War greatly affected the distribution of English and continental vessels sailing to the port; ships from areas at war with England (Artois, Picardy, and Normandy) rarely appeared at Exeter while vessels from regions allied with England (Brittany and the Channel Islands), almost doubled in importance.[89] Similarly, the growth of the south Devon carrying trade cut into the business of carriers from other English ports, reducing their presence at Exeter from 24 per cent to less than 9 per cent in the second half of the fourteenth century. Vessels from Cornwall were the only English ships to appear at Exeter in greater numbers in the later middle ages, an increase due in large part to the growth of the south-western fishing trade.[90]

Roughly 302 different ships can be distinguished in the total of 641 listed in the customs accounts. Differentiating them is difficult because of scribal idiosyncracies. For example, ships called *Goodyear* appear under English versions (such as *Godyer*) or French versions (such as *Bonan*), while ships named *Jonete* occur under no less than thirteen different spellings (some of which may also have meant *Jouette*). The *Margaret* of Exmouth was sometimes called the *Langbord*, perhaps to distinguish it from at least two other Exmouth ships also named *Margaret*. Scribal use of the definite article varied greatly as well; *la* was generally attached to female names and *le* to male names, but at times scribes appended either indiscriminately.[91] The identification of home ports could also be lax in that ships from smaller ports were sometimes listed under their head ports. The *Lyon* of Lymington (Hampshire), for example, was almost certainly the same ship as the *Lion* of Southampton since both were mastered by the same man.[92] This tendency to conflate smaller ports under their juris-

[88] For a longer discussion of coastal trade, see Kowaleski, *Local Markets and Regional Trade*, chapter 6, esp. table 6.1.

[89] In PCA 1350–99, only 1.2% of the ships at Exeter were from Picardy, Artois and Normandy, while just over 11% were from Brittany and almost 11% from the Channel Islands; the percentage from Spain and southern France changed little.

[90] In PCA 1350–99, 3.9% of the ships were from Cornwall, 1% from Dorset, 1.5% from Hampshire, and 2.9% from other English ports (*ibid.*, chapter 7, for the fish trade).

[91] For example, both *la* and *le* were used with ships named *Bartholomew* and *Notre Dame* (see below, pp 63, 111, 161, 176). Of the 641 ships, 94 appeared with no definite article, 193 with *le*, and 354 with *la*.

[92] Below, pp 158, 162. Other examples are the *Annoce* of Keyhaven and Lymington (below, pp 183–4, 186), and the *St Louis* of Abbeville and St Valéry (below, pp 87, 112).

dictional head port was especially common for ships from the Exe estuary; scribes often listed Exmouth as the home port of all estuarine vessels even though the ships may have been attached to Kenton, Topsham, Lympstone, or *Pratteshide*.[93]

Ship names with religious connotations were especially numerous; those called after saints enjoyed particular favour. *Notre Dame* was the single most common appellation, appearing on about eighteen different ships. The popularity of some names may have resulted from local circumstances. The many Exe estuary ships called *Margaret* (or some version thereof) probably derived from Topsham's parish church dedication to St Margaret, while the popularity of French ships named *St Louis* perhaps reflected devotion to the sainted King Louis IX (1226–70).[94] There were also at least twenty different ships with some version of the name *Nicholas*, the patron saint of mariners. Names descriptive of the ships themselves were also prevalent, such as *Long Batel*, *Langbord*, *Petite Nicholas*, *Vertbois* (green wood) and *Red Cog* (cogs were a type of ship). Others were simply known by the names of their owners, such as the *Rith'vele* (probably owned by the Rixthiveles, a wealthy Exeter family).

The accounts reveal little information about the size and type of the ships since this information was of little relevance to the customing process. The amount of wine carried by ships, however, offers a rough idea of ship size since the wine tun (of 252 gallons) was generally employed as the basis of measurement for ship capacity in medieval England. At least twenty ships exceeded 100 tuns, including the *St Mary cog* of Teignmouth which arrived with a cargo of 151 tuns, the *Goodyear* of Exmouth and *St Cruz* of Portsmouth which carried almost 140 tuns, and the *Alne* of Teignmouth, *St Mary cog* of Exmouth, and the *Notre Dame* of Exmouth which unloaded about 120 tuns.[95] The *Barthelemeu* of Lyme, with a cargo of over 1000 quarters of grain, must also have been fairly substantial. These large ships, however, were exceptional; most medieval trading ships were considerably smaller, averaging 50 tuns or less.[96] Few of the foreign ships specializing in lighter cargoes (such as dyestuffs, garlic, onions and canvas) and few of the coastal vessels transporting overseas goods from the bigger English ports to Exeter were as large as the ships that plied the wine route between Bordeaux and England. Many of these larger ships (about 50 of the 302) were cogs, the cog being a bulk carrier whose length-to-beam ratio (3:1) caused it to be termed a "round"

[93] For example, the *Jonete* of Exmouth and *Jonete* of Lympstone were both mastered by William Cok while the *Margaret* of Exmouth and *Margaret* of Topsham were both mastered by David le Rede (below, pp 74, 79, 98, 106).

[94] All five ships named *St Louis* came from France. The popularity of the ship name *Margaret* in the Exe estuary may also be related to the chapel of St Margaret established at Exmouth sometime before 1374, while the popularity of the ship name *Sauve* might refer to the earlier St Saviour's chapel there (Weddell, 'The Excavation of Medieval and Later Houses', p 115).

[95] Below, pp 53–4, 56, 123, 133, 188.

[96] For the capacity of fourteenth-century Devon ships, see also Kowaleski, 'Port Towns', table 7.4; and Ian Friel, 'Devon Shipping from the Middle Ages to c1600', *The New Maritime History of Devon*, pp 73–8, esp. table 8.2.

ship by some. Several other ships from Brittany and Guernsey were labeled a *holhop*, perhaps a reference to a sloop.[97] Aside from these appellations and one reference to a barge (an oared sailing vessel, usually smaller than a cog), the accounts mostly used some variation of the words ship (*nau, nav', nawe, nef, neof*) or boat (*batel, bot*) to describe the vessels.[98]

Slightly more information about the crews that manned these vessels can be gleaned from references to portage, a customs exemption claimed by mariners who were carrying their own merchandise on board ship in lieu of part or all of their wages. Some associated with portage were shipmasters and a few were merchants (who paid mariners for the privilege of using the space on the ship they were allotted), but most were common seamen.[99] Many remained nameless, referred to as "the crew", "the mariners", or alluded to only in a general fashion in lists of goods brought in under portage. But many were named and appear several times in the accounts. They include Richard Edmund, who declared one tun of wine for portage on the *Goodyear* of Exmouth on two different voyages, and also served as one of 28 mariners hired to accompany the *St Mary cog* of Exmouth on naval service to Scotland. Roger Aleys, Benedict Edmund, Richard Edward, Richard Gille, Peter Godlok, Walter Hardy, and Walter de Ilfridecomb were other mariners who claimed portage at Exeter and also served in the royal navy with Richard Edmund.[100] Foreign mariners appeared in the accounts claiming portage as well, although the goods they brought were more likely to be onions or garlic than wine. Mariners also seem to have exercised this option more often on some ships than others. Sidmouth ships, for example, especially the *St Giles cog* (usually mastered and probably owned by Ralph le Sanger), often had large numbers of mariners choosing this method of wage remuneration.[101] Portage claims slowed to a trickle, however, in the second half of the century, an indication that mariners could no longer afford this option.[102]

---

[97] Other variations which appear in the accounts are *halop, hollouw, hollok*, and *holoc*; see the Index for references to all occurrences. The words seem to be related to the Dutch sloop from which the French *chaloupe* and English *shallop* also derived; see *Nouveau glossaire nautique d'Augustin Tal*, vol 7, Paris, 1992, p 858. The last two versions may also refer to a hulk, a ship which rivalled the cog in carrying capacity by the late fourteenth century, although the spelling variations argue against this.

[98] For the barge, see below, p 178. The *Buzard* from Normandy (below, p 48) may also have been an allusion to the *buss* or *buza*, a cargo ship with less capacity than a cog; for descriptions of all these vessels and a discussion of how they changed over the course of the middle ages, see Richard Unger, *The Ship in the Medieval Economy 600–1600*, London, 1980, esp. pp 136–44, 163–72, 204–8.

[99] For this custom in maritime law, see above, notes 80 and 81.

[100] For their portage at Exeter, see the references under their names in the Index. For their naval service in 1310, see DRO, ECA ED/M/214 (printed in Michael Jones, 'Two Exeter Ship Agreements of 1303 and 1310', *Mariner's Mirror*, liii (1967), p 317).

[101] Below, pp 96, 102–3, 131–2, 189.

[102] For the much higher prices of wine and freightage in the later middle ages (largely a result of warfare in wine-producing regions, war-time piracy, and privateering on the high seas), see Margery James, *Studies in the Medieval Wine Trade*, Oxford, 1971, pp 37, 64–9, 151–5.

The most important mariners were shipmasters; responsible for freighting the ship, directing the mariners, and sailing the ship and its cargo into port safely, they received more recognition and profit than common seamen. Many shipmasters regularly imported goods on ships they mastered, although their cargoes were never as large as those of the bigger merchants.[103] But within their own coastal communities, shipmasters could be relatively prominent. Many appeared in the lay subsidies (which taxed only the wealthier section of the population) paying taxes as high as 5s.[104] Some invested in ships as well as mercantile ventures; Peter Godlok, who mastered at least five different Exmouth ships, and Richard le Wayte of Topsham, who mastered at least three ships, were also part owners of two of these ships, the *St Mary cog* and the *Sauveye* of Exmouth.[105] The occupation also had a strong familial cast; fathers, sons, and brothers often became shipmasters, probably receiving their training on voyages captained by close relatives. Examples include the Edmunds of Topsham (Walter, Richard, and Robert), the Doos of Dartmouth (Gilbert and Hugh), the Bolts (Giles, Julian, and Roger) and Payns (Roger, Thomas, and William), both of Teignmouth, and the Sangers of Sidmouth (Ralph, Roger, and William).[106]

Common mariners, such as Benedict Edmund of Topsham, also hailed from these families. The attraction of life at sea for residents of coastal settlements like Benedict and his shipmaster kinsmen can be seen in such mariners' surnames as de Gernemuth (Yarmouth), Hardenesse (in Dartmouth), de Slapton, de Torre (in Torbay), de Waymuth (Weymouth), and de Wynchelse (Winchelsea). The sea also occasionally lured men from such land-locked areas as the Dartmoor manor of Ashburton, the home of Thomas Knollying, a villein who sought manumission from his lord so that he might more freely practice his *ars navalis*.[107] Employment opportunities for mariners were limited only by the number of ships available. Highly mobile because of the nature of their occupations, many mariners probably settled in ports far from their native homes; surname evidence suggests, for instance, that men from Winchelsea served on Dartmouth and

---

[103] In this period, their wine cargoes were rarely over 7 tuns. In 1381–91, they represented about 15% of all importers but were responsible for importing only 5% of the iron, 6% of the wine, 9% of the salt, but 31% of the fish (Kowaleski, *Local Markets and Regional Trade*, chapter 6).

[104] The following shipmasters appeared in the 1332 lay subsidy; Richard Mugge of Teignmouth (5s); John Luverich of Dartmouth (4s); Richard Harvest of Kenton and Gilbert Whetepayn of Teignmouth (2s); John Luverich of Teignmouth (18d); John Avery of Topsham, Richard Gillot of Dartmouth, and Robert Stanbrigg of Topsham (12d); Adam Slegh of Powderham (10d); and Walter Parys of Topsham (8d); (*Devonshire Lay Subsidy of 1332*, pp 51, 56–57, 93, 111, 122).

[105] DRO ED/M/214.

[106] Paris Edmund was probably an alias for Walter Edmund (also called Walter Parys) rather than a fourth relative. William Sanger appears in these accounts as a common mariner but by 1326 he (and Hamelin Sanger) had become shipmasters (*CCR 1323–7*, p 609).

[107] *The Register of John de Grandisson, 1327–69*, ed. F. C. Hingeston-Randolph, 3 vols, London and Exeter, 1894–9, ii, p 1159.

Exmouth ships, men from Slapton and Spain worked aboard Teignmouth and Dartmouth ships, and a man from Ilfracombe in north Devon mastered an Exmouth ship.[108] Crew sizes for purely mercantile voyages were rarely recorded, but can sometimes be estimated from the number of mariners claiming portage on a particular voyage. The ten to twelve mariners aboard the *coc Cler* of Dartmouth (which freighted 96 tuns of wine) and the *St Gyles cog* of Sidmouth (116 tuns), for example, were probably close to the total number of mariners carried by these ships.[109] Cogs in particular did not demand much in way of skilled handling and were favoured for both their large capacity and relatively low labor costs.[110] It is not surprising, therefore, that cogs were particularly prominent on the wine routes between France and Exeter.

THE IMPORTERS

Importers' names, like those for ships, were often inconsistently recorded in the customs accounts. The translation of French and English names into Latin accounts, the varying languages and dialects spoken by shipmasters and importers, and the many different scribes and officials involved in the customing process all created difficulties. A surname like Cook can appear as *Coc, Cok, Cocus, Keu, Ku*, or *Qu* and the surname Skinner as *Peleter, Pellipar'*, or *Skynnere*. Further problems arise from the use of aliases. Joel de Bradecrofte was probably the same person as Joel le Taverner, just as Kyde of Pratteshide may have been the same as Philip Kyde.[111] Identification of importers is also hindered because the place where they resided was only occasionally recorded by the scribes, largely to draw attention to the custom status of the importer or to distinguish importers with similar names.[112] Importers well known to the local authorities, notably Exeter inhabitants and those regularly doing business at the port, were almost never identified in terms of their place of residence. More positive identifications can be made, however, by standardizing surnames and matching references in other documents to clues offered in the accounts themselves (such as dates of activity, custom status, importing activities, occupations, partners, ships employed as carriers, and so on). A preliminary analysis of the importers along these lines allows us to distinguish about 1071 different importers among the 2439 names in the accounts of 1302–21; about 70 per cent (748 of the 1071) can be

[108] E.g. below, pp 58, 180.

[109] Below, pp 96, 105.

[110] Unger, *The Ship in the Medieval Economy*, pp 139, 148–9.

[111] For the identification of Joel de Bradecrofte as a taverner, see below, p 73. For Kyde, see below, pp 66, 123.

[112] For example, the identification of Topsham and Taunton importers was probably due to disputes about their custom status at Exeter (below, pp 78, 127, 133). Note also that Martin, Richard, and William Cook of Bridford actually lived in Exeter but were identifed in this fashion to distinguish them from other Exeter residents with a similar surname.

identified in terms of residence, but this group owned 85 per cent of the cargoes.[113]

Residents of Exeter accounted for 19 per cent of the individual importers, but they owned over half of the cargoes.[114] The vast majority of the Exeter importers were wealthy members of the town's ruling elite, having served at one time or another as mayor, steward, or councillor.[115] The most prominent Exeter importer was Philip Lovecok, who was elected mayor ten times and was probably the richest man in Exeter.[116] In the surviving accounts of 1302–21, he imported 1060 tuns of wine and 745 quarters of grain, as well as herring, salt, wax, alum, canvas, iron, saffron, almonds, pitch, and salt-cellars. Not all Exeter residents imported on such a large scale; most traded in a more limited way and specialized in one or two imports. Wine was the most common specialty, followed by herring. Among the less prominent Exeter importers were men like John Whitebrother, who only imported herring on the cheaper coastal routes and who, unlike Philip, never served in high municipal office. John did not even gain admittance to the exlusive freedom organization until several years after he had begun importing goods and paying custom for doing so.[117]

The participation of Exeter merchants in the import trade was actually far more extensive than the accounts indicate since they purchased in bulk many of the goods brought in by foreigners and other non-residents who did not want to retail imports themselves. Exeter importers like William Brewer and John de St Nicholas, for instance, made large purchases from the Rouen importer, Adam Sage, while Richard de Spaxton, an Exeter wine importer, bought wine in bulk from James de Bertram of Bordeaux.[118] Similarly, Nicholas Lydeford,

---

[113] For the standardized surnames, see the Index, where Exeter residents are also identified. Residences were established by carefully matching details offered in the accounts with information found in other documents. The particularly good extant records for Exeter, Dartmouth, and Teignmouth (together home to more than half of the identifiable importers) made this task much easier. Most useful were *Devonshire Lay Subsidy of 1332; CCR; CPR*; the royal port customs accounts (PRO E 122/40/1–1A; E 122/40/3, /5, /7; E 122/78/3A; E 122/156/8); Exeter MCR (which include all the civic elections); Exeter mayor's tourns (a yearly market or leet court); Exeter deeds (many printed in *Exeter Property Deeds 1150–1450*, ed. P. R. Staniforth and J. Z. Juddery, Exeter Museums Archaeological Field Unit Reports Nos. 90.45–48, 1991); *Exeter Freemen*; Hugh R. Watkin, *Dartmouth*, Devonshire Association Parochial Histories of Devonshire, no. 5, 1935; ECL D&C 2946 (Teignmouth records, including a 1314 rental).

[114] A cargo consisted of all the goods one importer owned on one ship; Exeter residents owned at least 1414 of the 2939 cargoes and comprised 201 of the 1071 importers. These are minimum figures since the preliminary analysis only assigned residences when names were unambiguous and identifications could be corroborated by at least two different pieces of evidence.

[115] The fortunate survival of almost all annual elctions in the MCR makes such identification possible; see also Appendix 2, below.

[116] He paid the highest subsidy in Exeter in 1332 (*Devonshire Lay Subsidy*, pp 50, 110, 127 where John de Fenton's tax should be 40d. not 40s.).

[117] *Exeter Freemen*, p 9.

[118] MCR 1311/12, mm. 44–44d; 1313/14, m. 3d.

an Exeter merchant and skinner, only directly imported herring but purchased over £40 worth of Walter Launde of Winchelsea's cargo of 300 quarters of wheat and rye.[119] Nicholas either retailed much of this grain himself, or sold it to inland merchants who marketed it to others. Exeter merchants further deepened their involvement in maritime commerce by participating in the export trade. Hides, cloth, and a small amounts of wool were exported by Exeter merchants, all of whom also engaged in the import trade.[120]

About one quarter of the importers came from coastal settlements in Teignmouth, the Exe estuary, and Sidmouth. Teignmouth importers such as John de Bovy, Gilbert in the Combe, and William Ralle were particularly active, focusing largely on wine imports. Few importers came from inland locations, in contrast to the later middle ages when importers from inland towns in east Devon and Somerset were more prominent.[121] Three Taunton merchants imported goods at Exeter during this period, concentrating on the importation of woad, a blue dye used in the cloth industry.[122] Importers from elsewhere in England came almost exclusively from port towns. Most resided in Dorset, Hampshire, or Yarmouth, but some came from Cornwall, London, Winchelsea and other places. At least five importers resided in Southampton, including one of the town's wealthier burgesses, Henry de Lym, whose agent in Exeter, Peter de Exebrigg, improperly claimed Henry's custom-free status when selling his own imports of woad, potash, and corn.[123] Yarmouth importers, not surprisingly, brought mostly herring to Exeter. The Londoners included Adam Burgoynge (who also imported wine to London), William Fratre (importer of a wide range of goods at Exeter), and William Trente, alderman and king's butler.[124]

Foreign importers were not often identified as such in the Exeter accounts, although surname evidence and information recorded in the mayor's court rolls and the national customs accounts provide more definitive information on their origins. The most active foreign importers at Exeter came from Picardy, Normandy, and Gascony. Foremost among them was Peter le Monier of Amiens who imported 65 cargoes in 30 different ships between 1302 and 1321. Dyestuffs (woad, weld and potash) dominated his cargoes, although in the famine years of 1317–21 he imported large amounts of corn. He was responsible for the single largest grain cargo to medieval Exeter: 1023

---

[119] Below, p 193; MCR 1320/1, m. 26d.

[120] PRO E122 as listed above, n. 113. Cloth exports by denizens were not recorded in these accounts, but the many dyestuff imports and debt cases (MCR passim) referring to cloth sales point to the importance of this trade among Exeter merchants.

[121] Kowaleski, *Local Markets and Regional Trade*, chapter 6; E. M. Carus-Wilson, *The Expansion of Exeter at the Close of the Middle Ages*, Exeter, 1963.

[122] Philip Chepman, Robert Russel, and Nicholas le Webbe.

[123] MCR 1300/1, m. 2d; Colin Platt, *Medieval Southampton: The Port and Trading Community, A.D. 1000–1600*, London, 1973, pp 73, 248–9.

[124] Gwyn A. Williams, *Medieval London from Commune to Capital*, London, 1970, pp 119–20, 146, 154.

quarters of corn, peas and barley in 1320.[125] John and Thomas Petit of Amiens (who was John's son and the nephew of Peter le Monier) often acted as his agents in Exeter, marketing woad to local dyers and conducting business with tanners who probably sold Peter some of the hides he exported.[126] The Petits themselves also exported hides and imported woad, weld, and corn to Exeter. From Rouen came Adam and John Sage who employed Thomas Fartheyn, one of the most influential officeholders in Exeter, as their attorney in commercial debt suits tried in the borough court.[127] Gascon merchants imported wine, usually in far larger consignments than most importers handled. Bernard Andru of Bordeaux, for example, imported almost 90 tuns in two cargoes only seven months apart, while William Dyne regularly shipped wine to Exeter, including 69 tuns in 1316/17.[128] In return, these foreign merchants exported cloth, hides, tin and wool from Exeter.[129]

Besides casting light upon place of residence, the customs accounts also occasionally state the occupation of importers or point to their clerical status. Servants of wealthy merchants (who probably acted as the travelling commercial agents of their masters) at times imported goods in their own names, as did men described as a baker, carpenter, cutler, mercer, sarger, soaper, tailor, and taverner.[130] The clerics included well-off canons of Exeter Cathedral, such as Robert de Veteri Terra (Oldland) and the treasurer, Thomas de Henton.[131] The bishops of Exeter and Bath and Wells, and the archdeacons of Exeter and Wells also imported goods, as did the rector and chaplain of Thorverton (near Exeter). Most of the clerics restricted their imports to wine with the exception of the prior of Otterton who brought in one ton of salt, the vicar of Kenton who imported spurs, and Master Nicholas de Fovyle of Rouen who imported what appears to be Caen stone. Female importers were rare, numbering only fifteen in 1302–21. Most were widows or wives of wealthy male importers in Exeter or Topsham; Alice daughter of Gilbert atte Combe of Teignmouth was one of the few exceptions. Most if not all of these women were substituting for male relatives when they were recorded as importers, either because their husbands had died or were away on business.[132]

[125] Below, p 69. He also occasionally imported onions. He may have been related to the Peter le Monier of Amiens who had settled in Wells by 1340; see A. J. Scrase, 'A French Merchant in Fourteenth-Century Wells', *Somerset Archaeology and Natural History*, cxxxiii (1989), pp 131–40.

[126] MCR 1312/13, m. 4d; 1314/15, m. 44d; PRO E 122/40/7 for this and the following.

[127] MCR 1311/12, mm. 44–44d. Fartheyn was a royal custom collector (Robert L. Baker, *The English Customs Service, 1307–1343*, Philadelphia, 1961, p 66) and regularly served as a city steward (MCR elections) but only occasionally imported goods.

[128] Below, pp 173, 175 for Andru. For Dyne, see also PCA 1323/4 and PRO E 122/40/7A, 7B.

[129] PRO E 122 as in n. 113, above.

[130] For example, see below, pp 72–3, 77, 100, 104, 113, 140, 143, 196.

[131] John Le Neve, *Fasti Ecclesiae Anglicanae, 1300–1541*, vol. ix, *Exeter Diocese*, ed. Joyce M. Horn, London, 1964, pp 10, 22, 24.

[132] They are listed in the Index under women. Exeter importers who travelled abroad for business included William Brewer (MCR 1309/10, m. 32d); Walter Fraunceis (*CPR 1281–92*, pp 201, 211), Henry de Rixthivele (MCR 1299/1300, m. 4); Michael Thoraud (MCR 1301/2, m. 37d), and Thomas de Tettebourne (MCR 1317/18, m. 19d)

THE IMPORTS

Most of the goods arriving at the port of Exeter probably came via coastal routes. In the late fourteenth century when direct comparisions can be made between coastal and overseas trade, only 30 per cent of the vessels docking at the port employed direct overseas routes; most of these were wine ships from Bordeaux or smaller ships from the Channel Islands and Brittany.[133] By coastal routes came both native English goods such as fish (especially herring), coal, and corn, or foreign goods transshipped from re-export centres like Southampton. The large number of Hampshire ships recorded at Exeter indicates how often foreign goods were freighted first to Southampton, then re-loaded onto coastal craft for shipment to Exeter and other English ports. Dartmouth and Plymouth served a similar role (especially in the late fourteenth century) since they, like Southampton, had better harbours and more valuable exports (such as tin) to lure vessels directly from continental ports.[134] In the last two decades of the fourteenth century, 90 per cent of the valuable trade in foreign dyestuffs, linen cloth, canvas, garlic, onions, and spices arrived by coast from such re-distribution centers. Even wine, the import most likely to arrive directly from overseas, was frequently freighted first to ports like Southampton before being shipped by coast to Exeter.

Wine dominated the list of commodities arriving at the port of Exeter, accounting for about 53 per cent of the imports in 1302–21 (see Table 2). Annual imports averaged 964 tuns in this period, but ranged from 1557 tuns in 1305/6 to only 691 tuns ten years later.[135] Exeter merchants owned at least half of these cargoes and at least 56 per cent of the tunnage.[136] By purchasing and then reselling the wine cargoes of non-resident importers like Philip Rurde of Dartmouth or Robert le Lumbard of Gascony, Exeter merchants further extended their share of this important commerce.[137] Their role as middlemen brought them substantial profits when they marketed wine to other merchants and taverners in the hinterland (such as Elias William of Cadeleigh) and in Exeter, on occasion taking advantage of their better access to bulk supplies to cheat their customers.[138] Many of the most prominent Exeter wine importers employed their own taverners to retail wine on terms favourable to the importer.[139] Indeed, the grip

---

[133] For this and the following, see Kowaleski, *Local Markets and Regional Trade*, chapter 6, esp. table 6.1.

[134] For canvas transshipped from Plymouth to Exeter, see below, p 77.

[135] These figures do not include the imports of 1303/4 when the account covering September-May is missing. They do include the 724 tuns imported in 1320/1 when part of the account is also missing.

[136] In the surviving accounts of 1302–21, 10,924 tuns of wine were imported of which at least 6374 tuns were owned by Exeter residents.

[137] MCR 1287/8, m. 4d; 1288/9, m. 33d; 1289/90, m. 9d.

[138] For example, MCR 1302/3, m. 7; 1304/5, m. 12; 1306/7, m. 20; see also Kowaleski, *Local Markets and Merchants*, chapter 6 for other examples.

[139] MCR 1291/2, m. 4d; 1296/7, m. 31; 1300/1, m. 23. This arrangment seems to have died out by the second half of the century.

TABLE 2: COMMODITIES IMPORTED AT EXETER, 1302–21

Import	No. of Imports	Total of Imports	% of Total
WINE		1858	53.0
FOODSTUFFS		841	24.0
Fish (Herring=245)	258		
Grain	223		
Onions	97		
Salt	79		
Garlic	70		
Almonds	35		
Spices	33		
Figs, raisins, fruit	15		
Bacons, livestock	8		
Lard, grease	8		
Other	15		
DYESTUFFS & CLOTH INDUSTRY		354	10.1
Woad	152		
Potash	75		
Weld	71		
Alum	33		
Archil	9		
Other	14		
RAW MATERIALS		236	6.7
Iron	145		
Coal/charcoal	16		
Lead, copper, tin, steel	13		
Rosin, pitch, tar	15		
Wax	12		
Hides, skins, leather	24		
Building stone, glass, wood	8		
Other	3		
MANUFACTURED GOODS		217	6.2
Canvas	72		
Linen cloth	25		
Other cloth & mercery	48		
Clothing & domestic linens	13		
Domestic utensils	25		
Spurs, horseshoes	15		
Millstones, mortars	6		
Other	13		
TOTAL		3506	100.0

Source: PCA 1302/3–1320/1. Commodities imported by partners are only counted once. The figures reflect only the number of times a commodity was imported, not its volume or value.

of rich Exeter merchants on this valuable trade was partly responsible for the complaints in 1320 about excessively high wine prices in Exeter and other towns in Devon and Cornwall.[140] The greater familiarity of Exeter importers with the local market could also work to the disadvantage of foreign importers. In 1319/20, for instance, Robert le Carpenter of Bordeaux accused Richard le Seler of Exeter and Bernard Andru of Bordeaux of holding back some of the wine of his kinsman Bruni le Carpenter for so long that its value decreased significantly.[141]

Other foodstuffs made up 24 per cent of the imports in 1302–21; herring accounted for about one-third of these goods, followed by grain, onions and garlic, salt, and "luxury" items such as almonds, dried fruit, and spices (Table 2). Salt imported at Exeter probably came mostly from Brittany and the Bay of Biscay, although salt from Normandy is mentioned once and English sources also provided some of this essential commodity.[142] Most of the onions and garlic originated in Brittany (and some from Normandy), as did anise, vetches and the one cargo of butter. From the Channel Islands came fish (especially mackerel), bacon, oxen, and eggs. Mediterranean products included dried fruit (figs, raisins), nuts, oil, rice, spices (cumin, liquorice, pepper, saffron) and sugar.

The accounts printed in the present volume are particularly valuable for the light they cast on the importation of grain during the "Great Famine" that affected England (and most of Europe) in 1315–22.[143] Rainy weather and other problems during this period severely reduced the amount of grain harvested, leading to widespread shortages and very high prices. No grain was imported at Exeter in 1315/16, but 341 quarters came in the following year and the astronomical amount of 11,783 quarters arrived in 1319/20.[144] Since this quantity was far more than Exeter itself could consume in a year, much of the grain must have been sent to locations in the hinterland. Most of the imported grain was wheat. At least half (and probably more) came from the continent, particularly northern France, but some, imported by men from Chichester, Winchelsea,

[140] *Rotuli parliamentorum ut et petitiones et placita in parliamento*, 6 vols., London, 1783, i, p 375.

[141] Below, pp 68–9.

[142] For example, the salt arriving on a ship from Lutton (below, p 000), a Lincolnshire coastal settlement that produced salt in this period (H. E. Hallam, 'Saltmaking in the Lincolnshire Fenland during the Middle Ages', *Reports and Papers of the Lincolnshire Architectural and Archaeological Society*, new series, viii (1960), pp 87, 98–9; I am grateful to Derek Keene for pointing out this reference).

[143] Ian Kershaw, 'The Great Famine and Agrarian Crisis in England 1315–22', *Past and Present*, lix (1973), reprinted in *Peasants, Knights and Heretics: Studies in Medieval English Social History*, ed. R. H. Hilton, Cambridge, 1976, pp 85–132; Henry S. Lucas, 'The Great European Famine of 1315, 1316, and 1317', *Speculum*, v (1930), pp 343–77.

[144] For this and the following, see Maryanne Kowaleski, 'The Grain Trade in Fourteenth-Century Exeter', in *The Salt of Common Life: Essays Presented to J. Ambrose Raftis*, ed. Edwin B. DeWindt, Kalamazoo MI, forthcoming.

Sandwich, and Norfolk, also arrived from eastern England.[145] Exeter merchants played an important role in this trade as owners of at least 26 per cent of grain cargoes and 22 per cent of the grain by volume. As with wine imports, their role as purchasers and distributors of the grain imported by others gave them control over a much larger percentage of the trade than these figures indicate. Indeed, several times during the early fourteenth century customers vociferously complained that their unfair commercial practices led to excessively high prices for corn and other victuals.[146]

Dyestuffs comprised the third largest group of imports (Table 2). They included archil (a red or purple dye made from lichen), copperas (a dye and mordant made from iron sulphate), ochre (iron hydrate oxide that produced yellow to brown colors), weld (a plant yielding a yellow dye), and woad, as well as mordants like alum and potash.[147] Woad was the most valuable as well as the most common of these imports, accounting alone for almost one-half of dyestuffs arriving at Exeter in 1302–21. Produced from the leaves of a plant grown all over Europe, it could be permanently affixed to wool fibres without a mordant and could also serve as a base for other dyes to produce green, purple, black, brown, and other hues. Most woad imported to England at this time came from Picardy.[148] At Exeter, merchants of Amiens were especially prominent in this trade, including Bartholomew Bygge, Leonard (and probably John) de Cuntyf, Peter le Monier, John and Thomas Petit, John de Quarel, and John le Queynte, all of whom concentrated almost exclusively on the importation of woad.[149] The value of this trade at Exeter was recognized in the annual election of woad assayers (usually dyers) who measured and tested the quality of all imported woad in order to set its selling price. Although Exeter merchants as well as foreign and other English merchants had a say in this election, accusations of favouritism, false assessments, and outright fraud regularly cropped up.[150] Exeter merchants only accounted for about 20 per cent of woad importers in 1302–21, and their average cargo was generally less than that of foreign importers of woad, but the regulation of the trade in Exeter clearly promoted their acquisition of the supplies imported by foreigners. For example, the city forced woad importers who were not members of the freedom to offer their woad for sale to Exeter

[145] For these English imports, see also below, pp 51, 111, 129, 193–4; MCR Roll 1, m. 4 (1265); PCA 1322/3, 1332/3.

[146] *CFR 1307–19*, p 139; *CPR 1334–8*, p 445; *CPR 1338–40*, p 64; *CPR 1345–8*, p 320.

[147] Saffron could also be used to produce a yellow colour but it was probably more often employed as a spice at Exeter. Cork may also have been used as a dye.

[148] E.M. Carus-Wilson, 'La guède française en Angleterre: un grand commerce du moyen age', *Revue du nord*, xxxv (1953), pp 93–102.

[149] Bygge and Queynte were identified as from Amiens in the accounts (below, pp 101, 188). For the others, see MCR 1300/1, m. 28 (Cuntyf); 1305/6, m. 16d (Quarel); MCR 1314/15, m. 44d (Monier, the Petits). John Hangard (below, pp 172, 190; Carus–Wilson, 'La guède', p 99) was also from Picardy.

[150] MCR 1298/9, m. 33; 1319/20, m. 12d; 1328/9, m. 46d; 1334/5, m. 41d.

merchants for the first forty days before selling it to others.[151] Persons not in the freedom were expressly forbidden to participate in the trade in woad, weld, alum, and potash; as a result, the wealthier merchants and dyers of Exeter enjoyed the greatest profits from this trade.[152] The city also ordered that woad imports could only be sold in Exeter, heavily fining those found selling woad at Topsham or elsewhere.[153] Once in Exeter, woad could be carried out of the city for sale elsewhere, but it then was charged additional custom (although the woad importers from Taunton and Chard probably escaped this toll because of their customs exemptions).[154] All these regulations obviously favoured the Exeter merchant-middleman who could dominate sales to dyers and sell before his foreign competitors.

The city also attempted to place restrictions on the trade in weld, potash and alum but seems to have met with less success in this endeavour.[155] Weld and potash were handled by the same merchants who imported woad, although it is likely that much of the potash came from the Baltic area via Flanders.[156] Potash, called *cinerum* (ashes) in the accounts, was an alkaline substance prepared by leaching wood ashes. Used as a mordant to help fix dyes more permanently, it was imported in several forms: black, white, or mixed with some woad (which like potash could act as a mordant for other colours) or even weld. Alum, a mineral salt used as a mordant in dyeing as well as to taw or dress leather, was a Mediterranean import that probably reached Exeter from re-export centres like London and Southampton. Exeter merchants dominated this trade, accounting for over 73 per cent of alum importers in Exeter in 1302–21. Other imports related to cloth production were teasels (used to raise the nap of fabrics), Flemish clay (possibly used in the fulling process), yarn, and wool of Spain.

Iron was the raw material most often imported, comprising about 4 per cent of all imports at Exeter in 1302–21 (Table 2). At least some of this metal came from Spain. Lead, copper, tin and steel appear much less frequently. Other raw materials included coal, pitch, rosin, tar, and wax. Special types of leather (basan and cordwain) and imported furs (mostly rabbit and budge, lambskins imported from the Mediterranean) were relatively rare in this period compared to the later middle ages. Building materials (especially roofing slate and tiles) were also more common in the late fourteenth and fifteenth centuries. Their rarity in the earlier accounts reflects either their less frequent importation or their importation for immediate use rather

[151] MCR 1289/90, m. 19.

[152] MCR 1312/13, m. 7d; but see MCR 1310/11, m. 25d for the difficulty of enforcing this regulation.

[153] Below, p 47; MCR Roll 1, m. 2 (1265); 1285/6, mm. 9, 21; 1289/90, m. 10.

[154] Below, p 147; MCR Roll 1, m. 14d (1266). Philip Chepman and Nicholas le Webbe of Taunton, and John de la Hegh of Chard imported woad. For customs exemptions, see above, p 13.

[155] MCR 1312/13, m. 7d.

[156] T. H. Lloyd, *Alien Merchants in England in the High Middle Ages*, New York, 1982, pp 78–9.

than for resale. The fabric accounts of Exeter Cathedral, for example, note the arrival by sea of building stone from Beer, Salcombe, Purbeck, and Caen, as well as glass from Rouen, lead purchased at the Boston fair, and iron from Dartmouth, but because they were not saleable, their importation was not recorded in the customs accounts.[157] Yet the cathedral builders also bought such imported items as iron and lead at Topsham, and these purchases can sometimes be traced to specific cargoes.[158] At least one of the cargoes of Caen stone noted in the customs accounts may also have ended up in the hands of the cathedral builders.[159] The customs accounts also record two cargoes of glass, one imported by an Exeter merchant (William Brewer) and one by Adam Sage of Rouen. Timber and wood were imported by a merchant from Polruan (Cornwall), while plaster arrived on a Norman ship. The boards and nails imported by several Exe estuary shipmasters may have been intended largely as ballast although some of the imported boards were perhaps included among the "Irish and Welsh boards" occasionally purchased for the cathedral works.

Raw materials and manufactured items each accounted for about 6 per cent of the imported commodities (Table 2). As with building materials, manufactured goods were more common in the later middle ages when standards of living were higher and the South West was experiencing more economic growth. In the early fourteenth century, various types of cloth, especially canvas and linen cloth from Brittany, accounted for the bulk of imported manufactures. Items of clothing (hats, hose, caps) and domestic linens (tablecloths, tapets, towels, and quilts) only occasionally appear. Furnishings (chairs, chests, coffers, misericords), utensils (cooking-pots, cups, knives, lavers, pans, posnets, salt-cellars), and other domestic items (candles, lanterns, mirrors) were slightly more common; most were imported by Exeter merchants. Millstones, mortars, horseshoes, and spurs are also mentioned.

These imports offer valuable insights into the late thirteenth and early fourteenth-century economy of Exeter and its hinterland, especially when compared to what we know of imports in the late fourteenth and fifteenth centuries.[160] Dyestuffs in the early period were twice as prominent as they were in the late fourteenth century, although the later decline was due more to the interruption of continental supplies by the Hundred Years War than to any crisis in the local cloth industry. Woad continued to be imported, but in smaller

---

[157] *The Accounts of the Fabric of Exeter Cathedral, 1279–1353: Part I: 1279–1326*, ed. Audrey M. Erskine, DCRS, new series, xxiv (1981), passim.

[158] *Accounts of the Fabric*, pp 34, 42, 56, 77, 115, 117.

[159] The purchase of Caen stone at Topsham noted in *Accounts of the Fabric*, p 87 coincides with the importation of Caen stone by Gilbert Doo (below, p 149). Note also that the stone imported by Master Nicholas de Fovyle of Rouen was also probably Caen stone (below, p 163).

[160] For this and the following, see Kowaleski, *Local Markets and Regional Trade*, chapter 6; E. M. Carus-Wilson, *The Expansion of Exeter*.

amounts, and from Languedoc more often than from Picardy. Madder (a red dye) increasingly replaced woad as the most popular imported dye in the later middle ages. Devon cloth exports surged in the late middle ages, but consisted largely of russet and white (undyed) cloths. Cereal imports fell even more markedly than dyestuffs in the later period, a reflection of the more secure grain supplies available to a population reduced by both the Black Death and the recurrent epidemics of the following hundred years or more. Wine imports also dropped by about 2 per cent in the late fourteenth century, but this was a small decline when we consider how much smaller the population was after these demographic devastations. Indeed, rising standards of living in the later middle ages were reflected in the relatively stable, even rising level of imports of wine, canvas, linen cloth, fish, metals, and Mediterranean products such as honey, oil, and Spanish wine.

The impact of maritime trade on the fortunes of the city of Exeter can also be examined. In the earlier period Exeter merchants represented almost 20 per cent of importers, handled almost half of all cargoes, and owned 58 per cent of the wine tunnage. In contrast, during the late fourteenth century, they comprised only 8–10 per.cent of importers, handled but 29 per cent of the cargoes, and controlled about 44 per cent of the wine tunnage brought in. At first glance, it thus appears that Exeter merchants had by the late fourteenth century lost their previously firm grip on the port trade. Significantly, however, their share of the value of trade still hovered around a healthy 40 per cent while their control of the woad and iron trade grew. We should be wary, therefore, of assuming that these figures show an economic crisis in Exeter, especially in light of the evidence that Exeter prospered in the late middle ages when many other English towns were suffering decline.[161] The increasing presence of inland importers from Devon and Somerset in the later middle ages points to economic expansion in the hinterland, an expansion from which Exeter merchants clearly profited. As entrepreneurial middlemen in the networks that linked local, regional, and international trade, Exeter merchants were poised to take advantage of economic expansion in both inland and maritime commerce.

---

[161] On urban decline, see Alan Dyer, *Decline and Growth in English Towns 1400–1640*, London, 1991.

THE DOCUMENTS

Local port customs accounts survive for only a few English ports in the middle ages.[162] Although the earliest extant accounts date from the thirteenth century, port customs were levied by local lords and towns on ships and their merchants from as early as the Anglo-Saxon period.[163] From the twelfth to the fourteenth centuries, many towns acquired these rights from the king as part of their grants of fee farm. Administered separately from the national customs system controlled by the king's exchequer, local port customs were also distinguished from the national system by the tolls they charged on coastal trade: a commerce ignored by the national customs accounts which recorded only overseas trade.[164] In ports like Exeter, where coastal trade comprised as much as 70 per cent of all shipping traffic, local customs accounts often supply a completely different picture of the local maritime economy than that furnished by the national customs accounts.[165]

The local customs accounts extant for medieval English ports vary widely in scope and form. Most towns taxed both incoming and outgoing traffic, although not all distinguished between imports and exports or even between coastal and overseas trade. Only a few (Southampton and Yarmouth) occasionally indicated the direction of trade in their accounts.[166] Most levied different rates on different commodities, and some also assessed other port-duties (such as anchorage and keelage on ships mooring at the port), shore-duties (such as cranage and wharfage charged for the use of a crane or wharf), or murage and pavage granted temporarily by the king. Of the few accounts which survive before 1300, only those of Exeter, Sandwich and Winchelsea provide many details about ships, importers, or their

---

[162] The surviving accounts are listed and discussed in Henry S. Cobb, 'Local Port Customs Accounts Prior to 1550', *Prisca Munimenta*, ed. Felicity Ranger, London, 1973, pp 153–210. Local accounts in print may be found in Gras, *Early English Customs*, pp 153–210 (Sandwich, Scarborough, Southampton, Yarmouth, Winchelsea); *The Port Books of Southampton, 1427–1430*, ed. P. Studer, Southampton Record Society, xv (1913); *The Local Port Book of Southampton of 1435–36*, ed. Brian Foster, Southampton Record Series, vii (1963); *The Local Port Book of Southampton for 1439–40*, ed. H. S. Cobb; *The Port Books of Southampton for the Reign of Edward IV (1469–81)*, ed. D. B. Quinn, 2 vols., Southampton Record Society, xxxvii and xxxviii (1937–8); H. Bush, *Bristol Town Duties*, Bristol, 1828, pp 17–25 (an account of 1437/8); *Chester Custom Accounts, 1301–1566*.

[163] Such customs were levied by right of prescription or by charter; for a history of local customs, see Cobb, 'Local Port Customs Accounts', and Gras, *Early English Customs*, esp. pp 21–37, 153–216. For an example of such customs in the Anglo-Saxon period, see above, n. 8.

[164] For descriptions of the national customs system in medieval England, see Gras, *Early English Customs*; and Wendy R. Childs, 'Introduction', *The Customs Accounts of Hull 1453–1490*, Yorkshire Archaeological Society Record Series, cxliv (1986), pp xi–xxix.

[165] This figure is derived from a comparison of the trade enumerated in the particular accounts of the national customs and that in the local customs of Exeter for roughly five years from 1383 to 1411; see Kowaleski, *Local Markets and Regional Trade in Medieval Exeter*, table 6.1.

[166] Cobb, 'Local Customs Accounts', p 228, n. 135.

cargoes.[167] With the notable exception of the Exeter accounts, all surviving local customs records also suffer from two distinct limitations:
there are many gaps in their series, and merchants and cargoes
exempt from town customs were rarely recorded.[168] Thus one of the
fuller series of extant local accounts, those of the port of
Southampton, begin only in 1426 and survive for fewer than twenty
years of the fifteenth century.[169] The customs exemptions enjoyed by
the burgesses of Southampton and other privileged towns, moreover,
means that their local accounts omit much of the denizen (i.e.,
English) trade.[170] Indeed, this practice of excluding exempt merchants and cargoes is probably the biggest drawback to the use of
local port customs accounts.

   The local port customs accounts of Exeter are distinguished from
other local accounts by their early date, high rate of survival, and
comprehensive record of all incoming (but not outgoing) ships that
unloaded goods in the Exe estuary. Enrolled on the dorses of the
mayor's court rolls from as early as 1266, they were recorded on separate rolls by 1302/3 and survive for about 70 per cent of the years
between then and 1498. Several periods contain remarkably few gaps
(such as 1315–46 and 1381–1433). Unlike the accounts of other
towns, they list almost every ship's name, home port and master; the
importers, their custom status and custom owed; and the type and
quantities of all goods imported. Of special importance is the
accounts' enumeration of the importers and commodities that did not
owe custom. As a result, the local customs accounts of Exeter furnish
an unusually complete record of the import trade of a provincial port
in medieval England.

   Although Exeter had been collecting town customs at its port from
at least 1178,[171] the first specific references to the docking of ships at
the port of Exeter occur on the first extant mayor's court roll in 1266.
A court of record, the mayor's court met every Monday and handled a
wide variety of pleas; it also recorded the annual muncipal elections,
admissions of freemen, testaments relating to real property, the assize
of bread, and other items of borough business. Given the scope of the
court's interests, it is not surprising that the civic authorities chose to

---

[167] For the Sandwich accounts, see Gras, *Early English Customs*, pp 167–72, 203–7;
Cobb, 'Local Customs Accounts', pp 216–17. The Winchelsea accounts (PRO SC
6/1031/19–25) begin in 1266 and are the most complete series of thirteenth-century
accounts. None of these accounts, however, provide as many details as the Exeter
accounts.

[168] Besides Exeter, only the lone surviving account for Bristol (Bush, *Bristol Town
Duties*, pp 17–25) seems to have included custom-free merchants in the accounts.

[169] *Local Port Book of Southampton 1439–40*, p 111. The earlier accounts (1339–42) in
PRO E 122 137/8, 10–12; 193/10, are summary accounts that offer few details.

[170] The liability of all merchants at Southampton for cranage (paid on goods such as
wine and oil stored in tuns or pipes that had to be lifted with a crane) means that
denizen trade in these items were better covered by the accounts (Cobb, 'Introduction',
pp lxiii–lxvii).

[171] Above, n. 2; see also *CPR 1216–25*, p 248.

enter memoranda in its rolls regarding the landing of ships.[172] Three notes about ship arrivals were specifically labelled *memorandum*, three similar entries were recorded because of fines paid by merchants for unloading cargoes in the wrong place or without proper authorization, and one was noted in an inquisition concerning the sale of wine. The fact that all but 11 of the 99 entries recording specific ships were written on the dorses, usually at the bottom of the membrane, also points to the memoranda-like nature of these entries.

Our knowledge of the thirteenth-century maritime traffic at Exeter depends largely on the survival of these notes about ship arrivals recorded in mayor's court rolls. After the first court roll (which mostly contains courts dating from 1264 to 1266), no rolls are extant until 1285/6.[173] In the years following there were several entries about ship arrivals recorded in each surviving court roll until the start of Customs Roll 1 in 1302/3.[174] Thereafter the court-roll entries about ships largely disappear, with the exception of two memoranda in 1302/3, five entries in 1312/13, and two in 1319/20; three of these later entries were also inscribed on Customs Roll 1.[175] The form of the entry in the court rolls changed little over the years. Most start by noting the name of the ship, its home port, and the shipmaster before listing the individual importers, their imports, and notes about the custom and pledges. Most also give a summary of the cargo prior to listing the importers. Before 1300/1, the shipmaster was normally listed before the individual importers; thereafter his name usually appeared after the importers, the format followed throughout the accounts in Customs Roll 1. By 1287/8 almost all entries began with the phrase "Ship that is called [ship name] of [home port] docked at Topsham with ...", a formula also employed in the later customs accounts.

Only seven of the court-roll entries provide direct statements as to when the ship docked at the port.[176] For the remainder, the date of the court under which the entry was recorded offers the only evidence about the timing of the ship's arrival. But since the seven dated entries were all enrolled under courts which occurred within a few days of the date noted in the entry, there is good reason to believe that most ships actually arrived (or were customed) very close to the

---

[172] Other items of financial interest to the town were also sometimes placed on these rolls; see, for example, references to the receipt of various city revenues (MCR Roll 1, m. 17 (1266), 1308/9, m. 30d) and expenses (MCR 1290/1, mm. 16d, 24d). These types of items later appeared on the annual city accounts (CRA) which are extant from 1304, not far removed from the date of the first extant Customs Roll (1302).

[173] MCR Roll 1 contains courts from 1264/5 and 1265/6, as well as some from February–April 1271 and August–September 1307, along with one extract from June 1288. The next MCR (1285/6) contains courts from February–September 1286; thereafter all the mayor's court rolls cover one fiscal year running from Michaelmas to Michaelmas.

[174] No court rolls survive for 1291/2–1294/5.

[175] Below, pp 67–9.

[176] Below, pp 50, 65–9.

dates of the courts where they were first recorded.[177] The timing of seasonal cargoes also supports this supposition; large consignments of vintage wines were normally mentioned in courts dated between late October and December, herring in courts dated between November and February, and grain in courts dated between March and June. Presumably the purpose of the enrolment of the ship entries in the first place—to keep track of the incoming ships liable for custom— also caused ships to be recorded soon after they docked.

Although separate port customs rolls are extant only from 1302/3, they may have been kept even during the period when ship arrivals were regularly noted in the mayor's court rolls. One very interesting membrane from the court of 1287/8 suggests that separate accounts were maintained that early; membrane 20 begins with a formal heading similar to those inscribed at the tops of the annual accounts in Customs Roll 1. The wording (*Adhuc de navibus applic' apud Topsham anno 16*) and placement of the heading at the top of the membrane, along with the fact that both the heading and two entries were crossed through, all imply that the membrane was originally part of a separate account. Unlike most of the other court-roll entries, more-over, those inscribed on this membrane contained annotations about custom payments that were clearly added later, a characteristic also found in the annual accounts bound together in Customs Roll 1. The enrolment of the entries at the top of the membrane, and on its front rather than the dorse, was also unusual and provides further evidence that this particular membrane had once been intended to form part of a separate customs account.[178]

Other features of the court-roll entries about ship arrivals also imply that they served as memoranda for later enrolments in more formal port customs accounts. Scribes crossed through six of the entries, an action they may have taken after entering the information in the port customs accounts. In one of these cases, the clerk wrote in the margin "because elsewhere" in Latin, a clear indication that the ship arrival had been recorded somewhere else.[179] By beginning an entry with "memorandum" or scribbling entries on the bottom dorses, scribes were also acting as if their annotations were notes kept on the rolls of the city's chief written record in preparation for transfer to other documents. The weekly nature of the entries may also reflect a weekly accounting that we know was customary in other early local customs accounts (such as those of Sandwich, Southampton, Win-

---

[177] The courts occur (in the order they appear) 2 days earlier than the dated entry, the same day (two entries), 1 day earlier, 4 days earlier, and 1 day earlier; the entry in MCR 1319/20, m. 14d (below, p 68) is not relevant since it concerns an inquisition. Note also that the local accounts tended to record ships earlier than the national accounts (below, p 40), another indication that the local customers did their job fairly quickly.

[178] The heading's implied reference to previous entries is also in keeping with the May arrival date noted in the two entries that follow (below, p 48).

[179] Below, p 49.

chelsea, and Yarmouth).[180] A similar situation may have existed at Exeter where the weekly accounts both helped the clerk compile the annual accounts and functioned as a kind of check or counter roll to the information enrolled in the annual accounts.

The first surviving local port customs roll contains seventeen annual accounts from 1302/3 to 1326/7, twelve of which are printed here.[181] The 31 membranes in this roll were bound up together at a later date; several of the membranes are out of chronological order and at least one (containing the first part of the account for 1303/4) is missing altogether.[182] After 1326/7, accounts generally survive in individual rolls, one for each year, except for some periods in the late fourteenth and fifteenth centuries when accounts for several years were again bound up together.[183] Until 1305/6 there was a single account for each year; by 1310/11 two accounts were formulated for each year, one for wine and one for other types of merchandise. This annual division into two accounts was the norm until the 1380s when all customs were again recorded in one annual roll. The separation of wine from other imports reflected both the overwhelming importance of the wine trade (which in the late fourteenth century accounted for roughly 70 per cent of the total value of imports) and the claim by the earl of Devon to one-third of the wine custom.[184]

The widely varying size and condition of the membranes also indicate that they were bound up together at a later date. Although normally 19–23 cm in width, the membranes range in length from 30 to 87 cm.[185] Several membranes are in very good condition, but others are marred by tears and stains, particularly on the edges and bottoms.[186] Headings appear at the start of most of the accounts, but vary

[180] An early fourteenth-century ordinance at Southampton explicitly dictated weekly accountings of the port customs (Cobb, 'Introduction', *Local Port Book of Southampton*, p lv). See also Gras, *Early English Customs*, pp 172–3, 176–91 (Sandwich and Winchelsea); PRO SC 6/1031/19–25 (Winchelsea); BL Additional Charters 14,976–86 (Yarmouth).

[181] It was thought convenient to end the edition before the gap in the accounts that occurs in 1321/2; the accounts from 1322/3 to 1326/7 (not printed here) are enrolled on mm. 1–10.

[182] Below, p 80, for the missing membrane of 1303/4. The first part of the merchandise account for 1323/4 (m. 7) may also be missing since the account has no heading and the first entry is dated 11 December 1323. It is also likely that the second part of the wine account for 1324/5 (m. 5) is missing since the last entry is dated 1 December 1325 and the account contains no details of the spring (racked) wines; a comparison with the national port customs accounts of this date also supports this possibility (below, n. 214). Arguing against this possibility is the fact that the customs totals and one-third share given to the earl of Devon are noted at the bottom of m. 5, and that the totals match those in the surviving portion of the account.

[183] Many of the sixteenth-century accounts are in book form; see the detailed list of customs rolls in the DRO for more details.

[184] For the wine trade, see Kowaleski, *Local Markets and Regional Trade*, table 6.6. The earls' claims are discussed at greater length above, pp 1–7.

[185] The shortest are mm. 29–30, the longest m. 11.

[186] The membranes most affected by damage are mm. 30, 23, 17, 13, 12, 11, and 4; the bottom part of m. 12 (1320/1) is completely torn away (below, p 189).

greatly in their wording.[187] Some refer to customs of ships, others to customs of wines, and still others to customs of woad and other merchandise. The dating clauses in the headings also vary; most note a regnal year but only a few record the beginning or terminal dates of the account. The ends of the accounts differ as well; six of the twelve accounts finish with summaries of the amount of wine custom paid, along with the amount of custom delivered to the earl of Devon for his one-third portion.[188]

The accounts contain many emendations and later additions which indicate both the care taken by the clerks to compile accurate accounts and the running nature of the accounting process. The scribes often corrected individual forenames, surnames, commodities and their amounts by crossing out or expunctuating the old version and inserting the correction, usually interlineated.[189] Superscript annotations were often employed to indicate the custom status of importers, the amount they owed, and whether they had paid or not; many of these notes were clearly made later, an indication that the accounts were regularly updated.[190] Most of the membranes were written in two or three different hands; even those accounts composed largely in one hand were compiled not at one time, but over the space of several weeks or months, as indicated by changes in the ink, variations in spacing and format, and later marginal or superscript annotations. Several times the scribe left a blank space for the name of the home port, a surname, or the exact amount of a particular import as if he intended to go back and fill in these items later.[191] These features all suggest that the accounts were kept as a running record rather than written up at the same time. This practice probably reflected the customs collection system whereby the city's agents at the port handed over their rough notes regarding ship arrivals and customs to the city clerk, receiver, or other officials who compiled the accounts from these notes.[192] It also paralleled the weekly enrolments of customs entries on the earlier mayor's courts.

Like the mayor's court rolls, the local port customs accounts run from Michaelmas to Michaelmas. With the exception of five years (1302/3, 1304/5, 1305/6, 1310/11, and 1312/13) the vast majority of the entries gave the day, month, and year of arrival.[193] Even in these

---

[187] The account of 1303/4 (below, p 80) lacks a heading since the first membrane is missing. There is also no formal heading at the start of the merchandise account of 1310/11 (below, p 118) or the merchandise account of 1323/4 (Roll 1, m. 7).

[188] Below, pp 85, 99, 113, 118, 134, 158.

[189] These are all indicated in the footnotes of the text, below.

[190] Additions to the accounts clearly inserted at a later date are enclosed in curly brackets in the text. Interlineations are enclosed in round brackets.

[191] For example, a home port and surname on m. 21 (below, p 139), and a measure and amount on m. 15 (below, p 172).

[192] For the compilation of the fifteenth-century Southampton port books from rough returns, see Cobb, 'Introduction', *Local Port Book of Southampton*, pp lvii–lviii. For more on the collection of custom at Exeter, see above, pp 8–10.

[193] In the twelve years, 396 of the 551 entries are dated; of the 155 undated entries, 148 occur in these five years.

five years, the occasional dates offered allow us to discern at least the season and often the month particular ships arrived because the entries generally followed in strict chronological order. The few entries placed out of sequence in the dated accounts were usually awry by only a few days or weeks; those awry by several months were almost always placed by scribes in blank spaces near the bottom of membranes when they ran out of room elsewhere.[194] Occasionally clerks made mistakes in dating by putting in the wrong regnal year or noting arrivals "on the same day" of an entry they had forgotten to date.[195] In general, however, they carefully recorded dates of arrival, going so far as to cancel whole entries and remove them to another account if they had not been included in the correct accounting year.[196]

The form and content of each entry differ little from the earlier entries in the mayor's court rolls, although they are even more formulaic. Almost all entries commence with the phrase "Ship that is called [ship name] of [home port] docked". Some continue with "at Topsham" as in the entries in the mayor's courts, while others add "at Exmouth" instead; in the accounts, the two locations were used interchangeably to refer to the jurisdiction of the port of Exeter rather than discrete landing places.[197] The date of the entry came next, followed by a summary of the cargo (for large cargoes of wine and other goods)[198] and then lists of the individual importers and their imports. After enumerating the cargo, the scribe noted the shipmaster's name, followed by information about the customs if owed. This final section also recorded the names of the pledges and annotations regarding collection and receipt of the sums owed. Similar comments about the collection of customs were also entered in the left-hand margin, along with the name of the main cargo.[199]

Besides the standard information about ships and imports offered in each entry, the accounts also contain other types of annotations. Miscellaneous scribal scribbles or notes appear on some membranes, referring to such matters as custom collected on woad carried beyond the city gate, a pending trespass case, or money received by the city clerk for one term.[200] A second group of annotations comments on the accounts themselves. They mark off sections of the account dealing

---

[194] For example, the entry of 19 August 1304 placed at the bottom of m. 30 (below, p 82) should have come at the end of m. 30d but the scribe ran out of room and so wrote this entry in the blank space remaining at the bottom of m. 30. A similar situation occurred for the August entry noted at the bottom of m. 19 (below, p 151).

[195] Below, p 96 and 140.

[196] Below, p 85.

[197] See the sample account in Appendix 1 for the variations in phrasing. See also above, p 33.

[198] Such summaries do not always match the contents of the cargo, an indication of the faulty arithmetic of the scribes or customs collectors.

[199] Since the marginal notations often repeated information in the text of the account, they have here been included in the custom section of each entry. See also Appendix 1, below, for examples of the marginal notes in the account of 1310/11.

[200] See below, pp 107, 134, 147; for the city clerk, see also Appendix 2, pp 211-12, below. Another such scribble is the *Universis* written at the bottom of m. 11 (p 196, below).

with vintage or racked wines,[201] give directions to look on the other side of the membrane for the continuation of the account,[202] note the number of membranes in the account for a particular year,[203] refer to a certain cargo of a particular importer,[204] point to difficulties collecting customs from certain importers,[205] or record the number of tresses (a measure) in a horseload to help calculate the custom owed on a cargo of garlic.[206] A third group of annotations refers to the regnal year of particular accounts and were generally written at the bottom of membranes. One in 1304/5 was accompanied by the name of Robert Newton, that year's receiver (the chief financial officer of the city who was ultimately responsible for the collection and reporting of the port customs).[207] The two longest dating annotations appear together on a piece of parchment sewn onto the end of membrane 19d to serve as the cover to Customs Roll 1 when rolled up. Both were written in a later hand, one of the fifteenth century and the other probably of the sixteenth; these annotations show that the customs rolls were examined in later times.[208]

The fourth group of annotations were also written at a much later date and are particularly interesting for the hints they provide as to why these accounts were preserved for so many centuries. All refer to a search made of the customs accounts for importers from Taunton in order to discern whether they were free of custom in Exeter. Three consist only of a hand with a finger pointing to an entry noting an importer from Taunton; a fourth such hand occurs on the bottom of one membrane with the note that this mark indicates Taunton importers.[209] Two other accounts simply contain the word "scrutinized" near the start of the account; one of these also ends with the

---

[201] Below, pp 113, 116, 142, 156, 174.

[202] Below, p 145.

[203] Below, p 85.

[204] Below, p 145.

[205] Marks, perhaps meant to be a single pointing finger, were drawn both over the names of some importers and in the left-hand margins of the wine accounts of 1322/3–1326/7 (mm. 10–10d, 8, 5, 4, 2, not printed here). They probably referred to importers from Topsham or Newton Abbot who, as noted at the bottom of m. 5, were not paying custom, thereby decreasing the amount the city rendered to the earl of Devon for his share of the wine custom.

[206] Below, p 82. The sum of £2,470 17s noted in the account of 1304/5 (below, p 89) was too large to refer to the local customs (which in any case were never assessed by value of the goods). It probably pertains to the new custom administered by the national customs system starting in 1303; this valuation would have rendered a custom of about £31 at the going rate of 3d in the pound (Gras, *Early English Customs*, p 66). See also below, pp 39–43 for the relationship between the local and national customs accounts.

[207] Below, p 99; for the other such dating clauses, see below, pp 111, 121, 130, 147, 164. For the role of the receiver in the collection of port customs, see also below, Appendix 2.

[208] Below, p 152. Note also the "Customs" written at the bottom of m. 31d (below, p 80) which contains the earliest account in the roll.

[209] Below, pp 127–8, 130. Note also the memo on p 164 that simply states "Taunton" in the same late hand that wrote the other memoranda.

note "scrutinized and nothing found".[210] The hand of the annotations is much later than those that compiled the accounts; it probably dates from the fifteenth century, a time when Taunton merchants were complaining that they were unfairly being charged custom at Exeter.[211] Their complaints seem to have led to a legal suit which prompted the Exeter officials to search their old customs rolls for evidence; such suits and searches help to explain why the city kept its customs rolls for so long.

The local accounts of Exeter are fuller and considerably more accurate than the national port customs accounts, as a comparision of the two types of accounts illustrates. In the early fourteenth century, national port customs were only charged on certain goods: exports of wool, wool-fells and hides by both denizens and aliens, exports of certain goods like cloth and corn by aliens, and imports of wine and other merchandise by aliens. Since Exeter only kept track of imports and the royal customers only noted alien trade, comparisons must focus on alien imports and importers recorded in the two sets of accounts. The surviving national and local accounts for the port of Exeter overlap for only a few years during this period; they cover wine imports for two and one-half years from 5 March 1323 to 29 September 1325,[212] and other merchandise for slightly over three years from 3 February 1323 to 26 May 1326.[213]

All but three of the 54 alien importers noted in the national accounts can be located in the local port customs accounts; the three who are untraceable may have appeared in the two missing or torn

[210] Below, pp 80, 111, 135; a similar annotation appears at the top of PCA 1329/30 (wine account). An annotation in the margin of the account of 1322/3 (Roll 1, m. 9) regarding the liberty of Taunton may also have been written in the fifteenth century.

[211] Several Taunton residents wrote a petition, complaining about the unfair tolls they were charged at Exeter, to an unnamed bishop of Winchester who was also chancellor of England at the time; this probably refers to Henry de Beaufort c. 1413–17 (PRO C 1/6/329). Although Taunton was not specifically noted on the list of custom-free places kept by the city, its residents should have been free of custom by virtue of their status as tenants of the bishop of Winchester; see above, pp 13–14 for a discussion of toll exemptions at Exeter.

[212] The national accounts are in PRO E 122/40/7A/2 (5 March 1323–30 April 1324), E 122/40/7B/3 (30 April 1324–29 September 1324; printed in Gras, *Early English Customs*, pp 397–8), and E 122/40/7B/6 (27 November 1324–29 September 1325; printed in Gras, *Early English Customs*, p 398). The accounts do not cover the two-month period from 30 September–28 November 1324 (although they should have been included in Richard le Seler's account of E 122/40/7B/6), but they can otherwise be compared with the wine accounts in PCA 1322/3, 1323/4, 1324/5 (PCA Roll 1, mm. 5–10, not printed here). Note, however, that the second half of the local wine account of 1324/5 seems to be missing (above, n. 182 and below, n. 214).

[213] PRO E 122/40/7A/3 (3 February 1323 to 30 April 1324), E 122/40/7B/2 (30 April 1324 to 15 April 1325; printed in Gras, *Early English Customs*, p 395), and E 122/40/7B/4 (15 April 1325 to 26 May 1326; printed in Gras, *Early English Customs*, p 396). These accounts can be compared with PCA 1322/3, 1323/4, 1324/5 and 1325/6 (PCA Roll 1, mm. 3–10, not printed here).

sections of the local accounts.[214] Over half of the "arrival" dates of the alien cargoes in the national accounts match those given in the local accounts, but eleven are later (usually by a few days or weeks) and one is earlier.[215] The earlier dates noted in the local accounts suggest that the local customers (i.e., the customs officials) did their job more quickly than those assessing customs for the king. Similar discrepancies in the naming of cargoes also point to the greater efficiency of the local customers. Four of the fifteen wine cargos were underestimated in the national accounts,[216] and ten of the 35 merchandise cargos omitted commodities noted in the local accounts for these alien importers.[217] The national customs officials also had a tendency to conflate the cargoes of merchants who imported goods on several different ships in one year. For example, while the local customers carefully noted the three cargoes of corn imported by Astoricus de Sergynole on three ships that all docked at different times, the national customers listed Sergynole only once for a cargo of corn worth £176 (probably the aggregate value of all three grain shipments).[218]

The most compelling evidence of the relative accuracy of the local accounts, however, shows up in the large number of alien importers and their cargoes who were recorded in the local port customs, but escaped enumeration altogether in the national accounts. Many of

---

[214] Raymond Manent was charged custom for 10½ tuns of wine on 2 August 1325 (PRO E 122/40/7B/3); unfortunately, the wine account of PCA 1324/5 seems to be missing for the months of January–September 1325; see also above, notes 182 and 212, for the other inconsistencies in this particular E 122 account. An unnamed importer of 21½ tuns of wine on 23 September 1325 (PRO E 122/40/7B/6) would also have been on this missing portion of the account. Bertram de Campeneys was customed for woad worth £70 on 10 May 1326 (PRO E 122/7B/4); he may have been noted on a torn and illegible section of the wine account of PCA 1325/6 (PCA Roll 1, m. 4) which notes the arrival of several ships in May, at least one carrying woad (the *Nicholas* of Exmouth). See also below, n. 220, for another possible explanation of this missing cargo.

[215] The term used in the national accounts was *adduxit* while the local accounts employed *applicauit*; both refer to arrivals but probably relate to the day the ship and its contents were customed. In the one instance of an earlier "arrival" date in the national accounts, the local officials customed a cargo (PCA 1325/6) 23 days after it had been registered in PRO E 122/40/7B/4. In the eleven other cases, the dates in the local accounts were earlier by 3, 5, 6, 8, 14, 16, 17, 30, and 36 days, and twice by one year. In these last two instances (both in PRO E 122/40/7B/3), the day and month but not the year of arrival matched in both sets of accounts; it is probable that the customers noted the wrong regnal year, a likely occurrence in this mistake-ridden account which also notes smaller cargoes for two of the importers and includes one entry (for Raymond Manent on 2 August 1325) which cannot be traced in PCA 1324/5 (see above, n. 214).

[216] The discrepancies were of 1, 2, 10 and 20 tuns.

[217] These items were usually weld or linen cloth (both of which were subject to new custom); alum, bacons, spices, and canvas were other imports not recorded by the national customers but noted in the local accounts. Only once did the local accounts fail to name a commodity mentioned in the national accounts: garlic that accompanied a cargo of onions (that was noted). For custom on goods other than wine, the national accounts only named the commodity imported and its value so it is not possible to compare amounts as with the wine imports.

[218] PCA 1322/3 (Roll 1, m. 9); PRO E 122/40/7A/3. The royal customers probably grouped his imports together because the three ships arrived within days of each other and he was sole importer on all three ships.

these alien importers can be identified because they were customed elsewhere in the national accounts; thus the royal customers taxed Martin de Vermuwe (probably from Bermeo in Spain) for a cargo of fruit in 1326, but never noted his salt imports in 1323.[219] Similarly, they recorded two woad cargoes of Bertram de Campeneys in 1326, but failed to custom three other imports of woad under his name in 1324 and 1325.[220] The royal customers also omitted the 15 tuns of wine imported by Raymond de Vyngan of Bayonne, as well as the cargoes of many other importers whose surnames and trading activities make it likely that they were aliens rather than denizens.[221]

Many other examples of gaps in the national accounts could be given. Their omissions and inaccuracies may have been the result of fraud, collusion between collectors and merchants, or simply the neglect, inefficiency, and lack of supervision of the royal customs collectors.[222] The local men appointed to these unpaid offices (generally prominent citizens whose high positions in city government brought them to the attention of the king) had little to lose if their accounts were not particularly accurate.[223] Indeed, they had much to gain from temporarily using the money they collected for their own interests, charging special fees, accepting bribes to overlook customs owed, omitting their own customable cargoes from the accounts, and even committing embezzlement for their own profit. The three Exeter men who acted as royal customs collectors during this period were all wealthy members of the ruling oligarchy who served in the city's highest offices during the same years they were responsible for collecting royal custom at the port.[224] Thomas Fartheyn and Henry Lovecok served as royal customers for almost nine years, and Richard le Seler for two years, with no complaints lodged against them.[225]

---

[219] PRO E 122/40/7B/4; PCA 1322/3 (Roll 1, m. 9: salt imported on 22 June 1323).

[220] PRO E 122/40/7B/4; this account also contains a woad cargo belonging to Campeneys that could not be located in PCA 1325/6 (Roll 1, m. 4) for the reasons noted above, n. 214. It is possible that the national customers recorded an extra cargo of woad under his name to make up for all the cargoes they had missed in previous years; see PCA Roll 1, m. 7 (18 April 1324) and m. 6 (23 April 1325 and 12 May 1325). It is also possible that the customers conflated his various woad imports as they did for Astoricus de Sergynole (above, p 40).

[221] PCA 1324/5 (Roll 1, m. 5).

[222] Baker, *English Customs Service*, discusses these problems at length, although he concentrates primarily on the export accounts.

[223] Baker, *English Customs Service*, esp. pp 9–12, 20–23, 33. Before 1294, collectors were often appointed locally (Baker, *ibid*, p 7, n. 19); see MCR 1299/1300, m. 26 for the local appointment at Exeter of a searcher to supervise the traffic in money.

[224] PRO E 122/40/7A, 7B; Baker, *English Customs Service*, p 66. They were Thomas Fartheyn (elector 14 times, steward 8 times, receiver once, councillor once from 1307 to 1327), Henry Lovecok (elector 31 times, steward three times from 1304 to 1339), and Richard le Seler (elector 27 times, steward 4 times, councillor twice and mayor once between 1301 and 1343); see MCR election returns and below, Appendix 2. In 1332, Henry Lovecok paid 40d and Richard le Seler 10s in the lay subsidy (*Devonshire Lay Subsidy of 1332*, p 110).

[225] For the fraud of royal customers at Exeter later in the fourteenth century, see *CPR 1367–70*, p 52; PRO E 159/169 Easter recorda, m. 38 and E 159/171 Easter recorda, mm. 84–84d (failure to account for wool exports in 1391–2); E 159/171 Michaelmas communia, m. 1d (dispute on gauging wine in 1394).

Since they had limited personal involvement in maritime trade, they may have been more conscientious than their counterparts elsewhere who had more of a vested interest in the assessment of national customs.[226]

The local customs officials had better reasons to keep careful accounts. Their activities took place under the watchful eyes of fellow citizens who were ready to report inconsistencies or frauds that would decrease the amounts collected for the city. Indeed, the Exeter authorities were quick to fine any burgesses who infringed the city's privileges at the port, even if they were wealthy members of the city's ruling oligarchy.[227] The receiver, the civic officer ultimately responsible for reporting the sums collected from local customs, was also elected annually, thereby ensuring not only that he did not grow comfortable in office, but also that several men would be familiar with the duties attached to the post. The efforts taken by the city to secure customs jurisdiction over the whole Exe estuary also prompted extra vigilance on the part of local officials; indeed, given the control exercised by the city of Exeter over shipping along the entire length of the estuary, it is unlikely that many ships and cargoes escaped the notice of the authorities.[228]

The officials of the national customs system also seem to have recognized the greater accuracy of the local accounts, going so far as to check their own accounts against those compiled for the town customs. In the last part of the local wine account of 1322/3, for example, an X was placed over the names of alien wine importers, as if checking off their names and imports. These same importers were listed in the corresponding national account as well; the dates of arrival, ship names, home ports, importers, and tunnage match exactly, normally a very unusual occurrence.[229] Similar markings placed in the margin next to certain ships in the merchandise account of 1319/20 suggest the same practice, since they also accompanied

---

[226] In 1302–21, example, Fartheyn appeared once as an importer, Lovecok three times, and Seler five times. None of these men ever appeared in the extant national customs. Other local men appointed as royal customs collectors were, however, more actively involved in maritime trade; Walter de Langedon and Michael Toraud (*CFR, 1307–19*, pp 9, 78) are two examples. Toraud also served as city receiver (see below, Appendix 2).

[227] See, for example, the wealthy citizens assessed heavy fines for unloading wines at the wrong place in MCR 1288/9, m. 6d (below, p 49).

[228] Above, pp 1–7.

[229] These marks first appear in 24 April 1323 and go to the end of the account on 29 September 1323 (PCA Roll 1, m. 10); these dates correspond to those covered by the wine account in PRO E 122/40/7A/2 that starts 5 March 1323 and ends 30 April 1324. No such markings appear, however, in the wine account of 1323/4 (PCA Roll 1, m. 8) which covered the same period as this national account. It is also significant that the two alien wine shipments noted in this national account that appeared elsewhere (merchandise account of 1322/3 in PCA Roll 1, m. 9, and the wine account of 1323/4 on m. 8) were not marked with an X and were recorded as smaller shipments than noted in the local accounts.

entries about alien imports.[230] These marks on the local customs account clearly show that it was used to check the accuracy of the national account (or even to compile it in the first place). Other annotations in the local accounts, such as the customs valuation at the bottom of one membrane and the reference to a pledge for custom owed to the king, also show an overlap between the local and national customs systems.[231] Over 150 years later the national customs system again recognized the greater accuracy of the local customers at Exeter. In 1476, suspicious of the work of the royal customers in Devon, the royal exchequer ordered the city to send a copy of its local account to Westminster to allow them to use it as the controlment account (the account compiled by the controller to check the accuracy of the collectors' account) for that year.[232] This use of the local accounts by the royal customs system, like the searches conducted to find evidence for legal disputes, also helps to explain why the Exeter local port customs accounts were for so long retained by the city. The local accounts of Exeter thus not only provide unusual information about the coasting and overseas trade, but also detail this trade with unusual accuracy.

TRANSLATION AND EDITING PRACTICE

The translated accounts that follow are divided into two parts that correspond to the two types of sources recording the entries of ships. The first (pp 47–69) includes memoranda of ships unloading cargoes that were enrolled on the dorses of the Exeter mayor's court rolls. Because the ship entries recorded in these memoranda are usually short and laconic and because the style of enrolment was still evolving, the translation offered here aims to convey the format and wording of the originals as much as possible. Entries containing long lists of importers, however, are recorded in tabular form for easier comprehension. Since the entries were often scribbled at the bottom of the membrane and rarely noted when the ship had docked, the date of the court under which the entry was enrolled offers us the only clue as to when the ship arrived at the port.

---

[230] Five entries in the local account ranging in date from 25 February 1320 to 23 August 1320 contain an X in the left-hand margin; see below, pp 182–3, 185–6. Within this period, however, there were also alien importers who had no such mark near their entry; see, for example, the Caen importer on p 184. Unfortunately, no national account survives for this year so the correspondence between the two accounts cannot be checked. An X was also placed next to an entry in the wine account of 1318/19 (below, p 164) but the importers on this ship seem to include no aliens; the X may have been meant to draw attention to the unpaid custom noted there.

[231] For the valuation, see below, p 89 (and above, n. 206). For the pledge who stood for both local custom and "the new custom of the lord king if it ought to be rendered", see below, p 77. Both references came shortly after the new (and more complicated) custom of 1303 was introduced, which may account for the unusual intrusion of the national customs system into the local accounts.

[232] Izacke, *Remarkable Antiquities*, p 89.

The second part (pp 71–20) includes twelve extant accounts dated from 1302/3 to 1320/1 that appear in Roll 1 of the Exeter local port customs accounts. By this time the style of entry was established and the information offered was generally quite full, although arrival dates were still not always stated. From 1310/11, the accounts themselves were usually divided into two separate sections: one for wine and the other for woad and other merchandise. Because the entries had become so stereotyped, they are translated here into a tabular form that preserves the order of the entry, with two exceptions. First, the name of the shipmaster is given after the ship's name, whereas in the original it normally came after all the importers and their cargoes had been listed. The other exception concerns the custom section which here includes information drawn both from the very end of the entry (which usually offers the names of the pledges for the custom) and from the left-hand margin (which normally contains the amount of custom). No attempt has been made to distinguish marginal from textual annotations concerning custom pledges or amounts, in part because they often repeat the same information on the amount of customs and its collection. The membranes are also rearranged so that the entries appear, as much as possible, in chronological order, with the wine account preceding the merchandise account.

The following principles have been followed in editing both sets of accounts. *Names* of ships are preserved in the original Latin and italicized in the text. Some of their standardized equivalents may be found in the Index. The type of ship and the definite article preceding the ship's name are in lower case but the ship's name is capitalized. All places and forenames are anglicized and modernized, but surnames are left in their original spellings and unidentified or now lost places are italicized and spelt as they appear in the Latin original. The definite articles contained in some surnames are all given here in lower case. Forenames abbreviated by one letter have been left as they appear in the original, but the extended form of surnames ending in an apostrophe has been supplied when the spelling is known from other entries.

Numerals in the original appear as Roman but are here rendered in Arabic. Except for the halfpenny ($\frac{1}{2}$d) and farthing ($\frac{1}{4}$d), all sums of money are translated as they appear in the text. *Dates* in the translation are supplied in modern form, except for those stated in the headings to the individual accounts. Fiscal years are noted with a slash separating the two years (e.g., 1302/3); the city accounts and court rolls usually run from Michaelmas to Michaelmas.

Punctuation in the originals is very inconsistent and often lacking altogether. While some attempt has been made to preserve the spirit of the punctuation in the early mayor's court roll entries, punctuation is kept to a minimum in the translation of Roll 1 in favour of a more accessible tabular format.

Erasures and emendations to the text (such as words crossed out) are indicated in the footnotes, as are underlined words. Empty square brackets ([ ]) indicate places where the scribe deliberately left a black space in the manuscript.

Later additions to the text, normally written in another hand than that which wrote the original entry, are enclosed in curly brackets. It is unlikely, however, that all such additions have been identified since later insertions in the hand of the clerk who wrote the original entry are difficult to spot unless obviously written in a different ink. See below, Appendix 2, for a discussion of these additions.

Interlineations and superscript annotations are enclosed within round brackets and placed as close as possible to where they appear in the text. Those that were clearly inserted at a later date are enclosed in curly brackets.

Illegible or missing words are designated by three stops (...). When the transcription of a word is uncertain because of a stain or tear in the manuscript, a question mark enclosed in round brackets (?) follows the word. When the translation is uncertain, a question mark has been added at the end of the relevant translation and the Latin passage enclosed in square brackets.

Editorial insertions and extensions are enclosed in square brackets. Difficult or interesting words and passages are given in the original Latin, italicized, and enclosed within square brackets after the English translation.

Weights and measures have all been translated except for those with no known English equivalent. The C and M are used here to mean either the hundredweight and thousandweight, or the hundred and thousand by tale for commodities which are not expressed in any other measure; the original wording has been provided for ambiguous cases. Appendix 3, below, provides a glossary of weights and measures.

TEXT OF THE ACCOUNTS: I

LOCAL PORT CUSTOMS ENROLLED ON THE MAYOR'S COURT ROLLS (MCR), 1266–1320

MCR 49–50 HENRY III[1]

MCR 1265/6, m. 12d [court dated 3 February 1266]

Henry de Plimpton and Peter Clericus of Dartmouth [are] in mercy because they unloaded [*fecerunt Gywyndiare*] their wines at *Colepole* and Topsham without licence. Pledge, Thomas de Crandon'. In mercy, 4s.

MCR 1265/6, m. 13d [court dated 15 March 1266]

In *la Waygneben* of Pratteshide [are] 65 tuns and 1 pipe [wine]. Robert Eadmund [is] shipmaster.

In *la Alna* of Torre [are] 48 tuns [wine]. Robert Rolf [is] shipmaster.
  John de Fenton: 10 tuns
  Elias Palmerus [and] Herbert Piscator: 24 tuns of which 3 tuns [held] until [custom] paid [*unde iii dol' donec s'*][2] {paid}
  Pruz of Teignmouth [*de Teyngnemwe*]: 5 tuns
  Richard Mugge: 2 tuns, owes [custom],[3] Elias Palmerus, pledge [for the custom] {paid}
  Richard Schilling': 1 tun
  John Gascun and Richard Schilling': 6 tuns

MCR 1265/6, m. 18d [court dated 13 September 1266]

Peter le Rus is in mercy because he sold and unloaded woad [*weedam*] at Topsham [before being customed]. Geoffrey Frenel is in mercy for the same.

MCR 13–14 EDWARD I

MCR 1285/6, m. 26d [court dated 4 March 1286]

Walter Maynhere seeks a licence to unload corn from his ship and he has to make no custom? [*et ht' null' fac' cust'*].

---

[1] MCR Roll 1 binds together courts from 1264/5, 1265/6, Feb.–Apr. 1271, four membranes from Aug.–Sept. 1307, and one membrane from June 1288. All the other MCR contain the courts for one year, from Michaelmas to Michaelmas.
[2] *Of which 3 tuns [held] until [custom] paid* crossed through, probably to indicate that his account was settled.
[3] *Richard Mugge: 2 tuns, owes* crossed through, probably to indicate that his account was settled.

MCR 1285/6, m. 25 [court dated 9 September 1286]

Robert le Clergel of Genêts [*Genez*] in Normandy docked at Topsham with a certain *Buzard* loaded with garlic and onions; and he has licence to unload.

MCR 15–16 EDWARD I

MCR 1287/8, m. 20: [ACCOUNT] THUS FAR OF SHIPS DOCKED AT TOPSHAM UP TO NOW IN THE 16TH YEAR[4] [court dated 3 May 1288]

Ship that is called *Nostre Dame* of Dartmouth docked at Topsham with 82 tuns of wine and one pipe on which freight not paid. From which:
    William Buffet: 15 tuns
    Henry de Triccote: 9 tuns
    William de Wyk: 9 tuns
    Geoffrey de la Rythevele: 6 tuns
    Philip Rurde of Dartmouth: 20 tuns
    Robert, servant of the same Philip: 1 tun
    Walter Gayllard: 14 tuns of which 2 tuns for portage
    Simon Aubyn: 3 tuns of which 1 tun for portage
    Henry Rurde: 3 tuns of which 1 for portage
    Bartholomew Ahysling: 1 tun for portage
    Nicholas Gaylard: 1 tun for portage.
Master [is] Walter Gaylard. And the mainpernors for paying the custom are Henry de Triccote and Geoffrey de la Ryxthevele. Sum of custom, 5s 8d. {(Paid into the pyx by view of R. Alein.)}

Ship that is called *halop de Seynt Servan* docked at Topsham with wheat, barley and rye. And it is known that the granary is of canvas which owes custom [*Et sciend quod granar' est de canab' quod debet custum*];[5] mainpernor of custom [is] John Pitman.

MCR 1287/8, m. 43d [court dated 20 September 1288]

Ship that is called *la halop de Seynt Nicholas* docked at Topsham with garlic of which [there are] 2025 [*xx^c trac' & xxv trac'*] tresses; and the shipmaster is Ralph Manglynn. And the mainpernor for paying the custom is Ralph le Taverner.[6]

---

[4] This heading and the two entries that follow were written at the top of the membrane and then crossed through.

[5] Granaries aboard ship could be made of or covered with canvas; see *Calendar of Liberate Rolls, 1240–45*, London, 1931, p 185. I am grateful to Derek Keene for this reference.

[6] The entire entry is crossed through.

MCR 16–17 EDWARD I

MCR 1288/9, m. 6d [court dated 8 November 1288]

Unloaded [*Wynd'*] wines at *Colepole* against the ordinance[7] (statute) of the city; and [let there be] an inquisition if they bring a plea.

20s	—William de Buffet: 2 tuns
½ mark	—Roger Beyvin le Wheten: 1 tun
1 mark	—Henry de Triccote: 2 tuns
40s	—Vimanus Wille: 4 tuns
	—William de Gatepath[8]
	—Ralph de la Stapp'

MCR 1288/9, m. 33d [court dated 30 May 1289]

Ship that is called *la Barbere* of Port-en-Bessin [*Port*] docked at Topsham. Shipmaster [is] William de Port. From which:

William de la Hethe has 3 tuns woad, 16 C iron and 1 fardel of canvas

Drogo de Reins' has 12 pipes potash, 2 C and 1 quarter iron, customed

John de Smalecomb has 1 tun potash, 2 C iron, 1 C candles [*cand'*]

Mainpernor for paying the custom [is] William de la Heth.[9]

Ship that is called *la Godyer* of Exmouth docked at Topsham. The shipmaster [is] David le Rede. From which:

Walter le Cotyler has 1 tun woad, 1 sack potash

Ralph Frenel has 7 C iron, customed, and 3 tuns woad

William Cork has 7 C iron and 2 chests [*cist'*] (and 1 barrel glass [*verr'*]); he also has ½ C canvas, 1 dozen knives [*cnipul'*].

And all the rest belongs to John Soth.

Mainpernor for custom [is] Ralph le Freyns' skinner. Also W. de Carswill has 1 barrel oil.[10]

MCR 1288/9, m. 50d [court dated 12 September 1289]

Ship that is called *Nostre Dame* of Exmouth docked at Topsham; the shipmaster [is] Richard Bilbe of Exmouth. From which [there are] 5 frails and 25 M onions, 8 seams of garlic. Also wool [*Woll'*]. Also 5 tuns full of teasels [*card'*] which belong to Jordan de Venell' except for one tun of teasels. And the aforesaid goods belong to Alany le Cat. Also William Burel has 5 quarters of wheat. Mainpernor for paying his custom [is] Jordan de Venella.[11]

---

[7] *Ordinance* [*provisus*] is crossed through and *statute* is written above. This entire phrase appears on the right-hand side of the following column of names and fines.

[8] This name and the next have been crossed through.

[9] The entire entry is crossed through.

[10] The entire entry is crossed through.

[11] The whole entry is crossed through with *because elsewhere* [*quia alibi*] written in the margin, probably an indication that the entry was also enrolled in another document.

MCR 18–19 EDWARD I

MCR 1290/1, m. 44d [court dated 3 September 1291]

Memorandum that a boat of Plymouth docked at Topsham (on the Saturday after the Decollation of Saint John [1 September 1291]) with 9 tuns of wine which belong to John Reyner...[12]

MCR 23–24 EDWARD I

MCR 1295/6, m. 7d [court dated 14 November 1295]

Ship that is called *le Bayard* of Exmouth docked at Topsham with 4 lasts [of herring] of which 1 of *coripechon* [herring].[13] And the shipmaster is Nicholas Sele. And David le Rede of Exmouth has 3 lasts [of herring]; 1 last of *corpechon* [herring] [belongs to] John Hastolf, burgess of Yarmouth; of which the bailiff will have 1 C [herring for custom].

Ship that is called *le Bonan* of Teignmouth docked at Topsham with 6 lasts and 3 M of herring; from which:
   William de Smalecomb has 2 lasts 3 M
   John de Smalecomb: 2 lasts 2 M
   Philip Lovecok and Roger Lovecok: [1 last 5 M].
And the mainpernor for the custom [is] W. de Carswill.[14] {Quit.}

MCR 1295/6, m. 10d [court dated 5 December 1295][15]

Ship that is called *Nicholas* of the Isle of Wight docked at Topsham with 6 (lasts) 1 M of herring. And the shipmaster is Geoffrey de Insula. From which:
   John de Smalecombe has 4 (lasts) 1 M
   William de Smalecombe has 2 (lasts)
   The shipmaster has 2 M, of which the bailiff has 1 C herring [for custom]. John de Smalecombe [is] pledge [for the custom].

MCR 1295/6, m. 21d [court dated 5 March 1296]

Ship that is called *Seynt Nicholas* of Yarmouth of Dunwich [*de Hernemouth de Dumnewyc*][16] docked at Topsham with corn, viz., wheat and barley, and 1½ M of iron, [and] onions and garlic. And these are the goods of Philip Lovecok. [Custom] free.

---

[12] The last line of the entry is missing because the bottom portion of this membrane has been cut off.

[13] Herring that has been either gutted (with the head cut off, as in *corpion*, *OED*) or cured (from the Anglo-Norman *coriage*). If the latter, these herrings would be what are now termed kippers or bloaters: see also below, p 179.

[14] This sentence was actually inserted on the first line in the blank space that followed *Ship that is called le Bonan.*

[15] Unlike other entries, the one following was written upside down at the top of the membrane.

[16] The scribe may have forgotten to cross out *Yarmouth* after writing in *Dunwich*.

MCR 1295/6, m. 23d [court dated 2 April 1296]

Ship that is called *le Godher* of Sidmouth docked at Topsham with coal [*carbonibus*].[17] And the shipmaster is Ralph le Sangere. And he has licence to unload.

MCR 1295/6, m. 24d [court dated 9 April 1296]

Ship that is called *la Katheryne* of Guernsey docked at Topsham with 14 quarters of barley. And the shipmaster is William Harrepyn. And he has licence to unload.

Ship called *la Godebyyeate* of Lymington docked at Topsham with 21 quarters of wheat, 66 quarters of barley, 5 quarters of beans, 4 M of iron, 5 barrels of woad. And the shipmaster is Nicholas le Sout' and these are the chattels of Walter Tabernar' of Sandwich and John Syzok(?).

MCR 1295/6, m. 25d [court dated 16 April 1296]

Ship that is called *la Seynte Marie* of Romney docked at Topsham with black beans viz., 100 quarters. And the shipmaster is William Aryecanne. And he has licence to unload.

Ship that is called *le Seynt Michel* of Guernsey docked at Topsham with barley of an unknown number of quarters. It has licence to unload and the shipmaster is Nicholas le Corner.

Ship that is called *la Beatriche* of Sandwich docked at Topsham with 126 quarters of[18] beans [and] with 6 seams of wheat. And the shipmaster is Richard Beyane. He has licence to unload.

MCR 1295/6, m. 27d [court dated 30 April 1296]

Ship that is called *la Katheryne* of Guernsey docked at Topsham with 15 quarters of corn, viz., barley.

Ship that is called *Seint Marie* of Romney docked at Topsham with 30 quarters of wheat, 30 quarters of barley. And the shipmaster is John Coleman.

Ship that is called the boat [*le batel*] of Brixham docked at Topsham with 11½ quarters of wheat and 13½ quarters of barley.

MCR 1295/6, m. 31d [court dated 4 June 1296]

Ship that is called *Hamelin* of Exmouth docked at Topsham with 5 tuns of wine of which Roger atta Crosse has one half and John le Sangere the other half. And the shipmaster is the aforesaid Roger atta Crosse. And he pays 10d for custom on [his] one half because John le Sangere does not have to pay because [he is] in the liberty of Winchelsea. Paid all.

---

[17] Although this has been translated as *coal* throughout, it could also refer to charcoal.
[18] *Corn* is expunged and *beans* written in next.

Ship that is called *le Messeger* of Southampton docked at Topsham with 6 dozen frails of figs and 40 quarters of salt. And the shipmaster is Matthew le Cornwaleyes.

MCR 1295/6, m. 33d [court dated 18 June 1296]

Ship that is called *le Bon An* of Plymouth docked at Topsham with 12 tuns of wine. And the shipmaster is Henry Sampson. And the aforesaid wine belongs to said Henry and to William Boffet and J. Austin.

Ship that is called *la Blite* of Southampton docked at Topsham with 50 quarters of salt. And the shipmaster is Richard le Rede.

MCR 1295/6, m. 34 [court dated 25 June 1296]

Ship that is called *le Thomas* of Dartmouth docked at Topsham with 15 tuns of wine of which 2 [tuns] of William le Cotyler and John[19] de Smalecombe. And 13 tuns of Robert de Chalthewille. And the shipmaster is the same Robert. Custom, 4s 4d.

Ship that is called *la Fryse* of Bayonne docked at Topsham with (200 quarters) of salt. And the shipmaster is John de Artigelond.

MCR 1295/6, m. 42d [court dated 20 August 1296]

Ship that is called *la Seinte Croys* of Southampton docked at Topsham with salt, potash[20] 12 pipes and (1) tun woad. And the shipmaster is William de Insula. And the aforesaid goods belong to Peter de Lyouns.

MCR 1295/6 m. 43d [court dated 27 August 1296]

Ship that is called *la Godher* of Exmouth docked at Topsham with 50 quarters of white salt. And the shipmaster is David le Red and he has 1 C of iron on which he is customed 1d, [put] into the pyx.

MCR 24–25 EDWARD I

MCR 1296/7, m. 12 [court dated 10 December 1296]

Ship that is called *le Godher* of Exmouth docked at Topsham with 9 lasts [herring]. And the shipmaster is Walter Syde; from which:
John le Perour has 3 lasts
Richard Montein: 2 lasts
W. Carswill: 1 last
David le Rede of Pratteshide: 3 lasts
And the aforesaid David found security of 1 C herring. William de Carswill afterwards paid 6d for the herring.

---

[19] *Ph'* crossed through and *John* written next.
[20] It is unclear whether the *12 pipes* refers to the potash or the woad.

MCR 1296/7, m. 12d [court dated 10 December 1296]

Ship that is called *la Jowanete* of Teignmouth docked at Topsham with 4 lasts of herring. And the shipmaster is Richard le Rede. From which:
Nicholas Page has 3 M
John Innedehaye: 3 M
Thomas de Colepel: 4 M
William Boffet: 8 M
John le Saltere: 4 M
William de Smalecomb and John, his brother have 1 last
Thomas Codelep: 2 M
Nicholas le Skynnere: 1 last

Ship that is called *Jacob* of Teignmouth docked at Topsham. And the shipmaster is Henry Keych. And the ship has 30 lasts of herring of which:
William de Smalecombe has 5½ lasts
Stephen, his servant: 1 last
John de Smalecomb: 7 lasts and 1 M
Joan la Cotiller: 5 M
Philip Lovecok: 6 lasts
Alice Lovecok: 2 lasts
Richard le Skynnere: 1 last
Nicholas le Skynnere: 2 lasts
William Cork: 1½ lasts
William Kerdewill: ½ last[21]
John le Saltere: 3 lasts

MCR 1296/7, m. 39d [court dated 15 July 1297]

Ship that is called *la Alice* of Weymouth docked at Topsham [with] 20 quintals [*quinteaus*] of iron. And the mainpernor for the cargo is Vimanus Wille. And the shipmaster is Ralph Cole.

Ship that is called *Sancti Johannis* docked at Topsham with salt and 16 quintals [*quinteaus*] of iron (and 12 ox hides). And the shipmaster is John Luverig of Teignmouth. And the said iron belongs to Thomas de la Porche, and John Luverig has 2 quintals [*quinteaus*] of almonds. And for the custom on the iron (and almonds) Thomas de la Porch paid 9d into the pyx. All [paid].

MCR 25–26 EDWARD I

MCR 1297/8: m. 13d [court dated 7 April 1298]

Ship that is called *la cogge Sainte Marie* of Teignmouth docked at Topsham with 150 tuns and 2 pipes [of wine]. And the shipmaster is Thomas de la Borne. From which:
Walter Fraunceys: 18 tuns
William Cocus: 10 tuns
John le Perour: 25[22] tuns (2 pipes with) Botilston

---

[21] *1 last* crossed through and ½ last written in.
[22] *4* crossed through and the *5* in *25* inserted above.

Richard Mountein: 22 tuns
Goze, his servant: 6 tuns
Joel de Duk: 2 tuns
Philip Horn and Stephen de Boniham: 41 tuns 1 pipe
Peter atta Borne: 13 tuns wine
Paye Prouz of[23] Kenton: 8 tuns (of which Philip Rurde: 6 tuns)
Thomas atta Borne: 3 tuns, customed
Richard le Mareschall: 1 tun for portage
John Prust: 1 tun for portage.

Ship that is called *la Sawe* of Topsham docked at Topsham with 46 tuns of wine. And the shipmaster is Richard Wayte. From which:
Robert de Wodelegh: 14 tuns
Michael Toraud: 6 tuns
Walter le Teyngterer: 7 tuns
Robert de Hirlaunde: 8 tuns
William Saundr': 1 tun
H. de la Rixthivele: 1 tun
Geoffrey atta Rixthivele: 6 tuns
William de Smalecomb: 1 tun
Osbert le Sarger: 1 tun
William Arcediaken: 1 tun.
Quit [of custom] because in the freedom.

MCR 1297/8, m. 14d [court dated 21 April 1298]

Ship that is called *le Bongayn* of Plymouth docked at Topsham with 30 tuns of wine and 1 pipe. And the shipmaster is Richard Bod. Of which:
Richard le Skynnere [and] Matthew Peleter: 13 tuns and 1 pipe
John Saltere: 9 tuns 1 pipe
The shipmaster: 6 tuns 2 pipes.
And for the custom, Mathew Pellipar'. And 6 tuns are customed.
{Quit because of the Cinque Ports}.[24]

MCR 1297/8, m. 17 [court dated 12 May 1298]

Ship that is called[25] docked at Topsham with 5 tuns woad. And the shipmaster is Phelipe de Quatre Mars.

MCR 1297/8, m. 19d [court dated 9 June 1298]

Ship that is called *la Seinte Cruz* of Portsmouth docked at Topsham with 134 tuns of wine and 3 pipes of which:
Poncius de Quynto: 102 tuns 3 pipes of which 3 tuns [were lost] by
    leakage [*de Corizoun*]

---

[23] *Ty* crossed through.
[24] *6 tuns customed* also written in the left-hand margin but is crossed through with this later note written above it.
[25] The scribe left no space for the ship's name.

John Horsham: 32 tuns wine.
And the shipmaster is William Salwy of Portsmouth. And Robert de
Nymeton is for the custom. And 102 tuns of wine are customed.

MCR 1297/8, m. 21d [court dated 16 June 1298]

Ship that is called *la Jowanete* of Exmouth docked at Topsham with 12
tuns of wine and 1 pipe. And the aforesaid tuns belong to William
Brit. [Custom] free.

MCR 1297/8, m. 22d [court dated 23 June 1298]

Ship that is called *la Sauve* of Exmouth docked at Topsham with 46
tuns of wine... And the shipmaster is Richard Wayte. Of which:
  John Soth has 10 tuns
  Robert de Hirlaund: 10 tuns
  ... de Doune: 4 tuns
  Philip Lovecok: 2 tuns
  Henry Tricot': 1 tun
  G. de la Rixthivele: 5 tuns
  Henry, his brother: 1 tun
  W. Saundr': 1 tun
  Richard le Ercedyaken and W... his servant(?): 8 tuns
  Walter Gyrard: 3 tuns
  John Perour: 1 tun.[26]

MCR 1297/8, m. 24d [court dated 7 July 1298]

Ship that is called *la coge Seint Thomas* of Teignmouth docked at
Topsham with 68 tuns [wine] of which:
  Richard Stalon (shipmaster) has 2 tuns for portage
  Nicholas Bosse: 1 tun 3 pipes
  Master R. de Veteriterra: 3 tuns 2 pipes
  Master R. de Combe: 3 tuns
  H. de Bokerel: 4 tuns
  John Gerveys: 1 tun
  Walter Scote: 2 tuns
  John de Voleton: 5 tuns
  Peter de la Born: 5 tuns 1 pipe
  Ralph le Teyngterer: 3 tuns
  G. de Rixthivele: 2[27] tuns
  John Trapil: 7 tuns, customed
  R. Ercediaken: 4 tuns
  Thomas Chaille: 2 tuns
  John de Smal': 2 tuns
  Richard Longus: 2 tuns
  Arnulph Payn: 3 tuns, 1 for portage and 1 customed

[26] The right side of the membrane, which contains the end of this entry and the note
on custom, has been torn away.
[27] *1* crossed through and the *2* written above.

G. le Botor: 3 tuns
Osger de Kenton: 1 tun for portage
R. Gosse: 2 tuns
Benedict Morel: 1 tun for portage
Walter Dollyng: 1 tun for portage
Thomas Longus: 3 tuns, customed, 1 for portage
Lambard: 2 tuns, 1 for portage
William Was: 1 tun, customed.

And for the custom are N. Bosse and the shipmaster.

Ship that is called *la Alne* of Teignmouth docked at Topsham with 118 tuns [wine]. And the shipmaster is Richard Mortemer. From which:

William de Gathepath has 12 tuns
Ralph Lovet: 10 tuns
Michael Aurifaber: 24 tuns
Walter le Teyngterer: 3 tuns
Philip Lovecok: 5 tuns
William Cotiller: 4 tuns
William Steymour: 29 tuns
Hugh Osberntus of Topsham: 11 tuns
Stephen Steymour: 1 tun for portage
Walter de Molend: 1 tun for portage
William Bolle: 1 tun for portage
Parys Edmund: 1 tun for portage
Richard Edmund: 1 tun for portage
Richard Crawe: 3 tuns of which 1 for portage
Robert de Torre: 4 tuns of which 1 for portage
William de Forin: 1 tun for portage
Richard de Mortymer: 7 tuns of which 2 tuns for portage
Robert Slegh: 1 tun for portage.

And for the custom is William Steymour.

MCR 1297/8, m. 29d [court dated 18 August 1298]

Ship that is called *le Bon Gaug* of Plymouth docked at Topsham with 35 tuns ... pipes [wine]. And the shipmaster is Richard Uppehill. From which:

Philip Lovecok: ...
... Boffet: 2 tuns
William le Keu: 9 tuns
John ...
... le Saltere: 11 tuns 1 pipe
Robert ...
... for portage.

And ... 4d custom.[28]

[28] The right side of this entry has been torn away.

MCR 1297/8, m. 30d [court dated 25 August 1298]

Ship that is called *Sawe* of Dartmouth docked at Topsham with 55 tuns 2 pipes [wine]. And the shipmaster is Robert Wayte. From which:

Philip Rurde: 34 [tuns] 2 pipes
John Rurde: 8 tuns
Robert Hurteby of Dartmouth: 5 tuns, customed
Terry Bel of Dartmouth: 4 tuns [and] 4 tuns for portage.

And for the custom is P. Rurde; paid [to] N. Page per William Buffet.

MCR 1297/8, m. 32d [court dated 15 September 1298]

Ship that is called *le halop de Sancto Nicholao* docked with 14 C of anise [*de Ans*]. And the shipmaster is John de Lomemay. And for the custom is Ralph de Venella and William Pytteman.

MCR 26–27 EDWARD I

MCR 1298/9, m. 1d [court dated 13 October 1298]

Ship that is called *la Seinte Croys* of Lyme docked at Topsham with salt. And the shipmaster is William Godring. No custom.

MCR 1298/9, m. 4d [court dated 3 November 1298]

Ship that is called *la gogge Seint Thomas* of Dartmouth docked at Topsham with 42 tuns of wine and 8 pipes of wine. And the aforesaid wines, viz., 40 tuns 7 pipes, belong to ({Philip Rurde}). And the shipmaster [has] 1 tun and 1 pipe. Thomas who was with Nicholas Page [has] 1 tun [*Thom' q' sunt cum Nich'o Page i dol'*].[29]

Ship called *la Sawe* of Dartmouth docked at Topsham with 69 [tuns] and 2 pipes [wine]. And the shipmaster is Robert Wayte. From which:

Philip Rurde: 21 tuns and 1 pipe
John Rurde: 4 tuns
Thomas, servant of N. Page: 4 tuns
John de Galmeton: 20 tuns 1 pipe
Terri Bel: 14 tuns of which 1 for portage
Robert Wayte [ship]master: 2 tuns for portage
Edward Terri: 1 tun for portage
John Andru: 1 tun for portage
Luke de la Yockele: 1 tun for portage
Ralph Rurde: 1 tun for portage.

And for the custom is Robert Wayte and Robert de Nymeton. And the sum is 11s 4d.

---

[29] This is probably the same Thomas noted as the servant of Nicholas Page in the following entry.

MCR 1298/9, m. 6d [court dated 17 November 1298]

Ship that is called *la Nicholas* of Exmouth docked at Topsham with 14 tuns 2 pipes [wine]. And the shipmaster is Walter de Hilfridecomb. And the aforesaid belong to:

    William de Carswill: 3 tuns
    John Innethaye: 3 tuns
    Robert de Hirlaunde: 4 tuns
    Henry de la Rixthivele: 4 tuns 2 pipes.

No custom. Free.

Ship that is called *le Godyer* of Exmouth docked at Topsham with 9 lasts of herring; of which the shipmaster [is] Harlewin Bolt. From which:

    Ralph de Neweton the mercer: 3 lasts
    William de Smalecumb: 3 lasts
    The child [*puer*] of Roger Lovecok: 2 lasts
    Philip Lovekoc: 1 last.

W. Lovecok responds for the custom of the child.

Ship that is called *le Bayard* of Exmouth docked at Topsham with 12 lasts (3 M) [herring]. And the shipmaster is Nicholas Sele. From which:

    Walter le Cotiller: 1 last
    Reginald atta Porch: 10 M
    Henry le Skynnere: 3 lasts
    John Horn: 1 last
    Nicholas Pellipar': 2 lasts
    William Carswill: 1½ lasts
    Matthew Coffin: 1½ lasts
    Henry Tricoth: 1 last
    William Steymour: 2 M
    Matthew Pellipar': 2 M
    The shipmaster: 1 M.

Free [of custom].

Ship that is called *le Bonan* of Exmouth docked at Topsham with 28 tuns 3 pipes [wine]. And the shipmaster is David le Rede. From which:

    John Bosse: 2 tuns
    Nicholas Bosse: 6 tuns
    Ralph Lovet: 2 tuns
    Hugh Osbern: 10 tuns 1 pipe
    William Steymour: 3 tuns 1 pipe
    David le Rede: 3 tuns of which 2 for portage
    Richard Bilbe: 1 tun for portage
    Blaunchard le Hopere: 1 tun, for portage 1 pipe.

And for the custom is, if they ought to pay, William Steymour.

MCR 1298/9, m. 9d [court dated 15 December 1298]

Ship that is called *la Rith'vele*[30] of Topsham with 3 tuns of wine and 1 pipe. And the shipmaster is Richard Wayte. From which:
    Hugh de Toppesham: 2 tuns 1 pipe
    William Pellipar' of Dartmouth:[31] 1 tun, customed.
And for the custom on 1 tun is Hugh and Richard Wayte. William Cork [has] 1 ton of barley? [*Ord...*]. Custom, 4d.

Ship that is called *Seint Julyan* of Guernsey docked at Topsham with 300 tresses of garlic (and 500 tresses onions). And the shipmaster is Richard de Gardin. And 1 seam canvas. From which:
    Simon de la Stane: 2 parts of the garlic and onions
    The shipmaster: the 3rd part
    Peter Viger: 1 (seam) canvas
    Peter Denly brings 50 pounds of onion seed.
And for the custom are Ralph Tabernar and William Piteman. Free [of custom].

MCR 1298/9, m. 17d [court dated 16 March 1299]

Ship that is called *le halop Seint Nicholas* of Le Vivier [*Wyver*] docked at Topsham with 1400 tresses of anise (and 25 of onions)[32] [*xiiii*[c] *des anys (et xxv cep' tracis)*]. And the master is Gillame Porcher. And the aforesaid goods belong to Gillame Gere. And for the custom is Ralph de Venell' {paid 2s 11d, quit}.

Ship that is called *Nostre Dame* of Le Vivier [*Whithier*] docked at Topsham with 1000 tresses of anise [*anys*] and 200 tresses of onions. And the aforesaid goods belong to Robert de Lyvet. And for the custom, Ralph de Venella {paid, quit}. {All paid, 2s 2d.}

MCR 1298/9, m. 23d [court dated 4 May 1299]

Ship that is called *la Blide* of Exmouth docked at Topsham with 80 tuns of wine and (1 tun) 5 pipes. And the shipmaster is Thomas Chaille. Of which:
    Philip Lovecok: 20 tuns 2 pipes
    Henry de Tricote: 3 tuns
    William Steymour: 3 tuns
    John le Perour: 2 tuns
    John Horn: 2 tuns
    William Boffet: 1 tun
    John Rurde: 1 tun
    Philip Horn [and] William Cocus: 11 tuns of wine and 1 pipe
    John Petibon: 1 tun (paid 4d custom)
    Robert de Nymeton: 12 tuns
    Nicholas le Saltere: 9 tuns

[30] This ship was probably named after the Rixthivele family who were active importers at this time.
[31] There is a blank space here.
[32] *And 25 onions* crossed through and *tresses* written in next.

Stephen de Smalecomb: 3 tuns
Philip Steymour: 1 tun, customed (paid 4d into the pyx)
Philip Rurde: 1 tun
Walter le Cotiller: 1 tun
Ralph Lovet: 1 tun
Elias Horlok: 1 tun for portage and 1 pipe
Robert de Wynchilesee: 1 pipe (paid 4d [to] Page)
The shipmaster: 2 tuns
John de Pouderham: (2)[33] tuns, customed
William Hardyng: 1 tun for portage
Geoffrey le Butor: 1 tun
Walter Fraunceys: 1 tun
John Smalecomb: 1 tun.

And 2 tuns are customed. And for the custom is Thomas Chaille.

Ship that is called *le Bon An* of Sidmouth docked at Topsham with 46 tuns (5)[34] pipes [wine]. Whence the shipmaster [is] Ralph le Sanggere. Of which:

Nicholas Bosse: 13 tuns 3 pipes
Robert atta Wodeleg': 7 tuns 1 pipe
Henry de Tricoth: 3 tuns
John Baron and[35] (Ralph le) Sanggere: 10 tuns, customed of
    which 2 for portage
William Portreve of Lyme: 7 tuns
Thomas atta Borne: 1 tun
The Prior of Otterton: 1 tun
William Frere: 1 [tun] for portage
Roger Sanggere: (2) tuns (of which) 1 for portage
Jordan Vairlond: 1 tun for portage
John Cocus: 1 pipe for portage.

And 10 tuns are customed. And Henry de Tricote is for the custom. And 7 [tuns] are in dispute because they are in the freedom of Lyme, as it is said [*Et vii sunt in calupn' q' sunt in libertate de Lym ut dr'*].

Ship that is called *la Sawe* of Exmouth docked at Topsham with 46 tuns [wine]. And the shipmaster is Richard Hobel. From which:

Thomas, who was the servant of N. Page: 8 tuns
Nicholas Page: 2 tuns
Richard le Ercediaken: 4 tuns
Geoffrey atta Rixthivele: 2 tuns
Robert de Hirlaunde: 6 tuns
Walter le Teyngterer: 3 tuns
Robert de Doune: 2 tuns
John le Perour: 5 tuns
Henry de Tricote: 4 tuns
William Steymour: 2 tuns

---

[33] *1* crossed through and the *2* written above.
[34] *3* crossed through and the *5* written above.
[35] *John Baron* written in again and underlined, with *Ralph le* written above.

Henry atta Rixthivele: 4 tuns
Roger Barri of Bridport: 4 tuns.
And 4 tuns are customed; and H. de Rixthivele is for the custom.

MCR 1298/9, m. 25d [court dated 1 June 1299]

Ship that is called *Seint Nicholas* of Le Vivier [*Verver*] docked at Topsham with 1100 tresses of anise [*Anys*]. And for the custom is William Pytman and Adam Motoun.

Ship that is called *Sancti Johannis* docked at Topsham with 18 tuns woad. And [with] the aforesaid are 4 bales of alum, 2 C of archil, 4 C iron, 5 dozen knives. And [for] the custom is Richard le Noreys.

MCR 1298/9, m. 26d [court dated 15 June 1299]

Boat that is called *Wynnegod* of Teignmouth docked at Topsham with salt. And the shipmaster is John Grigor'. And the aforesaid salt belongs to John Innedehay and Robert ...cent'.[36]

MCR 1298/9, m. 27d [court dated 22 June 1299]

Ship that is called *la Blide* of Plymouth docked at Topsham with 42 tuns of wine (1 pipe). And the shipmaster is Richard Bod. And the aforesaid wines belong to Girard de Vilers, and Richard Bod [has] 2 tuns for portage. And for the custom of the aforesaid is Peter Stoyt(?). And 40 tuns and 1 pipe of wine are customable [*custumabl'*].

MCR 1298/9, m. 28d [court dated 29 June 1299]

Ship that is called *la cogge Sancti Spiritus* of Bayonne docked at Topsham, of which the shipmaster is Garsins Arnulph, with 70 M of iron and 2 M almonds, 1 M[37] of wax, 4 M[38] of cumin [*comyn*], 15 C of liquorice, 4 bales of wool yarn weighing 6 C [*fill' lanut' pond' vi^c*]. Also 9 rolls of cloth for veils [*ix rote de tele pro velis*]; Cosinet, a certain mariner of the ship, 4½ M of iron.[39]

Ship that is called *la Sawe* of Exmouth docked at Topsham with 46 tuns 1 pipe of wine. And the shipmaster is Richard Hobel. Of which:
Philip Lovecok: 18 tuns
William Cocus: 6 tuns
John Petibon: 1 tun, customed
William Steymour: 6 tuns
Henry Tricote: 4 tuns

[36] The manuscript is torn here.
[37] *10 C* crossed through before *1 M*.
[38] *30 sacks* crossed through before *4 M*.
[39] It is unclear whether Cosinet was the importer of the previous goods or just the 4½ M of iron.

Robert de Herlond: 4 tuns
Henry de la Rixthivele: 4 tuns 1 pipe
Geoffrey de la Rixthivele: 2 tuns
Walter le …: … tuns.[40]
And customed are 1 tun [ ] 4 tuns; 4d paid [to] Carswill.

MCR 1298/9, m. 31d [court dated 20 July 1299]

Ship that is called *Sawecors* of Barfleur docked at Topsham with …,[41] plaster [*implaustrum*], pitch? [*pis*]. And the aforesaid goods belong to … .

MCR 1298/9, m. 32d [court dated 27 July 1299]

Ship that is called *la Nichollas* of Sidmouth docked at Topsham with 400 quarters salt; and the shipmaster is Nicholas Blone.

Ship that is called *le Bonan* of Sidmouth docked at Topsham with 47 tuns 5 pipes [wine]. And the shipmaster is Roger le Sangere. Of which:
John Baron: 2 tuns
Bertrand le Gascoyn: 1 tun
… le Sangere: 3 tuns (1 pipe), customed and 2 tuns for portage
Nicholas le Saltere: 10 tuns 1 pipe
…urde: 9 tuns
Richard Ercediaken: 4 tuns and 1 pipe
Henry Tricote: 3 tuns
… Lovecoc: 2 tuns
John de Smalecomb: 2 tuns
Nicholas Page: 3 tuns
Thomas Gathcoche: 5 tuns 2 pipes
Robert de Hirlaunde: 1 tun.
And 5 tuns are customed, and for [the custom] is Henry de Tricote.[42]

MCR 1298/9, m. 35d [court dated 24 August 1299]

Ship that is called *Sancti Spirit* of Dartmouth docked at Topsham with salt. And the shipmaster is Bartholomew Aslyng.

MCR 27–28 EDWARD I

MCR 1299/1300, m. 1d [court dated 5 October 1299]

Ship that is called *Juenette* of Exmouth docked at Topsham with 8 tuns of woad, 1 tun of potash, 2 bales of alum, 1 C wax, 1 C rice [*rys*], 600 C of iron, 3 C of canvas; and no one owes custom; and the shipmaster is William le Bryt. And the said chattels belong to John, Michael Toraud, William Conk' and Richard Caperoun.[43]

---

[40] The manuscript is torn here.
[41] The manuscript is torn here (cutting off about four to six words) and at the end of the entry.
[42] Parts of the right and left sides of the manuscript are torn away.
[43] From *potash* to the end, the words of this entry are underlined. The bottom part of this entry was sewn onto the cover of the roll and is now separated from m. 1.

MCR 1299/1300, m. 5d [court dated 2 November 1299]

Ship that is called *le Bonan* of Exmouth docked at Topsham with 82 tuns 13 pipes [wine]. And the shipmaster is Richard Wayte. Of which:
    William Cocus: 13 tuns (2 pipes)
    Richard, his brother: 1 tun, custom paid into the pyx
    William de Gathpath: 3 tuns
    Robert Gosse: 2 tuns
    William le Brit: 5 tuns
    William Boffet: 2 tuns
    John de Smalecomb: 17 tuns 1 pipe
    Joel le Duk: 6 tuns 1 pipe
    Richard Ercedyaken and William, his servant: 11 tuns 3 pipes
    William Boffet: 1 tun
    Adam de Smalecomb and William Erkedyaken: 1 tun
    Richard Noreys: 3 tuns, customed (paid [per] Beyvin, into the pyx)
    Stephen Mounteyn: 3 tuns
    Robert de Wotton: 6 tuns 3 pipes
    H. Purpris: 8 tuns
    Richard Edmund: 1 tun for portage
    Hugh Gascoyng: 1 pipe
    Horloc: 1 pipe
    Richard Wayte: 1 tun
    John Cocus: 2 pipes
And William Cocus is for the custom. And 3 tuns and 2 pipes are customed. And [custom of] 1 tun paid into the pyx.

MCR 1299/1300, m. 8d [court dated 23 November 1299]

Ship that is called *le Bon An* of Sidmouth docked at Topsham with 48 tuns and 7 pipes of wine; of which the shipmaster is Ralph le Sangere. From which:
    Ralph le Sangere: 7 tuns and 1 pipe (5 [tuns] and 1 pipe customed)
    Stephen Uppehill: 1 tun, customed
    Robert de Nymeton: 7 tuns 2 pipes
    Philip Spryng: 10 tuns
    Arnolph Fenton of Gascony: 14 tuns 3 pipes, customed
    Roger Aleyes: 1 tun, customed
    Thomas de Catecotte: 7 tuns and 1 pipe
    Clement Tutor of Honiton: 1 tun
Sum of custom: 8s 4d; pledge, Philip Spryng. Paid all into the pyx.

MCR 1299/1300, m. 10d [court dated 14 December 1299]

Ship called *la goge Nostre Dame* docked at Topsham with 93 tuns and 8 pipes [of wine]. And the shipmaster is William atta Crosse. From which:
    Henry Tricote: 11 tuns
    Walter Tyngter: 1 tun
    Henry de Tricote and Walter: 1 tun
    P. Steymour: 1 tun and 1 pipe, customed

N. Bosse: 12 tuns and [1] pipe
G. le Butor: 3 tuns
Henry Tricote [and] W. Steymour [and] Codelep: 4 tuns
Michael Toraud: 5 tuns
William Austyn: 7 tuns
Thomas de la Porche and William Breuuer: 2 tuns
R. de Veteriterra: 1 tun 1 pipe
Robert Gosse: 1 tun
Richard Witheslegh: 1 tun
Reginald Sweygetel: 2 tuns (customed 8d, paid)
Hugh Osbern: 6 tuns
John Baroun: 5 tuns
Thomas Herberd of Plymouth: 7 tuns (customed)
William de Okampton: 9 tuns 1 pipe
Richard le Skynnere: 2 tuns
Nicholas, his brother: 2 tuns
W. de Okampton and Robert de Rixen: 3 tuns
John Kene: 1 tun for portage
Brounyng: 1 tun for portage
William Bovy: 2 tuns 2 pipes of which 1 for portage (paid 12d into
 the pyx)
John Isaac: 4 tuns of which 1 for portage (paid 12d into the pyx)
William de Corneworthy: 1 pipe for portage
And 17 tuns are customed. Henry Tricote is [the pledge] for the
remaining 3s [*est pro Remanent' 3s*]. 32d paid into the pyx.

MCR 1299/1300, m. 11d [court dated 14 December 1299]

Ship that is called *Nycolas* of Sidmouth of which the shipmaster is Cole
Rede docked at Topsham with 89 tuns (1 pipe) of wine. From which:
 Berteram Beraund has 59 tuns 1 pipe
 ...
 Nicholas Red': 15 tuns
 Nicholas Blouer: 3 tuns
 ... : 1 tun for portage[44]
Of which 6 [tuns] for portage. Philip Hor... [for the custom?].[45]

MCR 1299/1300, m. 12d [court dated 21 December 1299]

Ship that is called *Malyne* of Orwell Haven [*Horwill*] docked at
Topsham with 37 lasts and 8 M [of herring]. And the master is
Richard le Yungh. From which:
 John Perour: 5($\frac{1}{2}$) lasts
 William de Gathepath: $\frac{1}{2}$ last
 William Boffet: $\frac{1}{2}$ last
 Joel Tabernar: 1 [last] 8 M
 Robert Caym: 4 M
 William Smalecomb: 4 lasts

---

[44] *For portage* crossed through.
[45] This membrane is torn at the bottom where the entry appears.

Stephen, his brother: 1 last and 8 M
John de Smalecomb: 5 lasts and 8 M
P. Lovecok: 3 lasts
Nicholas Pellipar': 4 lasts
Joan Cotiller: 4 lasts
The son of Osbert le Sargere: 1 last
And John Perour is for the custom [on] 4 M.

MCR 1299/1300, m. 28d [court dated 13 June 1300]

Ship that is called *Beate Marie* of Barfleur docked at Topsham with 12
tuns of woad, 4 pipes of potash. And the shipmaster is Giffard de
Hoges. And William Corke is for the custom.

MCR 1299/1300, m. 38d [court dated 5 September 1300][46]

Ship that is called *la Nicolas* of Le Vivier of which the shipmaster [is]
Gerard Ryaunteel docked at Topsham with 1500 tresses of garlic and
100 [tresses] of onions. Of which 200 are free and the rest owe custom. And 1 C of canvas of William Buffet. And John Pycard received
the custom [and] paid R. de Newetone 3s 3/4d? [*r' de cons' sol' R. de
Newetone iiis ob q*].

MCR 28–29 EDWARD I

MCR 1300/1, m. 21d [court dated 13 March 1301]

Ship that is called *la Blitha* of Teignmouth docked at the port of
Topsham (with) 300 quarters of wheat, barley and peas and the corn
belongs to Walter le Cotiler and the shipmaster is Walter Godyng.

MCR 1300/1, m. 22d [court dated 27 March 1301]

Ship that is called *la Blythe* of Yarmouth docked (at the port) at[47]
Topsham on the Monday next after the feast of Palm (Sunday) [27
March 1301] with 86 tuns and 10 pipes [of wine] of which:
    William Buffet: 15 tuns and 1 pipe
    William de Carswille: 2 tuns
    William de Carswille sarger: 1 tun
    John in the Haye: 1 tun
    Henry de Rixthiwele: 3 tuns
    Walter Tynctor: 1 tun
    Robert de Hyrlond of Topsham: 3 tuns
    William Pellipar': 1 tun
    William de Gatepath: 5 tuns

---

[46] This court is dated Monday in the feast of St Gabriel. Bishop Walter Bronesombe
adopted St Gabriel as his patron saint and declared in 1278 that the feast was to be on
the first Monday in September (*Ordinale Exon*, ed. J. N. Dalton, vol i, Henry Bradshaw
Society, xxxvii (1909), pp xliv–v). For another ship entry dated by the feast of St
Gabriel, see below, p 79, n. 14.
[47] *At* is expunged.

Robert Gosse: 3 tuns
John de Busse:[48] 3 tuns
John de Busse and Geoffrey le Botour: 1 tun
Master John Dyrewyn and Joan, wife of Nicholas Busse: 1 tun
Master Robert de la Hollelonde: 2 tuns
Nicholas Busse: 7 tuns and 6 pipes
Thomas de la Burne: 2 tuns, customed
Joel Tabernar, servant of John le Perour: 2 tuns
Henry atte Forde: 2 tuns, customed
Thomas Fayrchyl and Richard Pellipar': 1 tun
Thomas Fayrchyl: 1 tun
Robert de Forde: 7 tuns and 1 pipe
William de Okampton: 9 tuns
William de Okampton and Robert, servant of the same William: 3
    tuns
Richard de Carswille: 1 tun
Richard de la More: 1 tun
Geoffrey de Rixthiwele: 2 tuns and 1 pipe
Kyde of Pratteshide: 1 tun, customed
William de Austyn: 5 tuns and 1 pipe

And the shipmaster is William Bround. Pledges for custom [are] Nicholas de Busse and Geoffrey de Rixthywele. Sum 2s 8d.

Ship that is called *la Sauee* of Exmouth docked at the port of Topsham on the Monday next after Palm Sunday [27 March 1301]; and the shipmaster is Richard le Wayte; with 94 (tuns of wine) and 2 pipes of which:

Philip Lovecok: 30 tuns and 1 pipe
John le Perour: 19 tuns and 1 pipe
Richard de Gatepath: 11 tuns
Robert de Hyrlond of Topsham: 6 tuns
Walter Tynctor: 4 tuns
Robert de Doune: 2 tuns
William Buffet: 2 tuns
Walter de Langeden: 1 tun
Richard Pellipar': 1 tun
Nicholas Pellipar': 1 tun
William de Carswille: 1 tun
William de Carswille sarger: 5 tuns
Richard de Gayte: 1 tun for portage
Thomas le Prouz: 1 tun, customed (paid)
Henry de Rixthiwele: 7 tuns
John in the Haye: 1 tun
Henry de Trycote: 1 tun.

And for the custom is Henry Rixthywele. {Sum 4d, paid, yet he inquires into it? [*summa 4d solv' tam' inq' cui*]}.

[48] *De* is expunged.

MCR 1300/1, m. 23d [court dated 10 April 1301]

A certain ship of Totnes docked at the port of Exmouth with 2 tuns [woad][49] and 1 pipe of potash which belong to Simon le Rey of Caen and 450 spurs [*de spurdon CCCC et di'*], customed, which belong to the same merchant; and 100 ells canvas. And for the custom is Jordan de Venell.

MCR 1300/1, m. 26d [court dated 8 May 1301]

Ship that is called *la Sauvee* of Dawlish [*Douelish*] docked at the port of Exmouth with 3 tuns of potash woad [*cinerum Wayd'*] and 2½ M of canvas and 1½ M iron and 3 C[50] of battery-ware which all belong to diverse men of the freedom. And the shipmaster is William Phelyp. No custom.

MCR 29–30 EDWARD I

MCR 1301/2, m. 17d [court dated 12 February 1302]

Ship that is called *le cog Seynt Thomas* of Dartmouth docked at port of Exmouth with 57 tuns of wine of which:
    Philip Rurde: 25 [tuns]
    William le Cok of Bridford: 7 tuns
    Gilbert de la Pole: 8 [tuns]
    John Peris: 12 tuns (of which 1 for portage) (paid all)
    Hugh Do: 5 tuns of which 1 for portage (11d paid)
Also in the same is ½ quintal [*quintowe*] of iron which belongs to Richard Holbeschort. Also ½ quintal of pitch which belongs to John Artour. And the shipmaster is Hugh Do. And for the custom is William de Brydeford called le Cook [*le Qu*].

[Custom Roll 1 starts here.]

MCR 30–31 EDWARD I

MCR 1302/3, m. 3d [court dated 15 October 1302]

Memorandum that on the Tuesday next after the feast of Saint Calixtus pope (in the present year) [16 October 1302] when Thomas de Halscumb and William de Stocbrigge, serjeants of the city of Exeter, were sent to Topsham by the mayor and bailiffs of the said city to prohibit the ship (of John le Webbe) that is called *la Nicholas* of Dartmouth from leaving the said port before the same John came and responded to his presentment concerning a certain concealment, Robert Poynz and other bailiffs of Lord Hugh de Curtenay came and strenuously did not allow the said serjeants nor any bailiffs of the aforesaid city to stop them from sailing away and forbade them from making any attachment or distraint on anyone there for whatever reason.[51]

---

[49] *Woad* is in the left-hand margin.
[50] *1 C* crossed through and *3 C* written in next.
[51] This entry is also recorded in PCA Roll 1 (below, p 71).

MCR 1302/3, m. 45d [court dated 2 September 1303]

Memorandum of 12d paid per the mainpernor of David le Rede of Sidmouth for 3 tuns of wine in the ship that is called *la cog Sancte Marie* of Sidmouth. Also for 6 seams of iron, 6d into the pyx. And the shipmaster is Dai Mongon.

MCR 6–7 EDWARD II

MCR 1312/13, m. 28 [court dated 30 April 1313]

Ship that is called *Charyte* of Boston docked at the port of Exmouth with 200 quarters wheat and maslin of Geoffrey de Bogh', William Jowe and others; and 2 *astr'* pitch [*pice*] of the same. And the master is John le Rede.

MCR 1312/13, m. 29 [court dated 7 May 1313]

Ship that is called *Notre Dame* of St Valéry docked on the 11th day of May with 26 tuns woad and 40 quarters wheat and 200 stones weld of Peter le Monyer; and the master is William le Breaunt.[52]

MCR 1312/13, m. 35 [court dated 25 June 1313]

Ship that is called *Rose* of Ravenser docked at the port of Exmouth with 64 quarters of wheat of which 4 quarters of wheat for portage, and 80 quarters of coal of Thomas Cacke; and the master is the same Thomas.

Ship that is called *la Joanette* of Whitton [*Wyneton'*] docked with 20 quarters wheat and 200 quarters coal of John de Wyneton' and the master is the same John.

MCR 1312/13, m. 43d [court dated 20 August 1313]

Ship that is called *la holhop Seynt Nicholas* docked at the port of Exmouth with 2000 C [*mm c*] garlic [and] 3 seams onions; and the master is Laurence Hugh'. 5½d [custom], pledge John de Sancto Nicholao.

MCR 13–14 EDWARD II

MCR 1319/20, m. 14d [court dated 7 January 1320]

Inquisition—[twelve jurors named] who say on their oath that a ship that is called *la Rode Cog* of Teignmouth, on which Henry Kech is shipmaster, that was freighted at Bordeaux with wines to go to Caan in Normandy, but because a tempest at sea came upon the said ship, docked at the port of Exmouth in the kingdom of England on the 19th day of the month of October in the thirteenth year of King Edward son of King Edward [1319] loaded with 91 tuns 3 pipes wine

---

[52] This entry is also recorded in PCA Roll 1 (below, p 128).

and there before the mayor and bailiffs of the city of Exeter the said ship was customed viz., in the name of:

Bernard Andru: 45 tuns 1 pipe

and in the name of Bruni le Carpenter of Bordeaux: 45 tuns 2 pipes

and in the name of the shipmaster: 1 tun.

Bernard sold all of his wine there to diverse men of the district viz., some tuns for a price of 5½ marks and some tuns for a price of 5 marks at least. And they say that the said Bernard and Richard le Seler of Exeter sold all the wine of Bruni le Carpenter there to diverse men of the district for the said price except for 10 tuns which remain to be sold because of the default of the same Bernard; and they say that the said Bernard could have sold these said 10 tuns viz., for 6 marks per tun but now they are worth but 2 marks per tun to the great damage of the same Bruni. And the aforesaid Robert[53] gave for having the inquisition as appears at the end; fine, ½ mark. Pledge, Robert de Wotton.[54]

MCR 1319/20, m. 36d [court dated 23 June 1320]

Ship that is called *le Berthelemeu* of Lyme docked on the feast of the birth of St John the Baptist [24 June 1320] with 1000 quarters corn of Peter le Moner and 20 quarters peas and 3 quarters of barley. And the shipmaster is Geoffrey Tony.

---

[53] This refers to Robert le Carpenter of Bordeaux, probably a relative of Bruni le Carpenter, who in the court preceding this entry (m. 14) brought a plea of account against Bernard Andru.

[54] This entry is also recorded in PCA Roll 1 (below, p 173).

TEXT OF THE ACCOUNTS: II

LOCAL PORT CUSTOMS ACCOUNTS (PCA), ROLL 1, 1302–1321

1302/3 (m. 31) EXETER—ROLL OF SHIPS DOCKING AT THE PORT OF EXMOUTH IN THE 30TH REGNAL YEAR OF KING EDWARD [I]

Ship called *le Andrw* of Christchurch
Master: Roger Kydenok
Cargo: Walter le Cotiler: 12 tuns 1 pipe woad and 2 tuns teasels
Custom: Gilbert, servant of said Walter for the custom; no custom

Boat called *la Mariote* of Beaulieu [*Beaulu*]
Master: Richard Pynnok
Cargo: 4 millstones and 4 tuns woad of which:
    Walter le Cotiler: 3 tuns woad
    Ralph[1] le Teyngturer: 1 tun woad
Custom: aforesaid Gilbert for the custom; no custom

Ship called *la Nicholas* of Dartmouth[2]
Master: John le Webbe
Cargo: Walter le Cotiler: 30 quarters woad, 1 frail onions
    Also are 4 M onions in the ship for portage
Custom: aforesaid Gilbert for the custom; no custom

Ship called *la cogg Seynt Thomas* of Teignmouth
Master: Henry le Lung
Cargo: 86 tuns 6 pipes wine of which:
    William le Cok of Bridford: 20 tuns (1 pipe)
    Walter le Cotiler: 2 tuns
    Richard le Cok: 4 tuns, customed
    Philip Lovecok: 20 tuns 1 pipe
    Stephen de Smalecomb: 20 tuns 1 pipe
    Philip Lovecok and William le Cok: 1 pipe
    Gilbert in the Comb and Henry le Lung: 20 tuns (2 pipes), customed except 3 tuns which are for portage
Custom: sum 7s, and Walter de Porte received all

Ship called *la cogg Sancti Thome* of Dartmouth
Master: Ralph Ponne
Cargo: 66 tuns 3 pipes wine of which:
    Philip Rurde: 30 tuns 2[3] pipes wine

---

[1] A *W* comes before *Ralph* and is expunged.
[2] This entry is also noted in an inquisition recorded in the MCR; see above, p 67.
[3] *Tuns* comes before *pipes* and is expunged.

Gilbert atte Pole: 17 tuns 1 pipe (of which Matilda de Langedene
  has 3 tuns 1 pipe), customed (of which 1 for portage)
John Peres: 14 tuns (customed, of which 1 for portage)
Hugh Do: 3 tuns (customed, 1 for portage)
Ralph Ponne: 1 tun (customed, 1 for portage)
Custom: Gilbert atte Pole for the custom; sum 10s, paid into the
pyx

Ship called *Seynt Anne* of Teignmouth
Master: Henry Kech
Cargo: 105 tuns 5 pipes wine of which:
  Nicholas Busse: 31 tuns 2 pipes (and from this
    Robert de Nymeton has 10 tuns
    Robert de Yoldelonde has 2 tuns (customed) and
    Robert Gosce has 2 tuns)
  Henry Treket: 20 tuns 1 pipe
  Walter le Teynturer: 3 tuns
  Andrew le Tayllur: 1 tun
  Thomas de Tetteburne: 2 tuns
  Robert de Wotdeton: 20 tuns 1 pipe
  Hugh Hosbern: 12 tuns 1 pipe
  Reginald Swengetil: 2 tuns (paid 8d custom)
  John Serle: 2 tuns (custom paid)
  John le Duk: 5 tuns (of which W. de Ochamton has 1 tun; 4 tuns
    customed)
  Thomas Colepole: 4 tuns of which 1 for portage (paid total [cus-
    tom])
  Henry Kech: 1 [tun] for portage
  Jordan Payn: 1 [tun] for portage
  Walter Kech: 1 [tun] for portage
Custom: Henry de Tricote and Robert de Wodeton for the custom;
sum 4s 4d of which 28d in the pyx. {Exonerated? [*ex'i*]}[4]

Ship called *la Savee* of Exmouth
Master: Richard Wayte
Cargo: 94 tuns 3 pipes wine of which:
  John le Perour: 15 [tuns]
  William de Kerswille senior: 6 [tuns]
  William de Kerswille sarger: 7 [tuns]
  Henry de Rixtivele: 15 (tuns) 1 pipe
  Robert de Irlonde: 17 tuns 1 pipe
  Ralph le Teyngturer: 8 tuns
  Walter le Teynturer: 6 tuns
  Robert de Doune: 2 tuns
  Thomas Prouz: 1 tun, customed

[4] The meaning of this annotation, which appears in the right-hand margin of certain
entries on this membrane only and was often written in later, is unclear. It may be an
abbreviation for *exonerati*, signifying that the cargo was unloaded from the ship or that
the customs debt had been discharged. It might also be an abbreviation for *extracti*,
meaning that the scribe extracted the entry from another document or that the money
owed for custom was paid or exacted.

William Buffet: 9 tuns
Henry de Tricote: 2 tuns
William Austyn: 4 tuns
Joel de Bradecrofte taverner: 3 tuns
Richard de Kerswille: 1 [tun]
Geoffrey de Rixtivele: 1 tun
Thomas de Tetteburne: 2 tuns (customed)
Custom: Henry de Rixtivele for the custom. {Sum, 12d; exonerated?
[*ex'i*]}

Ship called *la Blythe* of Exmouth
Master: Peter Godlok
Cargo: 81 tuns (5) pipes wine of which:
    Ralph Lovet: 11 tuns
    Ralph le Teynturer: 8½ tuns
    Jordan[5] de Venella: 6½ tuns
    Richard Caperoun: 3 tuns
    Richard le Peleter: 3 tuns
    Thomas Challe: 2 tuns (customed)
    John Gerard: 2 tuns, customed[6]
    Elias Horlok: 2 tuns 1 pipe
    Walter de Porte: 1 pipe
    Philip Lovecok: 11 tuns 1 pipe
    William de Gatepath: 3 tuns
    Thomas de Cadicote merchant: 13 tuns 2 pipes
    William de Ochamton: 10 tuns
    The same William and Robert de Rixan: 4 tuns in common
    Nicholas le Skynnere: 1 tun
    Walter de Grendel: 1 tun, customed
Custom: 4d in the pyx

Ship called *le Mich'* of Teignmouth
Master: Richard David
Cargo: 59 tuns (3) pipes wine of which:
    Ralph Lovet and Richard de Gatepath: 23 tuns
    John le Perour: 3 tuns
    Henry de Rixtivele: 2 tuns
    Michael Toraud: 15 tuns 1 pipe
    Walter Fraunceys: 2 tuns
    William Cork: 7 tuns
    Walter le Teynturer: 4 tuns
    Robert le Taverner: 1 tun
    David de Dupe: 2 [tuns] for portage
    Wymund Brytoun: 1 tun portage
    Richard in the Heye: 1 [tun] for portage
    Richard Bern: 2 (pipes) for portage of which 1 customed
Custom: 4d in the pyx

[5] *John* crossed through before *Jordan*.
[6] *Customed* is expunged.

Ship called *la Bon An* of Exmouth
Master: Walter de Ilferthecomb
Cargo: 134 tuns and 2 pipes (wine) of which:
    John de Smalecumb: 29 tuns
    Stephen de Smalecomb: 5 tuns
    Adam de Smalecomb: 4 tuns
    William le Cok: 13 tuns
    Richard le Cok: 5 tuns (custom paid)
    Walter le Cotiler: 1 tun
    William de Teyng: 1 tun, customed (paid)
    Richard le Archedekene and William le Archedekene: 21 tuns
    William de Strete: 1 tun (4d custom)
    Nicholas le Saltere: 7 tuns
    Thomas Codelyp: 6 tuns
    Adam le Espycer: 3 tuns
    Robert le Saltere: 1 (tun), customed (paid) Alured Horn: 13 tuns
    Hugh de Remmeston: 9 tuns
    Joan Cachefrench: 3 tuns
    Nicholas Busse: 2 tuns
    Robert de Yoldelonde: 1 [tun], customed (4d)
    Gilbert Schort: 8 tuns (of which Walter de Grendel [has] 1 tun, customed 4d)
    Thomas de Cadicote: 5 tuns[7]
    William de Ochamton[8]
    Henry de Rixtivele: 1 tun
Custom: William Archedekene and Walter de Ilferthecomb for the custom. Sum 40d, of which 2s 8d in the pyx; {exonerated? [*ex'*]}

Ship called *la Blythe* of Teignmouth
Docked: 9 November 1302
Master: Walter Godyng
Cargo: Peter Simoun: 55 tuns wine, 2 tuns woad
Custom: Walter de Porte for the custom; sum 18s 4d for the wine and 2s for the woad, received by W. de Porte; {exonerated? [*ex'*]}

Boat of John atte Wode of Plymouth
Master: John atte Wode
Cargo: The aforesaid John: 5 tuns wine
Custom: John de Sancto Nicholao for the custom; sum 20d [put] in the pyx by de Porte

Ship called *la Johannete* of Lympstone
Master: William Cok
Cargo: 4 lasts herring and 1 last for the men of the aforesaid ship in common for their dinner [*hominum predicte navis communie ad prandend'*] of which:
    William Cok: 2 mease
    Adam[9] Slegh: 2 mease

---

[7] Entry crossed through.
[8] Entry crossed through.

Other diverse men of the ship who are all customed except for the
  fifth last which belongs to Richard de Lenne; 16d in the pyx
Custom: sum 16d in the pyx; {exonerated? [*ex'*]}

Ship called *la Flory* of Le Vivier
Master: Guillaume Rydel
Cargo: 3 M onions or thereabouts [*vel circiter*], 1 seam garlic, both of
  which belong to John de Gwez
Custom: John de Sancto Nicholao for the custom; sum 4d in the pyx;
  {exonerated? [*Ex'*]}

Ship called *la Godyer* of Sidmouth
Master: Jordan de Fayrlond (customed)
Cargo: 10 lasts 5 M herring of which:
  Nicholas le Peleter: 4 lasts
  William de Ochamton: 2 lasts
  Richard le Peleter: 1 last
  William de Kerswille sarger: 1 last
  Matthew Coffyn:[10] 1 last 2 M
  Nicholas de Kerswille: 8 M
  Richard Wytbrother: 4 M
  Roger de Bury: 3 M
Custom: for the custom is [ ]; sum of custom 3d, in the pyx

Ship called *le Mich'* of Teignmouth
Master: Philip Tolle
Cargo: 15½ lasts herring of which:
  John le Perour: 4 lasts
  Robert de Ochamton: 1 last
  Richard le Peleter: 1½ lasts
  William de Ochamton: ½ last
  William de Kerdewille: 1 last
  William de Kerswille sarger: ½ [last]
  Richard his brother: 1½ lasts
  Matthew Coffyn: ½ last
  Nicholas de Kerswille: 8 M
  John Whytebrother: 8 M (customed)
  Richard Whytebrother: 6 M
  Nicholas Maynard: 2 M
  Philip Rurde: 2 lasts 3 M
  Robert de Nyweton: 3 M
Custom: Nicholas le Peleter for the custom; sum 3d in the pyx

Ship called *la Joanette* of Abbeville
Master: Hugh le Jeuene
Cargo: Hugh le Jeuene: 3½ frails onions (also 8 C onions), ½ seam gar-
  lic
Custom: Jordan de Venella for the custom; sum 4s 4d[11] all in the pyx

---

[9] *William* crossed through and *Adam* inserted above.
[10] *Le Peleter* crossed through and *Coffyn* inserted above.

Ship called *la Rose* of Yarmouth
Master: John Bartholomeu
Cargo: 38 lasts herring of which:
    Philip Lovecok: 5 lasts
    John le Saltere: 3 lasts
    Nicholas Page: 1 last
    Matthew le Skynnere: 2 lasts
    William de Criditon: 5 lasts
    William de Smalecomb: 5 lasts
    John de Smalecomb: 7½ lasts
    Adam de [Smalecomb] [*de eadem*]: ½ last
    Stephen de [Smalecomb] [*de eadem*]: 2 lasts
    Ralph de Nyweton mercer: 1 last
    John Bartholomeu and his fellows: 7½ lasts of which 3½ lasts for
        portage
Custom: Walter Lovecok for the custom; paid 40d, so all [paid]

(m. 31d) [**1302/3** account continued]

Ship called *la Jowanette* of St Valéry
Master: John de Goseford
Cargo: 6 frails onions, 1 seam garlic of which:
    Hugh Clabaut: the onions
    John de Goseford: the garlic and 18 harnesses [*heres*]
Custom: the aforesaid Hugh for the custom; sum 7s 0½d, in the pyx

Ship called *la Plente* of Dunwich
Master: Thomas Johanesone
Cargo: 10 lasts white and red [herring] of which:
    Thomas Jonesone and Walter Thursteyn: 8 lasts
    Basil de Donewych: 1 last
    Dennis le Buff: ½ last
    John de Donewych: ½ last
Custom: Guy le Peleter for the custom

Ship called *la Blythe* of Lyme
Master: William Faber
Cargo: 98 tuns 1 pipe wine of which:
    John ate Heye: 71 tuns
    Thomas de Chesilburge: 21 tuns 1 pipe (W. de Porte debited [*on'*] 7s)
    William Faber: 3 tuns
    Henry de Ryel: 2 tuns
    Richard Bers: 1 tun
    Richard le Bars: 4 quintals iron, 80 pounds almonds
Custom: Hugh Hosbern of Topsham for the custom on 22 tuns; and
    in dispute [are] 71 tuns because [the importer claims the freedom]
    of Chard [*Cherde*]; sum 31s[12] {paid 7s; exonerated? [*ex'*]}

---

[11] *4d* crossed through.
[12] *Sum 31s* crossed through.

Ship called *la Sauvee* of Saltash
Cargo: 51 tuns wine of which:
  David de Kont: 42 tuns
  Reginald Attaburgh: 3 tuns viz., 1 for portage and the others customed
  Simon Atirewynn: 4 tuns of which 1 for portage and the others customed
  John Ham': 1 tun for portage
  Robert Atteburgh: 1 tun for (portage)
Custom: John Horn for the custom and the same for the new custom of
  the Lord King if it ought to be rendered; sum 15s 4d; {exonerated [*ex'*]}

Ship called *la Johannette* of St Valéry-sur-Somme [*Summe*][13]
Cargo: Leonard de Cuntyf and John, his brother: 20 tuns woad
  The same Leonard: ½ frail onions, customed
Custom: Jordan de Venella for the custom; sum 20s; also 7d in the
  pyx; all [paid]

Ship called *la Blithe* of Seaford
Master: Richard Peytevyn
Cargo: Walter le Cotiller: 50 quarters woad, estimated [because] in
  graner, 40 stones weld, 2 frails onions
Custom: the said Walter for the custom; no custom

Ship called *la Bayard* of Exmouth
Master: Nicholas Sele of Pratteshide
Cargo: 20 tuns woad of which:
  Robert Pauch': 10 tuns, customed
  John de la Hegh' of Chard: 10 tuns, customed
  And 3 M and 5 C iron, 100 stones weld
Custom: Robert Pouch' for the custom who pays 11s for his part and
  mainperns for [ ] to satisfy for the part of John de la Heghen before
  24 June [1303]; sum 25s; 11s in the pyx and the rest quit because
  free [*per libertat'*]; {exonerated? [*ex'*]}

Ship called *la Seint Johan* of Exmouth
Cargo: 8 tuns 1 pipe woad, 2 tuns potash, 6 seams canvas, 6 bales
  alum, 1 cade archil [*Argoyl*] and another [cade] of ochre of which:
  Walter le Cotiler: 4 tuns woad, 1½ tuns potash, 2 seams canvas, 2
    bales alum
  Gilbert, his servant: 1 bale [alum], 1 C canvas viz., 1 seam [canvas]
    [imported] along with N. and Richard le Skynner), 1 cade ochre,
    6 pans [*patella*]
  Stephen de Smalecumbe: 1 bale alum
  (R.) Caperoun: 1 seam canvas (from the port of Plymouth)
  (T. de Caticote: 1 bale alum and 1 pack canvas)
  Ralph de Nyweton: 4 tuns 1 pipe woad
  Aforesaid Ralph and W. de Smalecumbe: 1 seam canvas, 1 bale alum
  Richard le Noreys: ½ tun potash
Custom: 4d paid into the pyx

[13] Although the home port reads only *Summe*, the ship's name, master, and type of
cargo all match that of a ship from St Valéry-sur-Somme, the port at the mouth of the
Somme river in Picardy. Similar evidence exists for other ships with this home port (see
below, pp 92, 107, 162).

Ship called *la Godyer* of Exmouth
Docked: 17 April [1303]
Master: Richard Harvest
Cargo: 24 tuns woad of which:
    Walter le Cotiller: 7 tuns
    Gilbert Short and his fellows: 7 tuns
    William le Brewere: 3 tuns
    William de Okampton: 2 tuns
    Nicholas le Webbe of Taunton: 5 tuns (customed), 12 garbs weld, 2
    bales almonds (customed)
    The Vicar of Kenton: 50 spurs [*L spordon*]
    John de Stonford: 50 knives [*knipuli*], 1 M mirrors [*specula*], 200
    cups [*ii^c ciphi*], and 200 cups of the same John
Custom: Thomas de Caticote merchant for the custom; 6s 9d; {exon-
erated? [*ex'*]}

Ship called *la Blythe* of Exmouth
Master: Peter Godlok
Cargo: 85 tuns 6 pipes wine of which:
    Philip Lovecok: 22 tuns 1 pipe
    Walter Lovecok: 4 tuns
    William called le Ku of Bridford: 17 tuns 1 pipe
    Richard, his brother: 4 tuns
    Alured Horn: 2 tuns
    Philip Rurde: 13 tuns 1 pipe
    Nicholas le Saltere: 10 tuns 1 pipe
    John de Smalecumbe and his fellows: 9 tuns 2 pipes
    John le Perour: 1 tun
    William Gregory: 2 tuns
    Nicholas de Carswille: 1 tun
Custom: no custom

Ship called *la Jowanette* of Teignmouth
Master: John Luverich
Cargo: 3 C salt, 10 M iron
Custom: W. de Porte for the custom

Ship called *la Bayard* of Exmouth
Master: Nicholas Sele
Cargo: 150 quarters salt

Ship called *Seint Jake* of Teignmouth
Master: Lambert de Riholm
Cargo: Lambert de Riholm: 1 piece of striped [*stragulati*] cloth

Ship called *la Godyer* of Exmouth
Cargo: 17 tuns woad
    Robert Poz: 9 tuns (paid custom)
    Nicholas Harier: 8 tuns (paid custom into the pyx)
    Robert Pouz: 2 tuns teasels [*teysl'*], 80 stones weld
Custom: Robert Pouz for the custom; paid custom into the pyx

Ship called *la James* of Teignmouth
Master: Jordan Ilberd
Cargo: 34 tuns 2 pipes wine of which:
  Ralph Wylem': 16 tuns
  Roger de Corn': 2 pipes
  William de Rue: 12 tuns
  Walter Cresci: 4 tuns, customed
  Roger de Corn': 1 tun (customed)
  Jordan Ilberd shipmaster: 1 tun
Custom: Ralph Wilem' for the custom, 20d; {exonerated? [*ex'*]}

Ship called *la Wayngnepayn* of Dartmouth
Master: William Lydon
Cargo: Walter le Spicer of Totnes: 1½ C salt, 6 M onions
Custom: Walter de Porte for the custom

Ship called *la Jowenette* of Exmouth
Master: William Coc
Cargo: 2 C salt with portage of the valet [*vallet'*]

Ship called *la Margarete* of Teignmouth
Master: Walter Hardi
Docked: 2 September [1303][14]
Cargo: Jordan de Venella and Robert de Nyweton: 3 fardels ultramarine cloth, and lead
Custom: no custom because in the freedom

Ship called *la Swan* of Teignmouth
Master: David in the Heye
Docked: 4 September [1303]
Cargo: Gilbert Short: 3 C salt, 100 yards linen cloth
Custom: no custom

Ship called *la Wynnegod* of Teignmouth
Master: John Grigge
Docked: 4 September [1303]
Cargo: woad and potash, viz.,
  John Soth: 2 bales alum, 4 C iron, 2 sugar loaves [*panes sucr'*]
  William Bruwere: 4 tuns woad, 1 tun potash, 2 bales alum, 600 C canvas, 2 pieces colored cloth
  Walter le Fraunceys: 2 bales alum, 2 pairs of millstones, 1½ dozens cordwain
  Thomas de Codelyp: 2 tuns woad, 1 pipe black potash
  Henry de Tricote: 1 tun woad, 2 bales alum
  John le Perour: 1 piece perse cloth, ½ piece green cloth
  Thomas Golde: 3 C canvas, 2 bales alum, 1 C battery-ware
  Richard le Noreys: 1 pipe black potash
  Walter le Deghere: 1 tun black potash, 1 tun woad
  William de Smalecumbe: 1 C canvas

[14] The date reads *in the feast of St Gabriel*; see above, p 65, n. 46.

J. de Sancto Nicholao: 2 C canvas, 25 pounds wax, 12 pounds cotton [*cotoun*], ½ C battery-ware
Custom: no custom

Customs[15]

1303/4 (m. 30) [No heading: account for April-August 1304][16]
{Scrutinized}[17]

Ship called *la Godyer* of Exmouth
Master: Harlewin Bolt
Docked: 5 April [1304]
Cargo: David le Rede of Pratteshide: 13 charges salt of which each
    charge [contains] 11½ quarters
Custom: William de Carswell sarger for the custom; no custom

Ship called *la Jouanette* of St Valéry
Master: Wulard de Taillie
Docked: 21 April 1304
Cargo: 17 tuns 1 pipe woad, 29 barrels potash, and weld[18]
    Robert Pouz: 17 tuns 1 pipe woad and potash[19]
    John de Bekere: 30 stones weld
Custom: Thomas Godwyne for the custom; Bartholomew Wyte paid
    .... for 6 tuns(?)...1 pipe woad which ...[20]

Ship called *la Bonan* of Exmouth
Master: W. de Ilfridecumb
Docked: 7 May 1304
Cargo: 129 tuns wine of which:
    Richard Brinye: (11 tuns of which 1 tun is distilled)
    Thomas de Caticote and G. Short: 10 tuns
    John de Smalecumbe: 9 tuns
    William de Trente: 10 tuns
    Nicholas Page: 3 tuns
    Roger Aleys: 1 tun, customed (for drink)[21]
    Thomas Belante: 3 tuns
    William Austyn: 3 tuns
    William de Criditon: 7 tuns
    Richard le Ercedeken: 4 tuns
    John Busse: 2 tuns

[15] Written in very large letters at the bottom of the membrane.
[16] The membrane containing the first part of this account (from 29 September 1303 to March 1304) is missing.
[17] Written in a later hand, probably of the fifteenth but perhaps the early sixteenth century; it refers to one of the searches made of the rolls, probably during a legal dispute (see above, pp 38–9). For similar annotations, see below, notes 73, 75, 110, 112, 118, 129, 177, 185.
[18] *29 barrels potash* written in twice; the first such entry is crossed through.
[19] *17 tuns and 1 pipe woad* underlined.
[20] The manuscript is torn here.
[21] *Customed* crossed out and *for drink* [*de beveragio*] inserted.

William le Ercedeken: 7 tuns
Philip Lovecoc: 11 tuns
Walter Lovecoc: 2 tuns
Henry Purpris: 3 tuns
William Cok: 2 tuns
Nicholas Lovecok: 2 tuns, customed
Hugh de Toppesham: 7 tuns
Reginald de Sueyngtel: 2 tuns, customed (in the pyx)
Jordan att Lane: 2 tuns
Elias Horlok: 1 tun
John Serle: 1 tun, customed
Walter de Langedene: 1 tun
Paya Pruz of Teignmouth: 2 tuns, customed
William de Okampton: 10½ tuns of which 1 [tun] distilled
William and Robert de Okampton: 4 tuns
Richard de Carswill: 1 tun
Joel de Bradecrofte: ½ tun
Robert le Taverner: 1 tun
John Hoigg: 2 tuns
Joel de Bradecrofte: 4 tuns of which 1 is empty
Custom: Richard Brimie and W. de Ilfridecumb for the custom; {20d
  into the pyx and thus 8d remains in the hands of the Receiver}

Ship called *la Belote* of Dartmouth
Master: Geoffrey Gilberd
Docked: 7 May [1304]
Cargo: 44 tuns 3 pipes wine of which:
  Robert de Nyweton: 15 tuns 1 pipe
  Durand de Momery: 12 tuns, customed
  Gilbert de Cumb: 12 tuns, customed of which 1 for portage
  Walter Beel: 1 tun for portage
  Geoffrey Gilberd: 2 tuns for portage and 2 pipes, customed
  Walter Rauf: 1 tun for portage
  Russel de Wynchelse: 1 tun for portage
  Peter Botsweyn: 1 quintal iron, customed
Custom: Walter de Porte for the custom; sum 8s 5d

Ship called *la Sauvee* of Exmouth
Master: Richard Wayte
Docked: 7 May [1304]
Cargo: 93 tuns 2 pipes wine of which:
  William Buffet: 10 tuns
  John le Perour: 5 tuns
  Andrew le Taillur: 2 tuns
  Adam le Spicer: 1 tun
  G. de Rixthivele: 1 tun
  Thomas le Furbur and John le Prute: 1 tun, customed
  Robert de la Rixen: 4 tuns (in his keeping of which
    J. le Perour and Joel de Bradecrofte: 1 tun
    William de Okampton: 2½ tuns

Robert de la Rixen: ½ tun)
Robert de Irlond: 12 tuns 1 pipe
Walter le Deghere: 3 tuns 1 pipe
John in the Haye: 3 tuns
Nicholas Busse: 3 tuns
John Busse: 2 tuns
John Girard: 3 tuns
Richard le Skynnere: 2 tuns
Elias Horlok: 1 tun
Thomas Challe: 2 tuns of which 1 tun for portage and the other
     customed
Stephen de Smalecumb: 8 tuns
John de Torre of Yarmouth: 7 tuns
Henry de Triccote: 8 tuns
Thomas Cotelip: 8 tuns
John, son of Henry de Triccote: 2 tuns, customed
John Cotelip: 1 tun, customed
Beatrix de Dodderigg: 1 tun
John le Cok: 1 tun, customed
John Gerveys: 1 tun
Walter[22] le Degher: 1 tun
Custom: Geoffrey de Rixthivele for the custom; sum 2s

Ship called *la holhop Seint Pere* of *Moun Doun*[23]
Master: Matthew Lamberd
Docked: 19 August 1304
Cargo: Stephen Moryn of *Moundoun*: 27 seams garlic, 7 seams
     onions, 2 seams honey
Custom: Alured le Clerk for the custom; 2s 7d which H. de Triccote
     received

(m. 30d) [**1303/4** account continued: May-August 1304]

24 tresses are [equal to] a horseload [*xxiiii trac' sunt summa equi*][24]

Ship called *la holhop Seint Pere* of *Moundoun*
Master: Matthew Lambert
Docked: 20 May 1304
Cargo: Stephen de Moryn, merchant: 200 (tresses) garlic, 3 C canvas,
     9 empty tuns
Custom: Thomas de Nyweton for the custom before the Mayor; sum,
     6d in the pyx

[22] *William* crossed through and *Walter* inserted.
[23] This entry is out of sequence; it should have come at the end of m. 30d but the
scribe ran out of room and so wrote this entry in the blank space remaining at the bottom of m. 30. *Moun Doun* (also *Moundoun* in this entry and below) was probably in
Brittany since Stephen Moryn is noted elsewhere as being "of Brittany"; the cargo
was typical of those from Brittany. If read as *Moun douu*, it might refer to Mont Dol in Ille-
et-Vilaine, Brittany.
[24] This equivalency probably refers to the cargo of garlic (measured in tresses) that
follows.

Ship called *la Nicholas* of Southampton
Master: William Vorthman
Docked: 21 May 1304
Cargo: Nicholas Haryer: 11 tuns woad and weld
Custom: Jordan de Venella for the custom; sum 11s

Ship called *la Seint Michel* of Teignmouth
Master: Henry Lom
Cargo: Henry Lome, William le Ku, J. le Perour, Nicholas Busse,
   Michael le Golsmyth: 3 C salt
Custom: no custom

Ship of Nicholas Peryn of Guernsey
Master: [Nicholas Peryn]
Docked: 15 June 1304
Cargo: Nicholas Peryn and his fellows: 12 M mackerel, 3 quarters
   linen cloth, 1 quarter canvas, 800 C Spanish iron, 350 spurs [*CCC
   di' esperdon*], 1 C licorice [*licorys*]
Custom: William de Carswill sarger for the custom; sum 23d {which
   H. de Tricote received}

Boat called *la Jowanette* of the Isle of Wight [*Wyght*]
Master: Richard Edward
Docked: 16 June 1304
Cargo: Peter de Lyouns, burgess of Southampton: 16 barrels potash
Custom: no custom

Ship called *Nostre Dame* of Santander [*Seint Andru*]
Master: Rue Peres
Docked 20 June 1304
Cargo: 15 tuns 6 pipes wine of which:
   John le Perour: 7 tuns
   Philip Lovecoc: 2 tuns
   William le Cok: 1 tun 2 pipes
   (Adam le Spicer: 1 tun)
   Richard de Gatepath: 6 tuns 4 pipes
   Also 1 ton iron, customed (in the pyx)
   Bernard Maynard (de Truro): [1] bale yarn [*filac'*] (1d in the pyx),
      20 pounds pepper (1d in the pyx)
   W. le Keu and R. Gatepath: iron
   Richard de Gatepath: 3 bales almonds
   Richard le Ku: 100 pounds sugar and spices [*pulver'*]
Custom: Richard de Gatepath for the custom; sum 6d in the pyx

Boat of Guernsey
Docked: 16 July 1304
Cargo: (Peter Hadyn): 20 M 850 C mackerel [*XX^{ml} DCCC & di' de makerel*]
   (Thomas de Tetteburn): 3 fardels linen cloth, 5 coffins rosin
   Peter Hadyn of Guernsey: 92 congers, 135 yards canvas, 6 M onions
Custom: Thomas de Tetteburn for the custom; sum 2s 6d

Boat of Richard Geneys of Guernsey
Master: Richard Geneys
Docked: 31 July 1304
Cargo: Gilbert de Nymet: 1 fardel canvas, 3 bales almonds, 1 fardel of
    cloth and knives [*knipulorum*], 2 bales almonds
  John de Sancto Nicholao: 1 fardel canvas, (2) dozen mortars, (2
    bales almonds)
  Thomas Golde: 1 fardel canvas, 2 bales almonds
  Luke le Mercer: 1 fardel canvas, customed (1d in the pyx)
  Thomas le Smyth: 1 fardel canvas, customed
Custom: Gilbert de Nymet for the custom; 1d

Ship called *la Nawe Deu* of Lyme
Master: William Lycher
Cargo: Gerard de Vilers: 20 quarters iron
  William Lycher: 20 pounds pepper
Custom: W. de Porte for the custom

Ship called *la Seint Benet* of Olonne
Master: William Berrochun
Docked: 15 August 1304
Cargo: 35 tuns 5 pipes [wine] of which:
  [25] (a certain man of Southhampton): 29 tuns 5 pipes
  Walter de Polgrun: 5 tuns, all customed (paid 20d to Alur'; after-
    wards received by H. de Tricote)
  The said John [Stonard]: 5 M tin [*stagmin'*]
Custom: Geoffrey de Ryxthivele for the custom

(m. 29) [**1303/4** account continued: September 1304]

Ship called *la Caterine* of Guernsey
Master: William Harepyn
Docked: 4 September 1304
Cargo: 1 seam garlic, 24 seams onions, 175 spurs [*c iii quart' esperdon*],
    300 yards canvas, 40 yards linen cloth and said if more, etc., [*& si
    plus dic' etc'*]
Custom: Thomas Cotlyp for the custom; 16d which H. de Tricote
    received

Ship called *la holhop Seint Nicholas* of Le Vivier
Master: William Pon
Docked: 7 September 1304
Cargo: Thomas le Clerian and Ives le Britoun: 60 seams onions, 2
    seams garlic
Custom: Ralph atte Lane and John de Sancto Nicholao for the cus-
    tom; sum 2s which H. received

Ship called *Sancti Nicholi* of Dieppe [*Dupe*]
Master: John Scarlet
Docked: 11 September 1304

---

[25] *John Stonard* crossed through but is noted as the last importer in this entry.

Cargo: John South, H. de Trucote, Thomas Cotelyp: 14 C iron, 1 tun 2 pipes potash, 6 carks (of alum) Richard Noreys: 1 bale alum,[26] (not customed [*non port' cust'*])
Custom: Richard Noreys for the custom: no custom

Ship called *la Jouanette* of Guernsey
Master: Richard Geneys
Docked: 21 September 1304
Cargo: Richard Geneys (and certain others unknown): 12 seams onions, ½ seam garlic
Custom: John de Sancto Nicholao for the custom; 9½d in the pyx

Sum of custom of wine for the year, 57s 2d. And 19s 0½d paid to Lord Hugh [Courtenay] for his third penny.

{Three membranes are contained in this file}[27]

1304/5 (m. 27) EXETER–ROLL OF CUSTOMS OF SHIPS APPEARING AT THE PORT OF EXMOUTH FROM THE END OF THE 32ND REGNAL YEAR OF KING EDWARD [I] TO THE BEGINNING OF THE 33RD YEAR

Ship called *la Florye Seint Nicholas* of Le Vivier[28]
Master: Nicholas le Rider
Docked: 8 October [1304]
Cargo: Stephen Moryn: 22 seams garlic, ½ C canvas
Custom: Henry Lovecoc and Alured Aylward for the custom; sum 22½d [put] in the pyx per the Mayor

Ship called *le Mesager* of Dartmouth
Master: Nicholas Swyft
Cargo: 90 tuns and 4 pipes wine of which:
  Philip Rurde: 40 tuns 2 pipes
  William le Ku cutler [*cotiller*]: 9 tuns 1 pipe
  Richard le Ku: 5 tuns
  Walter le Cotiller: 1 tun
  Philip Lovecoc: 15 tuns 1 pipe
  Robert de Wotton: 12 tuns
  Nicholas Swyft: 5 tuns of which 2 for portage and the rest customed
  Colewille: 4 tuns of which 1 for portage and the rest customed
  Ralph Rurde: 1 tun for portage
Custom: Philip Lovecoc and W. le Ku for the custom; and R. de N. received 2s for custom on 6 tuns of vendage wines

---

[26] *Customed* crossed through.
[27] This reference provides further evidence that the first of the three membranes containing the account for 1303/4 is missing (see above, n. 16). Also written at the bottom of this account but crossed through is the 8 October 1304 entry of the *Florye Seint Nicholas* that appears as the top of the 1304/5 account.
[28] This entry is also written at the bottom of m. 29 but is crossed through there.

Ship called *la Jouanette* of Teignmouth
Master: John Luverych
Docked: 18 October 1304
Cargo: 90 tuns wine of which:
  Ralph Lovet: 10 tuns
  William Ercedekene: 3 tuns
  Bernard atte Boghe of Barnstaple: 4 tuns
  John Luverich and Gilbert de Cumb: 27 tuns of which the shipmas-
    ter [has] 2 tuns for portage and Gilbert 1 for portage
  Master Robert de Oldelond: 3 tuns
  John Busse: 2 tuns
  Nicholas Busse: 16 tuns
  Thomas att Burne: 2 tuns customed (of which 1 for portage)
  Philip le Sopere: 4 tuns (of which 1 for portage)
  Henry Lange: 2 tuns (of which 1 for portage)
  Richard Hobel: 2 tuns (of which 1 for portage)
  Robert de Nymeton: 15 tuns
  Gilbert de Cumb: 14 quintals iron, 1 quintal almonds
  Thomas att Burne: ½ quintal almonds
Custom: Nicholas Busse for the custom; sum of custom on 30 tuns
  [wine] 9s 8d, in the pyx per W. de Porte; custom on iron 6d; cus-
  tom on almonds 2½d; sum of custom 10s 4½d, in the pyx per W. de
  Porte

Ship called *la Bonan* of Exmouth
Master: Richard Harvest
Docked: 18 October 1304
Cargo: 35 tuns 4 pipes wine of which:
  Philip Lovecoc: 9½ tuns 1 pipe
  Walter de Porte: 9 tuns 1 pipe
  Richard de Gatepath: 8½ tuns 1 pipe
  William Ercedekene: 2 tuns
  Alured Aylward: 1 tun
  William le Ku of Bridford: 1 tun
  And 3 tuns customed
Custom: Richard de Gatepath for the custom; 3 tuns customed, sum
  12d, which R. de N. received

Ship called *la nawe Notre Dame* of St Valéry
Master: Matthew le Dru
Docked: 20 October 1304
Cargo: 22 tuns 1 pipe woad of which:
  Robert Pouz: 9 tuns
  Bartholomew Byge: 13 tuns 1 pipe {R. de N. received 9s}, 100
    stones weld
  Matthew le Dru shipmaster and the crew: 27 M onions, customed
Custom: Robert Pouz for the custom; Bartholomew paid 13s into the
  pyx per W. de Porte and W. de Carswill; {R. de N. received 4s}

Ship called *Seint Lowy* of St Valéry[29]
Master: Hugh Gillard
Docked: 25 October [1304]
Cargo: Peter le Monyers: 9 tuns woad, 1 pipe potash
   Hugh Gillard shipmaster and the mariners: 11 seams onions
Custom: Adam le Degher for the custom; sum 9s 5d for woad and
   onions, in the pyx per W. de Porte and P. Den'

Ship called *la Seint Julian* of Harfleur
Master: Robert Felippe
Docked: 25 October [1304]
Cargo: Walter le Cotiller: 23 (tuns) 1 pipe woad, 4 seams onions
   Robert Felippe: 3 M onions
Custom: ½d in the pyx

Ship called *la Wynnegod* of Teignmouth
Master: {John}[30] Grigge
Docked: 28 October [1304]
Cargo: John Grigge: 1 C salt

Ship called *la Bonan* of Exmouth
Master: Walter de Ilfridecomb
Docked: 1 November 1304
Cargo: 121 tuns 1 pipe wine of which:
   William le Ku of Bridford: 11 tuns
   Richard le Ku: 5 tuns
   Nicholas le Ku: 1 tun
   Jordan atte Lane: 4 tuns
   W. le Cotiller: 2 tuns
   David le Rede of Pratteshide: 8 tuns, customed {2s 8d [which] the
      Receiver received}
   Richard Brinie: 11 tuns
   Hugh de Toppesham: 10 tuns
   Michael Toraut: 14 tuns
   Richard Gascoyng: 1 tun for portage
   Ralph le Sangere: 6 tuns, customed (Robert de Nyweton received 2s)
   Nicholas Busse: 2 tuns
   John de Smalecumb: 22 tuns
   Richard le Ercedekene: 8 tuns
   Adam de Smalecumb: 2 tuns
   Stephen de Smalecumbe: 11 tuns 1 pipe
   Walter le Cotiller: 1 tun
   William le Ercedekene: 2 tuns
   David le Rede: 2 C pitch [*pice*], 1 C seam [*C sagane*], customed
Custom: Richard Brinie and Adam de Smalecumb for the custom; 14
   tuns customed; all [paid]

---

[29] The entire entry is crossed through.
[30] *Nicholas* crossed through and *John* written in later.

Ship called *la Bayard* of Exmouth
Master: Nicholas Sele
Docked: 4 November 1304
Cargo: Nicholas Sele shipmaster and his mariners: 1½ C salt, 4 pipes wine
Custom: William de Carswill and Henry de Lywerne for the custom,
　…in the pyx

Ship called *la Alice* of Dover
Master: John de Salton
Docked: 22 April 1305[31]
Cargo: 19 tuns woad of which:
　Robert Pous: 12 tuns
　Matthew de Amyas: 7 tuns
Custom: Thomas Godwyne for the custom of Robert Pous, Joan la
　Cotiller for the custom of Matthew; {R. de N., Receiver, received
　19s}

Ship called *la Sauvee* of Lyme
Master: Robert de Ryhill
Docked: 2 November [1304]
Cargo: 78 tuns 2 pipes wine of which:
　Stephen Lambkyn of Rye: 75 tuns 2 pipes
　And 3 tuns for portage
Custom: no custom

la Seinte Marie cogge of Exmouth
Master: Peter Godloc
Docked: 2 November [1304]
Cargo: 60 tuns 5 pipes wine of which:
　William de Okampton: 10 tuns
　Alured Aylward: 1 tun
　William de Okampton and Robert de la Rixen: 7 tuns
　John Horn senior: 2 tuns
　Robert Gosce: 10 tuns 2 pipes
　Thomas Challe: 1 tun
　Philip Lovecoc: 10 tuns 1 pipe
　William de Trente: 8 tuns
　Nicholas Page: 3 tuns (1 pipe)
　Roger Aleys: 2 tuns, customed (in the pyx)
　Henry de Triccote: 1 tun
　Walter Lovecoc: 3 tuns
　Nicholas Lovecoc: 2 tuns, customed 8d in the pyx
　Robert de Stochaye: 1 pipe
Custom: Robert Gosce for custom; 4 tuns customed, 16d; of which 8d
　in the pyx; also 8d in the pyx

---

[31] This entry should have come at the end of m. 27d but the scribe ran out of room
and placed this entry in a blank space on m. 27 before continuing the rest of the
account on m. 28.

la Sauvee of Exmouth
Master: Richard Wayte
Cargo: 90 tuns 2 pipes [wine] of which:
    William Boffet: 7 tuns
    William de Carswill sarger: 8 tuns 1 pipe
    Geoffrey de Rixthivele: 2 tuns
    Henry de Tricote: 15 tuns
    Thomas de Tetteburn: 1 tun
    Elias Paye: 4 tuns
    Luverich de Combe (of Topsham): 2 tuns, customed[32]
    Joan de Rixthivele: 8 tuns
    Robert de Irlond: 17 tuns
    Robert de Doune: 1 tun
    William le Degher: 5 tuns
    John in the Heye: 3 tuns 1 pipe
    John Busse: 4 tuns
    Nicholas Busse: 2 tuns
    William Ercedeakene: 2 tuns
    John Girard: 1 tun
    John de Alfington: 5 tuns, customed {no custom}
Custom: G. de Rixthivele for the custom; ... custom

£2470 17s [*m'm' cccclxx li' xvii s'*][33]

(m. 27d) [**1304/5** account continued]

Ship called *la Sauvee* of Plymouth [*Sutton*]
Docked: 4 November 1304
Cargo: 49 tuns 8 pipes wine (of which 4 not customed), 1 ton avoir-
    dupois [with] 2 bales, and with 18 tuns wine of which:
    Joel de Bradecrofte: 8 tuns
    Henry de Triccote: 1 tun
    Thomas de Tetteburn: 1 tun
    Richard Pellipar': 1 tun
    Joel de Bradecrofte: 10 tuns 1 pipe
    Robert de Wotton: 2 tuns
    Gilbert de Ridmor: 1 tun
    The Archdeacon of Exeter: 4 tuns
    William de Criditon: 6 tuns
    Michael Aurifaber: 3 tuns
    Hugh de Toppesham: 3 tuns
    Robert Gosce: 2 tuns
    Robert de Nymeton: 2 tuns
    John le Ku: 4 tuns, customed[34] (not paid)
    The shipmaster: 9 tuns of which 2 tuns for portage and the rest
        customed

[32] *Customed* crossed through.
[33] This is written in at the very bottom of the tail of the membrane; it may be a customs valuation, perhaps for the royal customs of the king (see above, p 38 n. 206).
[34] *Customed* crossed through.

Roger de Foleford: 3 tuns 1 pipe (customed) of which 1 tun for
portage
John called Prust and William Willy: 3 tuns of which 2 tuns for
portage and 1 (tun) customed
Nicholas Bod: 2 tuns of which 1 for portage and the other cus-
tomed
John Denys: 1 tun for portage
William Berd: 6 pipes, customed
William de Criditon: 1 ton avoirdupois with 2 bales
Custom: Joel de Bradecrofte for the custom; {14 tuns customed, sum
4s 8d, [put] into the pyx by the hand of the Mayor}

Ship called *la Juliane* of Guernsey
Master: William Cokerel
Docked: 24 November 1304
Cargo: William Brewer: 7 tuns woad, 1 ton glass [*verre*], 1 tun potash,
7 barrels white potash, 1 bale alum, 200 spurs [*CC esperdon*]
Thomas Trapel: 1 fardel mercery, customed (2d in the pyx per R.
de Nyweton)
The mariners: 1 seam fish, customed (½d in the pyx)
Nicholas Levesk: ½ C iron, customed (1d in the pyx)
Aforesaid William [Brewer]: 1 C canvas
Custom: William Brewer for the custom; {in the pyx}

Ship called *la Portegoye*
Master: Wymund de Wyght
Docked: 26 November 1304
Cargo: 22½ lasts herring, 3 M[35] herring of which:
Philip Lovecoc: 5 lasts
William de Smalecumb: 4 lasts
Walter Lovecoc: 2 lasts
Nicholas Page: 1 last
John Perour: 1 last
Robert de Nyweton: 1 last
John de Botelston: ½ last
Adam de Middelcote: ½ last
Ralph de Nyweton: 4 lasts
William de Gatepath: ½ last
Robert de Wotton: 1 last
Adam, servant of Ralph de Nyweton: ½ last, customed, 2d in the
pyx
Richard Pruz: 1½ last
Wymund de Wyght: 3 M for portage (of which 1 for ship's victuals
[*staure navis*])
Custom: 2d in the pyx

[35] *C* crossed through.

Ship called *la Seinte Marie cog* of Dartmouth
Master: John Gorewet
Docked: 15 December 1304
Cargo: 21 tuns 1 pipe wine of which:
   Walter le Cotiller: 14 tuns 1 pipe
   John atter Burne of Teignmouth: 7 tuns
Custom: no custom

Ship called *la Andru* of Dartmouth
Master: Nicholas Loc
Docked: 10 January 1305
Cargo: 45 tuns wine of which:
   Robert de Wotton: 6 tuns
   Thomas de Catycote: 4 tuns
   Walter le Cotiller: 1 tun
   Walter Cork: 6 tuns
   Thomas Ladde: 3 tuns
   Nicholas Lok: 10 tuns of which 1 for portage
   John Isaac: 10 tuns of which 1 for portage
   Richard Gabriel: 2 tuns of which 1 for portage
   William de Fowy: 2 tuns
   John Reue: 1 tun for portage
   Nicholas Lok: 1 tun seam [*saym*]
   William Cork: 1 bale almonds
   Martin le Keu: 1 bale glass alum [*glas alym*]
Custom: William Cork for the custom; 21 tuns customed per W. de
  Carswill; 7s in the pyx

Ship called *la Mariote* of Teignmouth
Master: Coc Shipman
Docked: 29 January 1305
Cargo: John de Sandwico: 60 barrels potash woad, 6 striped cloths
Custom: no custom

Ship called *la Godale* of Yarmouth
Master: Roger Bacon
Docked: 30 January 1305
Cargo: Roger Bacon, William de Bekyngton, and Thomas Clement:
  20 lasts herring of which 11 lasts for portage
  Harvey Sciennce of Yarmouth: 3 lasts
Custom: Sum of custom 2s, [put] into the pyx by the hand of the
  Mayor

Ship called *la Lowetie* of St Valéry-sur-Somme
Master: Robert de Goseford
Docked: 4 February 1305
Cargo: (Robert de Goseford and) the mariners: 5½ frails onions, 6
  seams garlic for portage
Custom: Michael Toraut for the custom; and Walri le Gener' paid 7s
  4½d; {R. de N. received 7s 4½d}

Ship called *la Grace* of Yarmouth
Master: Thomas Salerne
Docked: 10 February 1305
Cargo: Thomas Salerne and other mariners (of Yarmouth): 9½ lasts
   herring of which all for portage
Custom: Matthew le Peleter for the custom; no custom

Ship called *la Jouanette* of St Valéry-sur-Somme [*Summe*][36]
Master: Robert Foley
Docked: 11 February 1305
Cargo: 24 tuns woad, 1 ton nuts, 50 M onions, 12(½) seams garlic, 20
   garbs weld of which:
   Adam de la Haye: 16 tuns woad {paid all [custom]}, 1 ton nuts
   John Moset: 4 tuns woad[37] {R. de N. received 4s}
   Bartholomew Byge: ... tuns [woad] {paid 5s(?) per...}
   Robert Foley has the rest
Custom: Henry Bokerel [and] Thomas C... for the custom; sum for
   garlic and onions, 18½d per P.; sum for woad, 24s

Ship called *la Nicholas* of Le Vivier
Master: Hamo Chatel
Docked: 28 February 1305
Cargo: Ives le Bretoun: 1 M garlic which contains 25 seams, 4 seams
   onions
Custom: Ralph de la Lane for the custom; sum 2s 3d; {[which] R. de
   N. received}

Ship called *le Blythe* of Yarmouth
Master: Adam de Doel
Docked: 28 February 1305
Cargo: 21 lasts herring
   Henry de Rochevale: 8 lasts, customed, but he is allowed to have 4
      for portage for 4 men on the ship
   Adam de Doel: 13 lasts of which 7 lasts belong to diverse men for
      portage
Custom: Matthew le Peleter for the custom; sum 3s 4d; {[which] R.
   de N. received}

Ship called *la holhop Seint Nicholas* of Le Vivier
Master: John Poleyn
Docked: 26 March 1305
Cargo: Stephen Moryn of Brittany: 30 seams garlic, 3000 seams
   onions, 20 yards canvas
Custom: Peter le Candeler for the custom; sum 3s 3d; {[which] R. de
   N. received}

Ship called *la Seint Lowys* of St Valéry
Master: Hugh ...
Docked: 31 March [1305]

[36] See p 16 n. 92, above.
[37] The phrases *16 tuns woad*, *1 ton nuts*, and *4 tuns woad* are all underlined.

Cargo: John de Querel junior: 12 tuns woad
Custom: Thomas Godwyne is for the custom; sum 12s

Ship called *la Jouanette* of Exmouth
Master: Adam Slegh
Docked: 14 April 1305
Cargo: Nicholas(?) le Skynnere and other citizens of Exeter: salt
Custom: no custom

Ship called *la Christismasse* of Exmouth
Docked: 21 April 1305
Master: John Gele
Cargo: ... tuns 3 pipes wine of which:
   Philip Lovecoc: 12 tuns 1 pipe
   Walter de Porte: 6 tuns
   Ralph Lovet: 3 tuns
   Richard de Gatepath: 11 tuns 2 pipes
   Robert de Irlond: 2 tuns
   John de Bayon: 1 tun 1 pipe
Custom: Philip Lovecoc for the custom, 4d; {[which] R. de Newton
   received}

Ship called *Seint Marie cog* of Teignmouth
Master: Peter Godloc
Docked: 22 April [1305]
Cargo: 70 tuns 2 pipes wine of which:
   Henry de Triccote: 16 tuns
   Philip Lovecoc: 23 tuns 1 pipe
   Richard le Skynnere: 1 tun
   Thomas de Tetteburn: 1 tun (1 pipe)
   Walter Lovecoc: 3 tuns
   Robert de Irlond: 5½ tuns (... tuns)
   William de Okampton (and Robert de la Rixen: 13 tuns)
Custom: no custom

Ship called *la Godyer* of Exmouth
Master: Richard Harvest
Docked: 22 April [1305]
Cargo: 26 tuns 3 pipes wine of which:
   Gilbert de Nymet(?): 23 tuns (1 pipe)
   John Busse: 1 pipe
   William Brewer: 2 tuns
   Richard Harvest: 2 tuns for portage
Custom: no custom

The 33rd year

{Neweton}[38]

(m. 28) [**1304/5** account continued: April-September 1305]

Ship called *la Sauvee* of Plymouth
Master: William Willy
Docked: 25 April 1305
Cargo: 66 tuns 7 pipes [wine] of which:
  The Bishop of Bath: 6 tuns
  Master Robert de Veteriterra: 2 tuns 1 pipe
  Andrew le Taillur: 1 tun
  Nicholas Busse: 30 tuns 3 pipes
  William de Trente: 10 tuns
  Nicholas Page: 2 tuns 2 pipes
  Roger Beyveyn: 2 tuns
  John le Perour: 2 tuns
  Alfred Horn: 1 tun
  Girard de Vylers: 10 tuns (customed)
  Roger Aleys: 1 pipe, customed
Custom: Roger Aleys for the custom; 10 tuns 1 pipe customed; sum
  3s 8d; {Gerard de Velars paid 40d}

Ship called *la Godyer* of Exmouth
Master: Walter de Ilfridecumb
Docked: 25 April 1305
Cargo: 123 tuns 2 pipes [wine] of which:
  William le Ku: 10 tuns
  Richard le Ku: 9 tuns
  John le Perour: 6 tuns 1 pipe
  Martin le Ku: 1 tun, customed
  Nicholas le Ku: 1 tun
  Philip Lovecoc: 1 tun
  Nicholas de Carswill: 1 tun
  Robert de Irlond: 1 tun
  John Luverich: 1 tun, customed
  John de Smalecumb: 27 tuns
  Richard le Ercedekene: 4 tuns 1 pipe
  William de Smalecumb: 2 tuns
  Adam de Smalecumb: 2 tuns
  Hugh le Gascoynge: 12 tuns
  Walter de Ilfridecumb: 3 tuns, customed
  John Serle: 2 tuns, customed
  William le Clerk of Pratteshide: 2 tuns (of which 1 for portage and
    the other) customed
  David le Rede: 1 tun, customed
  Richard Brynye: 8 tuns

[38] This refers to Robert de Newton who acted as city receiver in 1304/5; see Appendix
2, below.

Hugh de Nymeton: 1 tun, customed
Peter Jolyvet: 4 tuns, customed
Edward de Barnestaple: 2 tuns, customed
Michael le Goldsmyth: 5 tuns
William de Okampton: 2 tuns
W. de Okampton and Robert de la Rixen: 3 tuns
Walter de Grenedon and William [de Grenedon] [*de eadem*]: 2 tuns, customed (8d in the pyx per W. de Porte)
Joan de Rixthivele: 4 tuns
Henry de Triccote: 2 tuns
Walter le Degher: 2 tuns
Thomas de Tetteburne: 2 tuns
Custom: Richard le Ku and Robert de la Rixen for the custom; 16 tuns customed; sum 5s 4d {R. de N. received all}

Ship of Hastings
Docked: 24 April 1305
Cargo: 14 tuns woad of which:
  John Moset: 5 tuns {R. de N. received 5s}
  Walter de Haryer: 9 tuns
Custom: John Horn and John, son of Jordan de Venella for the custom; 14 tuns woad, sum 14s; {then 9s and so all [received]}

Ship called *la Nicholas* of Weymouth
Master: Vincent Gaye
Docked: 8 May 1305
Cargo: 45 tuns 7 pipes wine opf which:
  Girard de Vylers: 42 tuns 3 pipes (customed)
  Vincent Gaye shipmaster: 2 tuns for portage
  Hugh de Waymuth: 1 tun for portage
  Adam atte Nasse: 1 pipe, customed
  Walter de Porte: 2 tuns, of which 1 tun for drink
  Jordan de Venella: 1 pipe
Custom: Walter de Porte for the custom; sum, 42 tuns and 4 pipes customed; {R de N. received}

Ship called *la Jouanete* of Yarmouth [*Gern'*]
Master: Elias Chamberleyn
Docked: 3 June 1305
Cargo: Elias Chamberlayn: 200 quarters coal

Ship called *George* of Dartmouth
Master: Ralph Ode
Docked: 3 June 1305
Cargo: Walter le Cotiller: 42 quarters coal

Ship called *la Cristesmasse* of Yarmouth
Master: Fastel Cok
Docked: 3 June 1305
Cargo: 30 tuns 1 pipe wine of which:
  Joel de Bradecrofte: 18 tuns
  William de Criditon: 6 tuns

Gilbert de Rydmor and said William: 1 tun
Robert le Taverner: 2 tuns
Hugh de Rammeston: 1 tun 1 pipe
Benedict de Scrodeby: 1 tun for portage
Fastel Coki: 1 tun for portage
Custom: no custom

Ship called *le Messager* of Guernsey
Master: Peter Martin
Docked: 4 June 1305
Cargo: Thomas Golde: 600 C canvas and tapets [*tap'*], quilts [*quiltys*],
    knives, cups and empty tuns
  William Furment and Luke le Mercer: 2 seams (linen cloth), 175
    spurs [*1 centum et tribus quarter' esperdon*], 6 C garlic, 6 pounds archil
  Thomas de Beauchamp: 1 seam canvas and linen cloth (for which
    he paid 1d into the pyx)
Custom: Thomas Golde for the custom; sum of all, 4½d; all in the pyx

Ship called *la Godyer* of Ottermouth
Master: Richard Scote
Docked: 7 July 1305[39]
Cargo: Richard Scote: 27 charges salt

Boat of Luverich of Teignmouth
Master: Ralph Luverych
Cargo: Gilbert de Nymet, William de Criditon and Walter le Verour:
    46 quarters wheat, barley, and rye
Custom: no custom

Ship called *Seint Gylys cog* of Sidmouth
Master: Ralph le Sangere
Cargo: 35 tuns wine of which:
  Ralph le Sangere: 22 tuns of which 2 tuns for portage
  Richard Bodde: 1 tun for portage
  Benedict Edmund: 1 tun for portage
  Paris Edmund: 1 tun for portage
  John Vayrlond: 1 tun for portage
  William Spede: 1 tun for portage
  Jordan Paramour: 1 tun for portage
  Geoffrey Robyn: 1 tun for portage
  Adam Prat of Lyme: 1 tun
  Nicholas Blower: 1 tun, customed[40] (for portage)
  Robert Henry: 1 tun for portage
  John atte Pole: 1 tun for portage
  Richard Calewe: 1 tun for portage
  Ralph le Sangere: 4 C salt
Custom: 20 tuns, customed; 6s 8d [put] into pyx the by the hand of
  W. de Porte

[39] The scribe mistakenly wrote down the regnal year as *xxx* [1302] rather than *xxxiii*
[1305].
[40] *Customed* crossed through.

Ship called *la Godyer* of Exmouth
Master: W. de Ilfridecombe
Docked: 6 August 1305
Cargo: Richard le Ercedekene, William le Ku, John de Smalecumb,
   Henry Purpris, and Richard Brinie: salt

Ship called *la cog Seint George*
Master: Roger de Holecumb
Docked: 9 August 1305
Cargo: William and Pagan Brewer: 4 tuns woad, 4 tuns black potash,
   4 barrels white potash, 1 C canvas, 500 spurs [*D esperdon*], 60 stones
   weld, 1 piece striped cloth, ½ piece cloth
   Walter le Coteller: 1000 [*I*ᵐˡ] spurs, 650 taillies of iron [*DC di' tail'
   ferr'*], 2 pieces colored cloth, 2 pieces canvas
   Martin de Brideford: 9 yards colored cloth
   Thomas Codelip: 4 barrels potash, 400 spurs [*iiiiᶜ esperdon*], 1 barrel
   spices [*spicer'*]
   Stephen de Ellecumb: 1 C canvas, customed
   Walter Uppehull: 1 C canvas, 5 ells colored cloth, 50 pounds pans
   [*di' C li' patell'*]
Custom: 1d in the pyx

Ship called *la Welifare* of the Isle of Wight [*Whitht*]
Master: Walter Yve
Cargo: John Coulyng: 2 seams drapery (custom 8d, into the pyx)
   John Yve: 200 spurs [*cc spurdon*]
   John Trapel of Teignmouth: 1 seam canvas, 12 C iron
   Henry Triccote: 10 C iron
   Also 4 barrels potash, 2 C canvas
   Thomas Codelyp : 30 pounds weld
   Thomas Codelyp and Adam le Spicer: 1 barrel spices [*sperorum*]
   Alfred Horn and J. de St Nicholao: 1 fardel canvas which is 4 C, 1
   small fardel mercery
   Adam Sage of Rouen: 2 seams glass [*ver'*], [customed] 2d[41]
Custom: Thomas Cotelip for the custom; sum 3s (2)½d of which 8d is
   in the pyx; {all [received]}

(m. 28d) [**1304/5** account continued: September-October 1305]

Ship called *la Bonan* of Exmouth
Master: Richard Harvest
Docked: 18 October 1305[42]
Cargo: 35 tuns wine of which:
   Philip Lovecoc: 9½ tuns 1 pipe
   Walter de Porte: 9 tuns 1 pipe
   Richard de Gadepath: 8 tuns 1 pipe
   William de Goderington: 2 tuns

[41] *2d* crossed through.
[42] This entry is out of sequence; it should be the second entry of the account of
1305/6 which begins on m. 26.

William le Keu of Bridford: 1 tun
Alured Clericus: 1 tun
William le Brewer: 1 tun, and 3 tuns also remain in his custody, customed
Custom: Richard de Gadepath for the custom; 3 tuns customed, sum 12d; {R. de N. received}

Ship called *la Seincte Marie cog* of Exmouth
Master: Peter Godlok
Cargo: Philip Lovecok, Robert Gossce [and] Peter Godlok: salt

Ship called *la Mariote* of Teignmouth
Master: Giles Bolt
Cargo: 32 tuns 4 pipes wine of which:
    Richard Tolle: 28 tuns (2 pipes), of which 1 [tun] for portage
    Giles Bolt: 2 tuns (2 pipes for portage)
    Lamberton: 1 tun for portage
    Henry de Lyneton: 1 tun for portage
Custom: Walter de Porte for the custom; 10s 4d; {32 tuns customed and R. de N. received [the custom]}

Ship called *la Margarete* of Topsham
Master: David le Rede
Docked: 1 September 1305
Cargo: Peter le Monyer: 11 tuns woad, 1 tun potash
Custom: John Horn senior for the custom; sum {13s, R. de N. received all}

Ship called *la cog Seint Nicholas* of Le Vivier
Master: Julian le Clerk
Docked: 8 September [1305]
Cargo: Ives Julyane: 1000 tresses garlic, 1 seam canvas
    Stephen Gauter: 16 seams garlic
    Julian le Clerk: ½ seam garlic
Custom: sum, 3s 1d; [which] {R. de Neweton received}

Ship called *la holhop Seint Nicholas* of Le Vivier
Master: Lawrence Durant
Docked: 10 September [1305]
Cargo: Guillaume le Barber: 36 seams garlic
Custom: J. de Sancto Nicholao for the custom; 3s 6d [which] {R. de Neweton received}

Ship called *la Seint George* of La Rochelle
Master: Peter Bargoing'
Docked: 15 September [1305]
Cargo: 40 tuns 6 pipes wine of which:
    William le Ku: 18 tuns 2 pipes
    Walter de la Porte and Richard de Gatepath: 20 tuns 2 pipes
    Richard de Gatepath: 2 pipes
    Hugh de Remmeston: 2 tuns
    The said William, Walter, and Richard: salt

Custom: no custom

Sum of all custom of wine–66s 4d–of which Lord Hugh de Curtenay [has] for the third penny–32s 5¼d

1305/6 (m. 26) EXETER–ROLL OF CUSTOMS OF SHIPS APPEARING AT THE PORT OF EXMOUTH BEGINNING AT THE END OF THE 33RD YEAR OF KING EDWARD [I] TO THE 34TH YEAR

Ship called *la cog Seint Pere*
Master: John le Graunt
Docked: 10 October 1305
Cargo: Gerard Phelippe: 6 tuns muscadine wine [*musci*]
  Luke le Mercer: 2 C iron, 1 seam canvas
  The said Gerard: 3 pans [*patella*] weighing 10 pounds
Custom: Walter de Porte for the custom; 2s 2d, {all paid}

Boat of William Kyte
Master: William Kyte
Docked: 18 October 1305
Cargo: 21 pipes potash, woad, [and] Flemish clay with lime [*cleyes de calcar' flemming*]
Custom: Adam le Degher for the custom

Ship called *la Godyer* of Sidmouth
Master: John Irysh
Cargo: 40 tuns wine of which:
  Stephen de Smalecumb: 12 tuns
  William de Smalecumb: 3 tuns
  Ralph le Sangere: 5 tuns, customed
  Thomas de Cadicote: 9 tuns
  Richard Lovecoc: 7 tuns
  Alur': 1 tun (for portage)
  William Austyn: 1 tun
  Nicholas Page: 1 tun[43]
  William le Sangere: 1 tun 1 pipe, customed
  Gilbert Short: 1 tun
Custom: Stephen de Smalecumb for the custom; 2s 8d, {2s paid into the pyx; R. de N. received 8d}

Ship called *la Portegoye* of Teignmouth
Master: Richard le Lange
Cargo: 40 tuns 1 pipe wine of which:
  Nicholas Busse: 10 tuns 1 pipe
  John de Ilemin': 4 tuns
  Nicholas de Betteburgh: 5 tuns
  Ralph Lovet: 2 tuns
  Gilbert de Cumb: 12 tuns, customed (of which 1 for portage)

[43] Entry crossed through.

Richard le Lange: 1 tun for portage
Hugh le Gascoyng: 6 tuns
Custom: Walter de Porte for the custom; sum 4s 8d[44] , {all paid}

Boat of Walter Take
Cargo: Walter Take: 3 tuns wine
Custom: William le Keu cutler for the custom; sum 12d, {[put] into the pyx per R. de Neweton}

Ship called *la Seint Thomas* of Teignmouth
Master: Henry Lange
Docked: 1 November 1305
Cargo: 60 tuns 4 pipes wine of which:
    William and Richard le Keu of Bridford: 18 (tuns) 2 pipes
    William Buffet: 2 tuns
    Walter le Cotiller: 2 tuns
    Martin le Keu: 2 tuns, customed
    Henry Lovecoc: 1 tun
    Nicholas le Keu: 1 tun
    Philip Lovecoc and Walter Lovecoc: 26 tuns 2 pipes
    John de Bayon: 1 tun, customed
    Henry Lange: 3 tuns of which 2 tuns for portage[45]
    Thomas Challe: 1 tun for portage
    John Cosyn: 2 tuns of which 1 tun for portage[46]
    William Bonde: 1 tun for portage[47]
Custom: Philip Lovecoc and Richard le Keu for the custom; 5 tuns customed, sum 20d {[put] in the pyx per R. Beyveyn}

Ship called *la Jouanette* of Teignmouth
Master: Richard Hobel
Docked: 4 November 1305
Cargo: 87 tuns 3 pipes wine of which:
    Nicholas Busse: 19 tuns 1 pipe
    The Bishop of Bath: 6 tuns
    Master R. de Veteriterra: 4 tuns
    Hugh de Toppesham: 9 tuns
    (And Reginald Seingtel: 1 tun)
    Nicholas de Betteburgh: 11 tuns
    Ralph Lovet: 8 tuns
    Robert de Okampton: 2 tuns
    William le Ercedekne: 2 tuns
    David de Dupe: 1 tun 1 pipe
    John Luverych of Teignmouth: 15 tuns, customed (1 for portage)
    Thomas att Burne and John de Cottelegh: 3 tuns of which 2 tuns for portage[48]

---

[44] *8d* crossed through.
[45] *2 tuns for portage* underlined.
[46] *1 tun for portage* underlined.
[47] *1 tun for portage* underlined.
[48] *2 tuns* underlined.

John Dolling: 1 tun for portage
Nicholas de Slapton: 1 tun for portage
Richard Proute: 1 tun, customed
Richard Hobel: 3 tuns (1 pipe) of which 2 for portage[49]
Custom: Nicholas Busse and Walter de Porte for the custom; 19 tuns
customed, sum 6s 8d, {all paid}

Ship called *la nau Johan* of Southampton
Master: John Popel of Southampton
Docked: 6 November 1305
Cargo: 15 tuns woad, 40 garbs weld of which:
    Bartholomew Byg of Amiens: all the [weld and] (11 tuns) [woad][50]
    (John de Quarel: 4 tuns [woad], {paid 4s [custom]})
    William de la More: 5 M onions for portage
Custom: Richard le Noreys for the custom; sum 15s {Bartholomew
    Byge paid 11s to Philip Denebaud}

Ship called *la Rose* of Boldre [*Bolre*]
Master: William Boxy senior
Docked: 7 November 1305
Cargo: Walter le Cotiller: 24 pipes potash, 15 seams garlic
    William Boxi: 2 C iron, customed
Custom: for the custom is the servant of W. le Cotiller [who paid]
    according to the piece? [*secundam(?) pecciam(?)*];[51] {4d [put] into the
    pyx per Philip}

Ship called *la Bonan* of Exmouth
Master: Walter de Ilfridecoumb
Cargo: 128 tuns 2 pipes wine of which:
    John de Smalecumb: 32 tuns
    Richard le Ercedekne: 10 tuns
    William de Strete: 2 tuns
    William de Smalecumb: 1 tun
    Adam de Smalecumb: 6 tuns
    Walter le Cotiller: 18 tuns
    Walter de Langedon: 2 tuns
    William le Brewer: 4 tuns
    Pagan le Brewer: 2 tuns
    Martin le Keu: 3 tuns 1 pipe, customed (20d in the pyx)
    William le Keu: 9 tuns
    W. le Cotiller and W. le Keu: 1 tun
    Richard le Keu: 3 tuns
    Walter de Sancto Leonardo: 3 tuns
    Nicholas de Carswill: 1 tun
    William Buffet: 7 tuns

---

[49] *2 for portage* underlined.
[50] *Which all belong to* crossed through and *11 tuns* inserted above.
[51] This phrase comes at the end of the entry right after the phrase *servant of W. Cotiller* and must refer to the custom assessed on the iron, which could be measured by the piece. I am grateful for Derek Keene's comments on this reading.

John le Perour: 9 tuns
Thomas de Molton: 1 tun, customed (4d in the pyx)
Richard Brinie: 4 tuns
John Serle: 2 tuns, (not) customed
Richard Edmund: 1 tun 1 pipe, customed (of which 1 tun for portage)
William Burel of Pratteshide: 2 tuns, customed (of which 1 for portage; 4d in the pyx)
William le Clerk: 2 tuns of which 1 for portage ({4d in the pyx})[52]
William Gascoyng: 1 tun for portage
Geoffrey atte Will: 1 tun for portage
Walter de Ilfridecoumb: 1 tun for portage
Custom: The same Walter for the custom; ... tuns customed; sum 2s 8d

Ship called *Seint Anne cog* of Teignmouth
Master: Henry Kech
Cargo: 106 tuns 3 pipes (wine) of which:
Henry de Trucote: 24 tuns 1 pipe
Robert de Wotton: 22 tuns 1 pipe
Walter le Degher: 4 tuns
Robert de Irlond: 4 tuns
Henry de Trucote and Thomas de Codelip: 3 tuns
Thomas de Tetteburn: 2 tuns
W. le Degher and Henry de Trucote: 1 tun
Alured Aylward: 1 tun for portage
William de Okampton: 12 tuns 1 pipe
W. de Okampton and Robert de Okampton: 12 tuns
Richard le Skynnere: 3 tuns
Walter and William de Grenedon: 2 tuns, customed ({8d in the pyx})
Henry Kech: 3 tuns of which 2 tuns for portage ({4d in the pyx})
William Knight: 4 tuns of which 1 for portage[53]
Jordan Payn: 1 tun for portage
Thomas de Colepole: 2 tuns, customed ({8d in the pyx})
Nicholas atte Will: 2 tuns of which [1] tun for portage[54]
Thomas atte Burne: 1 tun, customed
Richard le Taillur: 1 tun, customed
William Vorn: 1 tun for portage
Henry de Trucote: 1 tun
Thomas de Codelyp: 2 tuns
Custom: Thomas de Tetteburn for the custom; ... tuns customed, sum 40d(?); 20d remains to be paid; {20d, all [paid]}

Ship called *Seint Gyles cog* of Sidmouth
Master: Ralph le Sangere
Cargo: 114 tuns 4 pipes wine of which:

[52] *1 for portage* underlined.
[53] *Of which 1 for portage* underlined.
[54] Entry crossed through.

Richard de Spaxton: 18 tuns, customed
William de Carswill sarger: 13 tuns
Alured Horn: 1 tun
Nicholas Page: 8 tuns
William Austyn: 4 tuns
The Master of Marsh Barton [Priory] [*Marisco*]: 1 pipe
Roger de Gynes: 1 tun for portage
Gilbert Short: 13 tuns
Ralph de Windesor:[55] 3 tuns, customed ({12d in the pyx per W. de
   Langedene})
Hugh le Gascoyng: 1 tun
Reginald de Seingtel: 1 tun, customed ({4d in the pyx per said
   William})
Ralph le Sangere: 28 tuns (2 pipes) of which 2 tuns for portage[56]
Robert Beaghe: 1 tun for portage
Benedict Edmund and Paris Edmund: 5 tuns of which 2 for
   portage[57]
Nicholas Blower: 2 tuns of which 1 for portage[58]
Robert Henry: 1 tun for portage
Walter Whyte: 1 tun for portage
Jordan Paramour and William Spede: 5 tuns of which 2 for
   portage[59]
Jordan Vayrlond: 1 tun for portage
Thomas de Cadicote: 1 tun
John atte Pole: 4 tuns of which 1 for portage[60]
Custom: Alured Aylward for the custom; {who paid 7s as mainpernor
   of Ralph [*pro manu Radulphi*] of which Philip [has] 2s; and the said
   Alured to pay 5s at Christmas term; he paid 7s 2d in advance which
   is in the pyx per the hand of H. de Trucot [*p' soluit 7s 2d q' sunt in
   pixidie per manum H. de Trucot*]}; {also 4s into the pyx}

Ship called *la Seinte Marie cog* of Exmouth
Master: Peter Godloc
Cargo: 61 tuns 1 pipe wine of which:
   Philip Lovecok: 16 tuns
   Walter Lovecoc: 3 tuns
   Henry de Triccote: 1 tun
   Robert Gosce: 13 tuns
   Michael Toraut: 15 tuns
   Hugh de Nymeton: 5 tuns, customed
   William le Ercedekne: 1 tun
   William Brewer: 2 tuns
   Thomas de Tetteburn: 1 tun
   Richard le Skynnere: 1 tun

---

[55] *Barn'* crossed through and *Windesor* inserted above.
[56] *2 tuns for* underlined.
[57] *2 for* underlined.
[58] *1 for portage* underlined.
[59] *Of which 2 for* underlined.
[60] *1 for portage* underlined.

Godlok: 1 tun for portage
Luverych in the Cumb: 1 tun for portage
Walter de Porte: 1 tun
Henry le Botur: 1 pipe for portage
Custom: Philip Lovecoc and Robert Gosse for the custom; ... custom
... paid to P. Denebaud

Ship called *la Wynnegod* of Teignmouth
Master: John Grigge
Cargo: 27 tuns 1 pipe wine of which:
Ralph de Nyweton mercer: 16 tuns
William Bruwer: 1 tun
Robert Rogem': 1 tun
Nicholas, rector of Thorverton church: 1 tun 1 pipe
Peter, chaplain of the same rector: 1 tun
Thomas Golde: 6 tuns
John Grigge: 1 tun for portage
Botemus atte Mede: ½ tun for portage[61]
Custom: ...

Ship called *la Sauvee* of Exmouth
Master: Richard Wayte
Cargo: 83 tuns 2 pipes wine of which:
Robert le Taverner: 4 tuns
Joel de Bradecrofte: 11 tuns of which 1 tun distilled[62]
John le Perour: 1 tun
Pagan Brewer: 1 tun
Benedict de Iplepenne: 1 tun
John Wele junior: 5 tuns, customed
William de Criditon: 13 tuns
John le Ku: 3 tuns
William atte Will: 1 tun
Robert de Alreton: 1 tun
Robert de Irlond: 12 tuns (1 pipe)
Walter le Degher: 4 tuns (1 pipe)
Joan de Rixthivele: 4 tuns
Alured Aylward: 1 tun
William Ercedekne, Roger Broun, John Busse: 4 tuns[63]
William Bufet: 6 tuns
John Gerveys: 4 tuns
G. de Rixthivele: 2 tuns
Goldene: 1 tun for portage
Paye Hardi: 1 tun for portage
Elias Slegh: 1 tun for portage
William Ercedekne: 1 tun
Gilbert de Nymet:[64] 1 tun
Custom: William de Criditon and Richard Wayte for the custom; ...

[61] *1* crossed through and ½ inserted above.
[62] *1 tun* underlined.
[63] *1 tun customed*, written after *Roger Broun*, crossed through.
[64] *Thomas de Tetteburn* crossed through and *Gilbert de Nymet* written above.

(m. 26d) [**1305/6** account continued]

Ship called *la coc Cler* of Dartmouth
Master: Adam Potel
Cargo: 95 tuns 2 pipes wine of which:
    Gerard de Vilars: 50 tuns (customed)
    Walter Raufe: 28 tuns (customed)
    Adam Potel shipmaster: 2 tuns for portage
    Bartholomew de Plympton: 1 tun for portage
    Henry Cane: 1 tun for portage
    Bartholomew Gabriel: 1 tun for portage
    Feraunt Spaygnel: 1 tun for portage
    William Cade: 1 tun for portage
    Gilbert Potel: 1 tun for portage
    Gilbert Cane: 1 tun for portage
    William Balste: 1 tun for portage
    Randolph Hardenesse: 1 tun for portage
    Geoffrey Gilberd: 1 tun for portage
    Henry de Coleputte: 1 tun for portage
    Bartholomew de Plympton and Bartholomew Gabriel: 5 tuns, customed
    W. de Porte: 1 pipe, 1 pipe for drink [*de beverag'*]
Custom: Walter de Porte for the custom; W. Ercedekene owes 9s 4d;
    83 tuns customed, sum 27s 8d {Walter de Porte paid 18s 4d}

Ship called *la Godyer* of Strood [*Strode*]
Master: Richard Springe
Cargo: John Coghte: 7 frails onions, 10 seams garlic, 20 seams cockles
    [*cokaille*]
    Richard Springe shipmaster and the mariners: 1 frail onions
    Richard Springe: 3 seams garlic for portage and 3 seams cockles
    [*cokaille*] for portage
Custom: John Horn senior for the custom; {sum 7s 4d received per
    the hand of R. de Nyweton}

Ship called *la Crsistesmasse* of Exmouth
Master: John Gyele
Docked: 18 December 1305
Cargo: 19 lasts herring of which:
    William de Smalecumbe: 2 lasts
    Philip Lovecok: 2½ lasts
    John de Smalecumbe: ½ last 2 M
    Walter Lovecok: ½ last
    Richard Archediakne: 1 M
    Philip Lovecok: 3 M
    William de Okampton: 9 M
    Richard le Skynnere: 9 M
    Nicholas le Skynnere: 3 lasts 3 M
    John Whytebrother: 1½ last of which the said last [belongs to] his
    brother Nicholas

The same Nicholas: 1 last
Richard le Whytebrother: 1 last
Richard de Carswell: 1 last
Peter le Chandeler: 4 M
Henry de Triccote: 2 M
John le Perour: 3 lasts
Adam de Middelcote: 4 M
John Gyele shipmaster: ½ last, customed
Custom: 6d in the pyx

Ship called *la Godyer* of Exmouth
Master: Richard Harvest
Docked: 28 January 1306
Cargo: Michael Bazeyn: 5 frails onions, 20 M onions
    Robert, valet of the same: 10 seams garlic
    The aforesaid Michael: 2 tuns 1 pipe woad
Custom: John (Horn) senior for the custom; owes 2s 6d[65] {paid 7s 1d
into the pyx in the presence of the Mayor; also 2s 6d [paid] per cus-
tom into the pyx}; {all [paid]}

Ship called *la Godyer* of Sidmouth
Master: John Irysh
Cargo: 41 tuns 2 pipes wine of which:
    Nicholas Busse: 12 tuns
    Stephen de Smalecumb: 12 tuns 2 pipes
    John de Smalecumbe: 10 tuns
    Richard le Ercedekne: 2 tuns
    The shipmaster: 2 tuns for portage
    Three crewmen [*vallet' eiusdem navis*]: 3 tuns for portage
Custom: no custom

Ship called *la Jouanette* of Dartmouth
Master: Robert Red
Cargo: Ralph le Degher: 4 tuns woad
    Henry de Lym, burgess of Southampton: 4 pipes potash
Custom: no custom

Ship called *la Margarete* of Exmouth
Master: David le Rede
Docked: 9 March 1306
Cargo: Richard Brynye and Ralph de Nyweton mercer: 60 quarters[66]
    maslin (½C(?) corn)
Custom: no custom

Ship called *la Godyer* of Teignmouth
Master: William atte Brigge
Cargo: Matthew le Skynnere: salt and 4 tuns wine
    William atte Brigge: 1 tun wine
Custom: Matthew le Skynnere for the custom; 4d, {received from N.
    the Receiver}

[65] *Owes 2s 6d* crossed through.
[66] *Wheat* crossed through.

Ship called *la holhop Seint Nicholas* of Le Vivier
Master: John Brian
Cargo: William le Barber and Richard de Cirestre: 13 C(?) garlic, 200
  tresses onions
  Luke Bocher: 106 pounds onion seed [*de semine oygn'*]
  William le Barber[67] : 18 pounds onion seed [*semine de oign*]
Custom: Thomas Golde and John de Sancto Nicholao for the custom;
  {sum 4s in the pyx}

Ship called *la Lowys* of Abbeville
Master: Hugh Gellart
Docked: 26 March 1306
Cargo: 27 tuns woad of which:
  John Comyn of Silchester [*Cilecestr'*]: 20 tuns woad (H. de Triccote
    received 20s)
  John de Quarel: 7 tuns [woad] {paid 7s}
  John Comyn: (100) stones weld
  Hugh Gellart: 9 quarters barley, 50 M onions
  Domyngius: 2 quarters wheat
  The same Hugh: 1 quarter beans
Custom: Bartholomew Bygge for the custom per W. de Porte; sum
  27s 6d; {6d in the pyx}

Ship called *la Katerine* of *Oyse* [Pontoise?]
Master: Giles Faderoun
Docked: 26 March 1306
Cargo: John le Yunge: 110 quarters wheat (and) maslin, 12 stones weld
Custom: Thomas Godewyne for the custom

Ship called *la Jowanette* of St Valéry-sur-Somme [*Summe*][68]
Master: Robert Folye
Docked: 26 March 1306
Cargo: 24 tuns woad of which:
  Bartholomew Bygge: 13 tuns {paid 13s}
  John Moset: 11 tuns [woad], 100 stones weld
  Bartholomew Byyge: 1 seam garlic (1d in the pyx), 14 quarters
    corn for portage? [*de p...*]
  And 5 M onions for portage (1d in the pyx)
Custom: Gilbert de Nymet for the custom; sum 24s; {all [paid]}

Ship called *la cog Seint Nicholas* of Le Vivier
Master: Robert Maunsel
Docked: 13 April 1306
Cargo: Nicholas le Graunt: 1000 (tresses) garlic, customed [*1 m' (de
  tracis) de allea cust'*], 1½ C canvas
  Geoffrey Bare: 2 C canvas
Custom: Walter de Porte for the custom; sum 2s 4d; {[which] P.
  received in part payment for his stipend of Easter term}

---

[67] *Nicholas* crossed out and then *said William le Barber* written in.
[68] See p 16 n. 92, above.

Ship called *Seinte Marie cog* of Exmouth
Master: Peter Godlok
Cargo: 60 tuns wine of which:
　Thomas le Furbur: 2 quintals iron (customed)
　Philip Lovecok: 14 tuns
　Walter Lovecok: 2 tuns
　John de Bayona: 1 tun, customed, [paid] into the pyx
　Thomas de Molton: 1 (tun), customed, [paid] into the pyx
　Nicholas Busse: 3 tuns
　John Girard of Topsham: 3 tuns
　Thomas le Furbur: 1 tun, customed
　Walter de Langeden: 1 tun
　Richard le Skynnere: 1 tun
　Peter Godlok: 2 tuns for portage
　Walter de Porte: 4 tuns
　Ralph Lovet: 4 tuns
　Richard de Gadepath: 8 tuns 1 pipe
　John le Perour: 10 tuns
　Adam le Perour: 2 tuns
　Robert de Irlond: 1 tun
　John Luverych: 1 tun (for portage)[69]
　Thomas Challe: 1 tun for portage
Custom: John le Perour for the custom; charged the sum of 5d

Ship called *la Sauvee* of Exmouth
Master: Richard Wayte
Cargo: 80 tuns wine of which:
　Henry de Triccote: 15 tuns 1 pipe
　… de Tetteburne: 3 tuns
　Richard le Skynnere: 1 tun
　Alured Aylward: 1 tun (for portage)
　Philip Lovecok: 15 tuns 1 pipe
　Walter Lovecok: 6 tuns
　John de Bayona: 1 tun, customed, [paid] into the pyx
　Robert de Irlond: 10 tuns 1 pipe
　W… le Degher: 3 tuns
　John in the Haye: 3 tuns
　Paye Hardi: 4 tuns
　Richard le Seler: 2 tuns
　Geoffrey de Boghe: 6 tuns
　Thomas le Furbur: 1 tun, customed {paid 4d}
　Geoffrey de Rixthivele: 2 tuns
　John Busse: 1 tun
　Richard le Wayte: 1 tun for portage
　John Averay: 1 tun for portage
　Adam Slegh: 2 tuns of which (1) for portage and … customed
　Goldene: 1 tun for portage
　Elias Slegh: 1 tun for portage

---

[69] *Customed* crossed through and *for portage* inserted above.

Harlewin Bolt: 1 tun for portage
Geoffrey Daumarle: 1 tun, customed {paid 4d}
Peter Edmund: 1 tun for portage and 2 tuns, customed
Custom: the shipmaster for the custom; charged the sum 20d

Ship called *la Godyer* of Exmouth
Master: Richard Harvest
Cargo: 39 tuns wine 3 pipes of which:
  William de Ochamton: 9 tuns 1 pipe
  Richard le Skynnere: 8 tuns
  Nicholas le Skynnere: 6 tuns
  Richard le Seler: 1 tun
  Alured Aylward: 1 tun
  William de Okampton and Robert de Okampton: 9 tuns 1 pipe
  William de Grenedon and Walter de Grenedon: 1 tun, [custom
    paid] into the pyx
  Walter Lovecok: 2 tuns
  Henry de Triccote: 1 pipe
  Richard de Gadepath: 1 pipe
  Geoffrey Daumarle: 1 tun, customed {paid 4d}
  Elias Hardi: 1 tun
Custom: Robert de Okampton for the custom; sum 4d

Ship called *Seinth Thomas cog* of Teignmouth
Master: Henry le Lange
Cargo: 75 tuns 3 pipes [wine] of which:
  William le Keu: 20 tuns 1 pipe
  Richard le Keu: 18 tuns 1 pipe
  Martin le Keu: 3 tuns, customed [paid] into the pyx
  Nicholas le Keu: 1 tun
  Jordan atte Lane: 3 tuns
  Philip Lovecok: 1 pipe
  John le Perour: 9 tuns
  Adam Perour: 4 tuns
  Michael in the Cumbe: 4 tuns, customed
  William Buffet: 3 tuns
  Henry le Lange: 9 tuns of which 7 tuns customed
Custom: John le Perour for the custom; sum 9 tuns; sum 3s received
  per Philip

Two boats
Cargo: Hugh Do: 14 tuns 1 pipe wine
  William de Exon': 3 tuns wine
Custom: William le Keu of Bridford for the custom; sum 17 tuns 1
  pipe; sum {6s in the pyx}

Ship called *la Nicholas* of Saltash
Master: Odo de Crutur
Cargo: William de Summe, a Picard: 100(?)[70] garbs weld

---

[70] There is a hole in the manuscript here; the amount may be 200.

Ship called *la Godyer* of Exmouth
Master: Roger atte ...
Cargo: 123 tuns 1 pipe [wine] of which:
  John de Smalecumbe: 15 tuns
  Sabina le Ercedekne: 3 tuns
  Adam de Smalecumb: 3 tuns
  Adam Osbern: 16(?) tuns
  Walter de Porte: 12 tuns
  William le Keu: 3 tuns
  Thomas de Molton: 2 tuns, customed (8d in the pyx)
  Richard de Spaxton(?): [10] tuns (customed, paid 40d)[71]
  Geoffrey de la Boghe: 2 tuns
  Richard Edmund: 2 tuns (of which 1) for portage
  Benedict Edmund: 2 tuns (of which 1) for portage
  William B... : 4 tuns (of which 1) for portage (paid 12d)
  William le Clerk: 4 tuns of which 1 for portage and others cus-
    tomed (paid 12d of which 10d for B...)
  Roger Broun: 1 tun for portage
  W... Papegay: 1 tun for portage
  Geoffrey atte Will: 1 tun for portage
  William Gascoyng: 1 tun for portage
  Robert He... : 1 tun for portage
  Geoffrey Daumarle (pledge, Jordan le Clerk): 3 tuns, customed
  Gilbert Short: 2 tuns
  Hugh de ... ton : 1 tun (4d in the pyx)
  Walter de Langdene: 6 tuns
  Michael Turaud: 6 tuns
  William Bruwer: 5 tuns 1 pipe
  Roger Bruwer: 3½ tuns
  Roger Beyvyn: 6 tuns
  Ralph le M... : 1 tun[72]
  Richard Dirkyn: 2½ tuns
  Richard le Keu [and] Nicholas le Keu: 1 tun
  Jordan de Venella: 1 tun
  John Serle of Topsham: 2 tuns of which the other for [portage]
  Thomas Toraud: 1 tun, customed (4d in the pyx per R. B.)
  John de Dodescumbe: 1 tun for his drink
Custom: John de Smalecumb and William le Keu for the custom; 24
  tuns customed, sum 8s; 16d remains to be paid; {all [paid]}

Ship of John de Holecumbe
Master: John de Holecumbe
Cargo: Henry de Lym, burgess of Southampton: 64 garbs weld, 10
  barrels potash
Custom: no custom

Ship called *la Katerine* of Yarmouth

---

[71] The number of tuns is illegible, but the custom paid indicates it must have been 10.
[72] Entry crossed through.

Master: Walter (de) Wrexham
Cargo: Roger de Norf' and John...: 150 quarters (corn) maslin
  The said Roger and John: 10 M teasels

{Scrutinized and nothing found}[73]

The 34th year

Philip received 4s 2d in the term of the Nativity of St John Baptist[74]

(m. 25) [**1305/6** account continued: May–September 1306]

Ship called *la Nicholas* of Ringmore [*Rydmor*]
Master: Robert Peverel
Cargo: 19 tuns woad of which:
  Robert de Pouz and John de Quarel: 9 tuns {all [custom paid]}
  John Moset: 5 tuns {paid 5s}
  Bartholomew Bygge: 5 tuns {paid 5s}
  Aforesaid Robert: 100 (stones) weld
Custom: Walter le Degher for the custom; sum 19s

{Scrutinized}[75]

Ship called *la Peter* of Hamble [*Hamele*]
Master: Walter Walkelyn
Cargo: William le Brewer: 100 stones weld, 7 barrels potash, 800 iron
  spurs [*DCCC ferri esperdon*], 800 taillies of iron [*DCCC tayl ferri*], 3 pos-
  nets [*poscenett'*], 1 laver with basin [*lavator cum pelve*], 11 bales alum
Custom: no custom

Ship called *la Godyer* of Watermouth
Master: Michael Fresel
Docked: 28 May 1306
Cargo: 44 tuns 5 pipes wine of which:
  Robert Pope of Lyme: 20 tuns (1 pipe)
  Nicholas de Crokerne: 20 tuns 2 pipes, customed, and 4 tuns 2
    pipes for portage
Custom: Henry de Triccote for the custom and afterwards Robert
  Gosse came and paid 16d to the Receiver for Nicholas de Crokerne;
  sum 7s 4d; {the Receiver received 16d from Robert Goce}

Ship called *la Berthelemeu* of Exmouth
Master: W. de Ilfridecumbe
Cargo: 15 tuns 2 pipes wine of which:
  Richard de Tetteburne: 10 tuns 2 pipes

[73] Written in a later hand, similar to that above (n. 17) and below (n. 75).
[74] Scribbled at the tail end of the membrane. *Philip* was probably the city clerk, Philip
Denebaud; see Appendix 2, below.
[75] Written in a later hand, similar to those above (see n. 17).

Gilbert de Ridmore: 5 tuns
Custom: no custom

Ship called *la Seint Lowys* of Abbeville[76]
Master: Hugh Gillard
Cargo: John le Perour: 2 fardels cloth
  Matthew le Skynnere: 1 fardel [cloth][77]
  Matthew de Brussele: 10 tuns woad, 60 quarters rye
Custom: John Moset for the custom; sum 10s; {5s in the pyx per R. Beyveyn}; {R. de N. received 5s}

Ship called *la Sauvee* of Rye
Master: Richard Box of Rye
Docked: 28 June 1306
Cargo: 44 tuns 2 pipes wine of which:
  Robert le Taverner: 6 tuns
  John Leverich of Teignmouth: 1 tun, customed
  Joan Busse: 2 tuns
  Joel le Taverner: 10 tuns (of which 1 distilled)
  Gilbert de Nymet: 10 tuns
  Walter Squier: 4 tuns
  John Wele, son of Master John Wele: 5 tuns
  John le Keu: 5 tuns 1 pipe
  Jobel le Taverner and Gilbert de Nymet: 1 tun 1 pipe
Custom: Joel le Taverner for the custom; 6 tuns customed, sum 2s in the pyx

Ship called *la Bonan* of Exmouth
Master: Roger atte See
Docked: 1 August 1306
Cargo: 128 tuns wine, 42 quintals iron of which:
  Richard Dyrkyn: 21 quintals
  Nicholas de Carswill: 21 quintals
  Reymund de Monte Bardone: 42 tuns 4 pipes, customed (14s 4d; of which 2 pipes [custom] free)
  John Favard: 22 tuns (7s 4d)
  Stephen Furvern: 20 tuns ($\frac{1}{2}$ mark), 1 pipe [custom] free, also 6 tuns for portage
  William Bruwer: 1 tun
  Philip Lovecoc: 1 tun
  Walter de Porte: 1 tun
  Richard de Gadepath: 1 tun
  Also for the crew's drink [*de beverag' navis*]: 1 tun
  William de Criditon: (11 tuns)
  William Den: 9 tuns, customed (3s in the pyx)
  Robert Waleys: 1 tun, customed (...)[78]

---

[76] An X is placed over the entire entry.
[77] *Peletry [peler']* crossed through so the import probably refers to cloth.
[78] *Customed* crossed through. The superscript phrase is unclear (it may read *qd' exp' rerum* or *qd' ex'p rep'*) and may run onto the next line (*Nicholas Busse: 1 [tun] distilled*).

(Nicholas Busse: 1 [tun] distilled)

Thomas de Tetteburne: 5 tuns, customed (20d in the pyx by view of Richard de Gadepath)

Nicholas de Carswill: 3 tuns

Richard Dirkyn: 4 tuns

And they say that 4 tuns or thereabouts are distilled

Custom: and for the custom, Richard de Gadepath ({paid 40d}), William le Keu (for the aliens), ({paid 40d}); and Thomas de Tetteburne for 3s; sum of all custom 33s; {R. de N. received 5s 8d}; {W. de Langedon owes 16s for Reymund de Monte Bardone and John Favard}[79]

Ship called *la Cristesmasse* of Exmouth
Master: John Gele
Docked: 13 August 1306
Cargo: John Gele and his fellows: 100 quarters coal
Custom: no custom; afterwards he comes and seeks a licence to unload at Pratteshide and gives a fine on condition that he can unload; 3d in the pyx

Ship called *la Petite Nicholas* of Sidmouth
Master: Cole Reade
Cargo: Cole Reade: 100½ quarters coal

Ship called *la Berthelemeu* of Exmouth
Master: Walter de Ilfridecumbe
Docked: 8 September 1306
Cargo: 13 tuns woad of which:
    William Brewer: 6 tuns
    Henry de Triccote and Thomas Codelyp: 6 tuns
    Adam Sage: 1 tun, customed
    Ralph de Nyweton and Walter le Ware: 4 bales alum
Custom: William Brewer for the custom, 12d; {R. de N. received 12d}

Sum of the custom of wine, £6 3s 8d of which Lord Hugh de Courtenay for his third penny [has] 41s 2½d with one third of a halfpenny

1310/11(m. 24) [CUSTOMS OF] WINES LANDED AT THE PORT OF EXMOUTH AFTER THE FEAST OF ST MICHAEL IN THE FOURTH YEAR OF KING EDWARD SON OF KING EDWARD

Vintage wines[80]

Ship called *le Godyer* of Exmouth
Master: John Morkyn
Cargo: 45 tuns wine of which:

[79] This last phrase is written at the top of the entry.

[80] Vintage wines normally arrived before Christmas so the following ships probably docked in Exeter between October and December. This heading is followed later by one indicating racked [*reek*] wines which arrived in the spring.

Richard le Keu: 11 tuns
William le Keu: 8 tuns
Martin le Keu: 8 tuns
William Buffet: 2 tuns
Adam Broun: 2 tuns
Thomas Toraud: 2 tuns
John Horn: 1 tun
Nicholas de Bradecrofte: 2 tuns, customed
Gilbert de Cumbe: 6 tuns
Walter de Porte: 3 tuns
Custom: 2 tuns customed; 8d in the pyx

Ship called *la Margarete* of Exmouth
Cargo: 50 tuns 4 pipes wine of which:
Philip Lovecok: 30 tuns 3 pipes
Walter de Hugheton: 1 tun
John de Bayona: 1 tun
Robert de Irlond: 10 tuns 1 pipe
And 8 tuns for portage
Custom: no custom

Ship called *Godyer* of Exmouth
Master: Richard Harvest
Cargo: 133 tuns 7 pipes wine of which:
John de Smalecombe: 21 tuns 1 pipe
Walter de Pourte: 6 tuns (1 pipe)
Hugh le Garscoyng: 4 tuns
Robert Gosce: 1 tun
Adam de Smalecombe[81]
Robert Belechere: 3 tuns
William le Ku of Bridford: 5 tuns 1 pipe
Martin le Ku: 7 tuns 1 pipe
John de Dodescomb: 1 tun
Gilbert de Cumb: 3 tuns
Nicholas de Bradecrofte: 1 tun 1 pipe (customed 8d)
John de Somery: 12 tuns (customed 4s)
Gilbert Pycard: 5 tuns 1 pipe (customed 2s)
Adam Peror: 10 tuns
William Boffet: 2 tuns
Thomas Forbur: 2 tuns
Thomas Toraud: 7 tuns 1 pipe
Michael Toraud: 2 tuns
Master Hamond: 1 tun (customed 4d)
William de Okampton: 3 tuns
Robert de Okampton: 9 tuns
John Horn: 3 tuns
Nicholas Busse: 3 tuns
Richard Harvest: 1 tun (for portage)

---

[81] *Adam de Smalecombe* crossed through.

Richard Golde: 1 tun (for portage)
John de Wreyford: 7 tuns (customed 2s 4d)[82]
Giles Bolt: 12 tuns (customed 4s)
Custom: 11s in the pyx

Ship called *la Sauve* of Exmouth
Master: Walter Edmund
Cargo: 86 tuns 10 pipes wine of which:
  Richard le Keu: 16 tuns 1 pipe
  William Buffet: (4) tuns[83]
  Gilbert de Cumbe: 3 tuns
  Robert de Okampton: 2 tuns
  John le Perour: 1 tun
  William le Keu: 1 tun
  Nicholas de Bradecrofte: 2 tuns, customed, in the pyx
  Matilda de Trickote and John de Trickote: 8½ tuns
  Thomas Tregony the baker: 10 tuns (3 pipes)
  Walter de Langeden: 1½ tuns
  Michael de Oxton: 1 tun
  Richard de Gatepath: 1 tun
  Robert de Criditon: 1(½) tuns, customed
  Thomas le Furbur: 1½ tuns
  William de Criditon, once servant of the Bishop: 1 tun, customed
  Geoffrey atte Boghe: 11 tuns 3 pipes
  Henry Lovecok: 1 tun
  William Arcedekne: 1 tun
  William Jobbe has in his custody 5 tuns 1 pipe of which:
    Alured Aylward: 1 pipe
    John David: 1 tun
  Richard Engelond: 5 tuns, customed
  Robert de Irlond: 3 tuns
  Henry le Megr': 2 tuns for drink [*de beverag'*] [and] p[ortage]
  Walter Edmund: 1 tun 1 pipe
  Henry le Carpunter: 1 tun for portage
  Luverych: 2 tuns 1 pipe of which 1 tun for portage[84]
Custom: 9½ tuns customed for which William le Keu received 3s and
  deposited it in the pyx

Ship called *la Grace Deu* of Dartmouth
Master: Nicholas Swyft
Cargo: 87 tuns 1 pipe wine of which:
  Philip Lovecok: 48 tuns 1 pipe
  Walter de Hugheton: 6 tuns
  John de Bayona: 3 tuns
  Nicholas Page: 7 tuns
  Thomas le Baker: 2 tuns
  William de Ridmor: 1 tun

[82] *Customed 2s 4d* crossed through.
[83] *5* crossed through and *4* written above.
[84] *Unde 1 tun* underlined.

William Austyn: 2 tuns
Richard de Spaxton: 7 tuns
Richard Dyrkyn: 2 tuns, and 1 tun, customed (4d in the pyx)
Robert Gosce: 3 tuns
William Mounteyn: 2 tuns, customed
And 2 tuns for portage; also 1 tun, customed, 4d in the pyx
Custom: Robert Gosce for the custom of William Mounteyn; 7 tuns
　　customed; in the pyx

Ship called *la Croys* of Dartmouth
Master: Roger le Pyper
Cargo: 24 tuns wine of which:
　　John Stiward: 8 tuns
　　John Bataille, burgess of Winchelsea: 16 tuns
Custom: no custom

Ship *Sancti Martini* of St Valéry
Master: William Blogoy
Cargo: John Mouset: 10 tuns woad, 160 stones weld
Custom: 10s; W. le Keu received 10s

Racked wines [*Rek*][85]

Ship called *la Sauvee* of Exmouth
Master: Paris Edmund
Cargo: Robert de Irlond, Geoffrey de la Boghe, Thomas de Tetteburn
　　and others: salt
　　And 8 tuns wine of which:
　　　　Robert de Irlond: 1 tun wine
　　　　Walter Edmund: 2 tuns[86]
　　　　Luverych: 2 tuns
　　　　William Jobbe: 2 tuns
　　　　Gascoyng: 1 tun for portage
Custom: no custom

Ship called *la Seinte Marie cog* of Exmouth
Master: Peter Godlok
Cargo: 93 tuns 19 pipes wine of which:
　　Walter de Porte: 8 tuns 5 pipes
　　Richard de Gadepath: 4 tuns 3 pipes
　　William de Gadepath: 3 tuns 1 pipe
　　John le Perour: 3 tuns
　　Adam le Perour: 3 tuns
　　Thomas le Furbur: 3 tuns
　　Robert de Criditon: 2 tuns, customed (8d in the pyx)

---

[85] This line contains the word *Rek* written five times in large letters; they refer to the
mature *reek* (racked) wines drawn off the lees (the dregs) in January and February and
normally sold in the spring. The following cargoes, therefore, probably did not arrive
in Exeter until March or later.
[86] *1 tun* crossed through.

Thomas de Tetteburne and John de Trickote: 15 tuns (2)[87] pipes
Geoffrey le Degher: 7 tuns, customed (2s 4d in the pyx)
Michael Toraud: 2 tuns
John Girard: 2 tuns
Peter Godlok: 1 tun
Paye Gosse: 1 tun for portage
Leticia de Ridmor: 1 tun
Philip Lovecok: 26 tuns 5 pipes
Walter Lovecok: 3 tuns
John Lovecok: 2 tuns 1 pipe, customed (8d in the pyx)
Walter de Hugheton: 4 tuns 1 pipe
John de Bayona: 3 tuns
William Ralle: 1 pipe (4d in the pyx)
Custom: 2 tuns 2 pipes [wine] customed for which Philip Lovecok received [4s]

Ship called *la Margarete* of Exmouth
Master: Adam Slegh
Cargo: 61 tuns 5 pipes wine of which:
   Philip Lovecok: 23 tuns 5 pipes
   Walter Lovecok: 3 tuns
   Walter de Hugheton: 2 tuns
   John de Bayona: 2 tuns
   Robert de Irlond: 6 tuns
   John Gayllard of Plymouth: 11 tuns, customed (challenged)[88]
   Vincent[89] Tak: 7 tuns
   Adam Slegh: 3 tuns of which 2 for portage [and the other customed] (4d in the pyx)
   Nicholas de Lideford: 3 tuns
   Roger Serle: 1 tun for portage
   Adam Slegh: 4 quintals iron (1d in the pyx)
   John Vissher: 2 quintals iron (1d in the pyx)

Ship called *le Bonan* of Exmouth
Master: Richard Harvest
Cargo: 61 tuns 12 pipes wine of which:
   William le Keu of Bridford: 5 tuns 1 pipe
   Martin le Keu of Bridford: 10 tuns 2 pipes[90]
   Richard (le Keu) of Bridford: 2 tuns
   William de Gatepbath: 2 tuns
   Gilbert Pykard: 2 tuns (8d)[91]
   William Dyne: 10 tuns 4 pipes (4s 8d)
   Richard de Tavystok: 1 tun (4d)

[87] *1* crossed through and *2* inserted above.
[88] Superscript reads *calumpnum*, implying that the importer disputed his custom status.
[89] *Robert* crossed through.
[90] *1 pipe* crossed through and *2 pipes* written in.
[91] A curving line is drawn over the top of this entry, as well as that of William Dyne, Richard de Tavystok, and Nicholas de Ryouns.

William le Bruere: 1 tun
John le Ercediakene: 4 tuns
John David: 3 tuns 1 pipe
Nicholas de Ryouns: 1 pipe (4d)
Robert de Irlond: 1 pipe
Richard de Gatepath: 2 pipes
John de Smalecomb: 13 tuns
Robert de Ochampton: 4 tuns
Robert Belechere: 3 tuns
William le Skynnere: 1 tun
John de Smalecomb: 1 bale almonds
William le Skynnere: 1 bale almonds
William le Bruere: 1 bale almonds
Adam Broun: 1 bale cordwain
Richard de[92] Stavystok and Adam Broun: 1 bale archil [*argoul*]
Custom: 6s, as appears in superscripts, which William le Keu received

Ship called *la Hynde* of Ipswich
Master: Pyk
Cargo: 80 tuns 4 pipes wine of which:
Adam le Perour: 4 tuns
Thomas le Foubour: 4 tuns
Giles Boolt: 10 tuns (1 pipe)
John Leverich: 7 tuns
John de Bovy: 10 tuns 2 pipes
Henry de Covyntre: 7 tuns
Gilbert in the Comb: 12 tuns 1 pipe
Walter de Porte: 6 tuns
Stephen Wyldlere: 8 tuns
And 12 tuns for portage
Custom: 19 tuns 2 pipes customed; and the custom is 7s which W. le
Keu received

Sum of custom of wine–33s 8d–of which Lord H. de Curtenay
[receives for his one-third share] 11s 2½d

1310/11 (m. 24d) [ACCOUNT OF CUSTOM OF OTHER MERCHAN-
DISE]

Ship called *Godyer* of Teignmouth
Master: William Chaste
Docked: 28 November [1310]
Cargo: Thomas Golde and Stephen le Bruere: 5 tuns woad, 6 pipes
potash, 7 quarters barley, 3 quarters beans
Walter de Morchard: 6 pipes potash, 4 quarters beans, 6 quarters
barley

---

[92] *Brydef'* crossed through.

Ship called *Seint Lowy* of Abbeville
Master: Hugh Gyllard
Docked: 4 December [1310]
Cargo: Peter le Monyer: 24 tuns woad
  And 15 M onions for portage
Custom: 24s which William le Keu received

Ship called *Godyer* of Ottermouth
Master: Richard Dollyng
Docked: 14 December [1310]
Cargo: Nicholas Busse and others viz., Giles de Tignemuth and other
  mariners: 180 quarters wheat
  The said Giles: 5 C onions, customed

Ship called *la Margarete* of Yarmouth
Master: Robert le Corteler
Cargo: 40 lasts herring[93] 10 M herring of which:
  Philip Lovecok: 5½ lasts
  Walter Lovecok: 5 lasts 3 M
  William de Smalecoumbe: 6½ lasts
  Nicholas le Skynner: 3 lasts 10 M
  Matthew le Skynner: 1 last 2 M
  William de Okampton: 1 last
  John Whytebrother: 3 lasts 2 cades
  Robert de Okampton: 1 last
  Guy Maynard: ½ last
  Thomas Fartheyn: ½ last
  Thomas le Furbur: 1 last
  Richard Gaudethon: 1 last
  Thomas de Molton: 2½ lasts
  Jordan de Venella: 1½ lasts
  Seman atte Sonde, burgess of Yarmouth: 6 lasts 3 M
  Nicholas le Skynnere: 3 M
Custom: no custom

Ship called *Benvenue* of St Valéry
Master: John de Goseford
Cargo: William le Brewer and Walter le War': 4 frails onions and
  weld [*wald'*]
Custom: no custom

Ship called *la Katerine* of Guernsey
Master: Robert de Genes
Cargo: Robert de Genes: 30 quarters barley, 1 quarter beans, 2½ quar-
  ters peas, 4 quarters oats, 40 M onions (5d in the pyx), 6 fresh rays
  [*ragad' friscis*]
  John de Sancto Nicholao: 20 quarters wheat

---

[93] *Herring* is expunged.

Ship called *la Margaret* of Romney
Master: John Laurenz
Cargo: 160 quarters beans and peas on which there is no custom
Custom: no custom

Ship called *Godale* of Gosport
Master: Stephen de Dagevill
Cargo: William le Brewer: 50 quarters maslin, 100 stones weld
Custom: no custom

Ship called *la Margarete* of Calais
Master: Copyn Harpe
Cargo: W. de Porte and Stephen de Smalecumb: 30 quarters wheat maslin
Custom: no custom

Ship called *Seynt Johanas cog*
Master: Peter la Cornayll
Cargo: Peter la Cornayll: 20 quarters wheat, 40 quarters barley, 2 quarters peas and beans, 1 quarter oats, 1 M salted mackerel
Custom: pledge for the custom, John de Sancto Nicholao; 1½d in the pyx

Ship called *la Floryete* of *Salune?* [*Salvin?*]
Master: Richard le Coverour
Cargo: John de Kent: 8 tuns woad
Custom: 10s, [which] William le Keu received

Ship called *la Lowys* of Abbeville
Master: Hugh Gyllard
Cargo: Peter le Monyer: 16 tuns woad, 100 stones weld
Custom: William le Keu received custom, 16s

Ship called *la holoc de St Lowis*
Master: John Rydel
Cargo: Pagan le Bruere and Stephen de Ellecombe: 80 stones weld, 4 bales alum, 36 hats [*capell'*], 100 knives, 15 lanterns
Pagan le Bruere: 2 small millstones
Walter de Morchard: 2 bales alum, 12 hats, 50 knives

Ship called *la Nicholas* of Calshot
Master: Robert Toppe
Docked: 3 July [1311]
Cargo: Ralph Burgeys: 4 tuns woad
Lawrence le Potyer: 15 C battery-ware
Custom: John Mozet for the custom; to be paid within the next 15 days; sum 6s 6d, [which] {William le Keu received}

Ship called *la Nostre Dame* of Louvières [*Loveris*]
Master: John Adam
Docked: 3 July [1311]
Cargo: Richard Mounteyn: 12 tuns woad, 20 stones of Caen [*petr' de cain*], 20 M teasels, 2 (pieces) serge cloth of Caen [*pann' sarg' de*

cain], 1 tun full of towels and table-cloths, 2 pieces linen cloth
Custom: William le Deghere and Gilbert de Nymet for the custom, to
be paid within the next 8 days; {William le Keu received 12s}

Ship called *la Osanne* of Cabourg [*Cabowe*]
Master: Richard Osanne
Cargo: Richard Osanne: 30 quarters wheat, 20 quarters barley, 1
millstone, 12 C mackerel [*xii^C*] (2½d in the pyx)

Ship called *la Floryete* of Cabourg [*Cabowe*]
Master: Peter de Geneyes
Cargo: William Cokerel: 36 quarters barley, 12 quarters wheat, 1
dozen stockings, ½ C canvas

Ship called *la holhop de St Lowys*
Master: John (Rydel)
Cargo: Nicholas le Graunt: 28 quarters wheat

Ship called *Seinte*[94] *Margarete* of Exmouth
Cargo: Philip Lovecok [and] Robert de Irlond: 2 C salt

Ship called *la cog Seint Lowys* of *Maullo* [St Malo?]
Master: Philip Peytevyn
Cargo: Thomas Lukeys: 55 quarters wheat and barley

Ship called *Seint Nicholas* of Le Vivier
Master: Lawrence Hughe
Cargo: Robert Russel: 2500 tresses garlic, 2 seams onions
Custom: John de Sancto Nicholao for the custom; 5s 3½d [which]
{William le Keu received}

Ship called *la Joanete* of Guernsey
Master: Richard Geneys
Cargo: Richard Geneys and his fellows: 30 seams onions, 20 yards
linen cloth
Custom: 15d in the pyx

Ship called *la cocke Seint Johan* of Le Vivier
Master: Gylyet Pycherel
Cargo: Ives le Britoun: 2500 tresses garlic, 40 yards linen cloth, 5
pots [*oll'*] butter
Custom: John de Sancto Nicholao and Alured Aylward for the cus-
tom; sum 5s 5d [which] W. le Keu received

Wine custom in the fourth year of King Edward [II][95]

---

[94] *Katerine* crossed through.
[95] Written in large letters at the bottom of the membrane.

1312/13(m. 23) VINTAGE [WINES]–EXETER–ROLL OF CUS-
TOMS OF WINE, GARLIC, ONIONS, WOAD AND
OTHER MERCHANDISE IN SHIPS LANDED AT THE
PORT OF EXMOUTH FROM THE FEAST OF ST
MICHAEL IN THE SIXTH YEAR OF KING EDWARD
SON OF KING EDWARD TO THE SAME FEAST IN THE
FOLLOWING YEAR[96]

Ship called *Seinte Marie cog* of Teignmouth
Master: Henry Kech
Cargo: 74 tuns 6 pipes wine of which:
　　Gilbert de Cumbe: 23 tuns ...
　　Sir Thomas de Henton: [2 tuns] ...
　　Walter de Porte: 16 tuns 1 pipe
　　Ralph, his son: 4 tuns
　　John de Bovy: 9 tuns (1 pipe)
　　John ...: 14 tuns, customed
　　Henry Kech: 1 tun, customed, and 5 tuns for portage
　　Gilbert de Cumbe: 4 caps of sindon [*capita de cindon*]
　　John de Beauforest: 3 caps of sindon (3d in the pyx)
　　John de Bovy: 2 caps of sindon
Custom: on 16 tuns, 5s 4d [which] J. de Smalecumb received

Ship called *la Margarete* of Exmouth
Master: Adam Slegh
Cargo: 60 tuns 4 pipes wine of which:
　　Philip Lovecok: 22 tuns 4 pipes
　　William le Keu: 5 tuns
　　Richard le Keu: 4 tuns
　　Martin le Keu: 3 tuns
　　John de Bayona: 5 tuns
　　William R... : [3 tuns] ...
　　Thomas Toraud: 2 tuns
　　Walter de Hugheton: 3 tuns
　　Robert de Irlond: 6 tuns
　　T... ... : 2 tuns
　　Adam Slegh shipmaster: 5 tuns of which 2 tuns for portage
Custom: Geoffrey atte Wille ... [for the custom?]; 5 tuns customed; J.
de Smalecumb received 20d

Ship called *Seinte Marie cog* of Exmouth
Master: Peter Godlok
Cargo: 100 tuns 8 pipes wine of which:
　　Philip Lovecok: 43 tuns 4 pipes
　　John de Bayona: 9 tuns
　　William Ralle: 2 tuns, customed
　　John le Perour: 3 tuns 1 pipe
　　Richard le Keu: 21 tuns 1 pipe (of which Adam Broun [has] 1 tun)
　　Thomas Toraud: 10 tuns 1 pipe

[96] Many parts of this membrane are torn or frayed.

Thomas le Furbur: 4 tuns
Robert le Carpunter: 2 tuns, customed
Philip Kyde: 3 tuns of which 1 tun for portage
Elias Sleghe: 1 tun for portage
Thomas Gesse: 1 tun for portage
Peter Godlok: 1 tun 1 pipe
Thomas Toraud: 1 bale almonds
Custom: 6 tuns customed; 2s [which] J. de Smalecumb received

Ship called *la Nicholas* of Teignmouth
Master: Wymund le Geg
Cargo: 38 tuns 1 pipe wine of which:
   Raymond de Vilearse: 37 tuns 1 pipe
   Nicholas B... : 1 tun
Custom: 37 tuns 1 pipe [customed]; 12s 8d, which J. de Smalecumb
   received

Ship called *la Sauvee* of Exmouth
Master: Paris Edmund
Cargo: 95 tuns 1 pipe of which:
   Walter de Hugheton: 32 tuns (1 pipe)
   Nicholas Busse: 22 tuns
   Richard le Keu: 20 tuns (of which:
      William Buffet: 6 tuns
      and G. de la Bogh': 4 tuns)
   Nicholas de Bradecrofte: 7 tuns
   Robert de Irlond: 6 tuns
   Paris Edmund: 3 tuns and 5 tuns for portage
   Walter de Hugheton: 1 bale almonds
Custom: 7 tuns customed; 2s 4d which J. de Smalecumb received

Ship called *Nunne* of Studland
Master: John Feg
Cargo: Robert de Okampton, William Jobbe and other men of the
   city of Exeter: 12 tuns wine, 1 M iron, 1 bale cordwain, 3 jars oil
Custom: no custom

Ship called *le Bonan* of Exmouth
Cargo: 133 tuns 7 pipes wine of which:
   Philip Lovecok: 24 tuns 1 pipe
   Walter Lovecok: 11 tuns
   John de Bayona: 5 tuns
   Martin le Keu: 15 tuns 2 pipes
   William le Keu: 5 tuns
   Richard le Keu: 3 tuns
   William de Okampton: 1 tun
   John le Noreys: 1 tun, customed (4d)
   William de Gatepath: 4 tuns
   Henry, his son: 6 tuns 1 pipe
   Thomas de Oxton: 3 tuns
   John de Smalecumb: 31 tuns 2 pipes

Adam Broun: 8 tuns
The same Adam and William Ralle: 1 tun
The same Adam and Gilbert Pycard: 1 tun (4d)
The same Gilbert: 4 tuns (16d)
Adam Broun and Walter Lovecok: 1 pipe
Richard de Tavistok: has 4 tuns in his custody
Richard Goldene: 4 tuns of which 1 tun for portage, (12d in [the pyx])
Richard Harvest: 1 tun for portage
Roger Clist: 1 tun for portage
Custom: 3s which J. de Smalecumb received

Ship called *Seint Poul* of Teignmouth
Master: John Hyne
Cargo: Walter de Hugheton: 18 tuns 1 pipe wine
　　And 1 tun full of iron of which 15 quintals iron [are] customed
Custom: none on wine; iron: 7½d, in the pyx

Ship called *la Margarete* of Exmouth
Master: Adam Slegh
Cargo: 49 tuns 8 pipes wine of which:
　　Philip Lovecok: 25 tuns 8 pipes[97]
　　Walter Lovecok: 2 tuns
　　John de Bayona: 7 tuns
　　William Ralle: 3 tuns of which 1 for portage (8d in the pyx)
　　Adam Perour: 1 tun
　　Thomas Furbur: 4 tuns
　　Adam Slegh: 4 tuns of which 2 for portage[98] (8d, which J. de
　　　　Smalecumb received)
　　Robert de Irlond: 2 tuns
　　Thomas le Barbur: 1 tun
　　Adam Slegh shipmaster: 24 C iron (6d(?) paid)
　　Geoffrey atte Wille: 2 quintals iron (for portage)
Custom: 4 tuns customed; Philip Lovecok[99] for the custom; {paid}

Ship called *Seinte Marie cog* of Exmouth
Master: Peter Godlok
Cargo: 100 tuns 8 pipes wine of which:
　　Philip Lovecok: 32 tuns 4 pipes
　　Walter Lovecok: 4 tuns
　　John de Bayona: 6 tuns
　　William Dyne of Bordeaux: 7 tuns, customed (Philip Lovecok
　　　　received 2s 4d which J. de Smalecumb received)
　　Thomas de Oxton: 8 tuns 1 pipe
　　Peter Godlok: 1 pipe
　　John le Perour: 13 tuns 2 pipes
　　Robert de Criditon: 3 tuns, customed (12d, paid to J. de Smalecumb)
　　Thomas le Furbur: 8 tuns

[97] *25 tuns 8 pipes* underlined.
[98] *4 tuns of which 2 for portage* underlined.
[99] *Philip Lovecok* crossed through.

Stephen le Wyller: 8 tuns, customed (2s 8d, paid to J. de Smalecumb)
Adam le Perour: 9½ tuns of which 2½ tuns customed (paid to J. de
  Smalecumb)[100]
(Adam Slegh): 1 tun for portage[101] (customed, 4d which J. de
  Smalecumb received)
Custom: 21 tuns customed; 7s which J. de Smalecumb received

Ship called *Godyer* of Sidmouth
Master: John Irysh
Cargo: Walter de Porte and Gilbert de Cumbe: 15 tuns 1 pipe wine
  And 8 pounds saffron, 3 sugar loaves, 6 tons iron
Custom: no custom

Ship called *la Sauvee* of Exmouth
Master: Walter Edmund
Cargo: 95 tuns 3 pipes wine of which:
  Elias de Hemeston: 32 tuns 1 pipe of which 1 tun customed[102]
  James le Gascoyng: 21 tuns, customed[103]
  Richard le Keu: 7 tuns 1 pipe
  Martin le Keu: 5 tuns
  Robert de Irlond: 5 tuns
  Walter Edmund: 6 tuns 1 pipe
  John Gregory: 4 tuns
  Nicholas de Bradecrofte: 5 tuns, customed[104]
  Benedict Edmund: 2 tuns and 4 tuns for portage
  Ralph de Todewille: 4 tuns, customed[105]
Custom: 31 tuns customed; 10s 4d which J. de Smalecumb received

Ship called *la Bonan* of Teignmouth
Master: Wymund Britun
Cargo: 16 tuns wine of which:
  Richard de Gatepathe: 7 tuns 3 pipes
  Thomas Golde: 6 tuns
  Thomas le Barbur: 2 tuns
  Thomas Toraud: 1 tun 1 pipe
  And 1 tun full of iron for portage
Custom: none

Ship called *le cog Seint Gyle* of Sidmouth
Master: Ralph le Sanger
Cargo: 108 tuns[106] 6 pipes wine of which:_
  Bernard Gascoyng: 67 tuns 6 pipes
  Ralph le Sanger: 29 tuns of which 2 for portage[107]

---

[100] *2½ tuns* underlined.
[101] *For portage* crossed through.
[102] *Of which 1 tun customed* underlined.
[103] *21 tuns, customed* underlined.
[104] *5 tuns* underlined.
[105] *4 tuns, customed* underlined.
[106] *98 tuns* crossed through
[107] *2 for* underlined.

Richard de Todewille: 5 tuns (of which) 1 for portage[108]
Robert Lode: 2 tuns of which 1 tun for portage
And 7 tuns for portage
Bernard le Gascoyng: 1 tun woad
Custom: 104 tuns [wine] customed, 34s 8d; J. de Smalecumb
received[109] all; woad: 12d [which] John de Smalecumb received

1312/13 (m. 23d) CUSTOM ON GARLIC, ONIONS, WOAD AND OTHER MERCHANDISE

Ship called *la cogg Seint Nicholas* of Le Vivier
Master: Geoffrey Lukeys
Cargo: William le Barbur: 2000 tresses onions, 1 M garlic
Custom: 2s 3½d [which] J. de Smalecumb received

Ship called *la holhop Seint Lowys* of Le Vivier
Master: John Rydel
Cargo: Peter le Vesk: 300 tresses garlic, 4 M onions
    The Prior of Otterton: 1 ton salt
Custom: 12½d [which] John de Smalecumb received

Ship called *Soper* of Wareham
Master: William Fog
Cargo: 29 lasts herring of which:
    John Whytebrother: 1 last 3 M
    William de Okampton: 1 last
    Geoffrey atte Boghe: ½ last
    Nicholas le Skynnere: 3 lasts 3 M
    Philip Lovecok: 1½ lasts
    Robert de Okampton: 1½ lasts
    Richard Gaudethoun: 1 last
    Thomas le Furbur: 1 last (4 M)
    Geoffrey atte Boghe: 1 last
    Thomas de Tetteburne: 1½ lasts
    William Buffet: 4 M
    Robert de Irlond: 4 M
    Ralph Lovet: 5 lasts
    Ralph de Nyweton mercer: 2 lasts ...
    Adam le Cynnge: 2 lasts
    Adam le Perour: ½ last
    Philip Lovecok: 1 last ...
    ... ... : 1 last
    Avicia Perour: 1 last

Ship called *Sauvee* of Sidmouth
Master: Richard Calewe of Sidmouth
Docked: 20 December 1312

---

[108] *1 for* underlined.
[109] *25s 8d* crossed through and *all* written in.

Cargo: Nicholas ... and Philip Chepman, burgesses of Taunton: 28 tuns woad, 2 frails onions, 10 stones weld
Custom: none[110]

Ship called *Nostre Dame* of Winchelsea
Master: Robert Germeyn
Docked: 31 December 1312
Cargo: 18 tuns woad of which:
  John le Poter: 12 tuns
  Matthew de Mees: 6 tuns
  Ralph le F...s: 3 frails 45 M onions (3s)
  Thomas de Mytanney: 2 frails 40 M onions (2s)
  Robert Germeyn shipmaster: 100 quarters wheat
Custom: John Mozet and Alured Aylward for the custom; 18s on woad, 4s on onions of which J. de Smalecumb received 10s, also 12s

Ship called *Margarete* of Exmouth
Master: The same John [Luverich?]
Cargo: 50 tuns 2 pipes wine of which:
  ... ...e : 6 tuns
  Ralph Lovet: 6 tuns
  John de Fenton: 6 tuns
  Philip Lovecok: 2 tuns
  John de Smalecumb: 6 tuns
  Richard de Gatepath: 6 tuns (1 pipe)
  John de Bayona: 4 tuns
  Henry(?) de Gadepath: 5 tuns (of which 1 customed, 4d)
  Luverych in the Cumb: 2 tuns (1 pipe) for portage
  William le Spicer: 1 tun
  ... Drogger: [4 tuns]
  John Horn senior: 2 tuns
Custom: 4d [which] Smalecumb received

Ship called *la Trinite* of Teignmouth
Master: John Hunte
Docked: 5 January [1313]
Cargo: 23 tuns woad, 5 pipes potash of which:
  John Fowyer: 12 tuns [woad]
  John de Kent: 11 tuns [woad]
  John Fowyer: the [5] pipes [potash]
  John de Kent: 1($\frac{1}{2}$) seams canvas
Custom: William[111] de Carswille and Alured Aylward for the custom; woad, 23s 1$\frac{1}{2}$d, which J. de Smalecumb received

---

[110] A hand with a pointed finger aimed at this entry is drawn in the left-hand margin. It refers to the search made later concerning the custom status of burgesses of Taunton, as does the hand drawn in the entry below concerning Nicholas le Webbe of Taunton. See also the annotation concerning this matter written at the bottom of this membrane and above, n. 17 for other annotations probably connected to this search.

[111] *John* crossed through.

Ship called *la Nunne* of Studland
Master: John Feg
Docked: 1 March [1313]
Cargo: Nicholas le Webbe of Taunton: 5 tuns 1 pipe woad, 2 frails onions
Custom: no custom[112]

Ship called *le holhop Seynt Nicholas*
Master: Lawrence Hugh'
Docked: 10 March 1313
Cargo: 13 C garlic, 60 M onions, 1 bushel [onion?] seed for portage
Custom: 3s 2½d which John de Smalecumbe received; pledge John de Sancto Nicholao

Ship called *la Joanette* of St Valéry
Master: Robert Folye
Docked: 11 March [1313]
Cargo: Philip de Quarel: 12 tuns woad, 80 quarters wheat, 12 seams garlic
And 18 M onions of which 15 M for portage, 80 stones weld
Custom: John Mozet for the custom; sum, 13s which J. de Smalecumb received

Ship called *Isac*(?) of Abbeville
Master: John Werres
Docked: 11 March 1313
Cargo: John de Werres: 2 frails onions, 40 M onions for portage
Custom: John Mozet for the custom; 2s 6d which J. de Smalecumb received

Ship called *la Nicholas* of Kingston-upon-Hull
Master: Robert Rotynheryng
Cargo: 200 quarters wheat

Ship called *la cogg Seint Nicholas* of Le Vivier
Master: Geoffrey Lukeys
Cargo: William Dyre: 19 C garlic
Geoffrey Lukeys: 20 yards linen cloth
William (Barry):[113] 3 seams canvas and linen cloth, 1 quarter barley
Custom: 4s 3d on garlic which John de Smalecumb received

Ship called *la Nostre Dame* of St Valéry
Master: William le Breaunt
Docked: 11 May [1313]
Cargo: Peter le Monyer: 26 tuns woad, 40 quarters wheat, ...[114]
Custom: 26s ...

---

[112] Another hand with a pointing finger is drawn in the left-hand margin, again an indication of the custom-free status of burgesses from Taunton; see above, n. 110.

[113] *Baryst'* crossed through and *Barry* written above.

[114] The entry of this ship was also noted in the MCR where the illegible portion reads *200 stones weld*; see above, p. 68.

Ship called *Bonan* of Exmouth
Master: Richard Harvest
Cargo: Philip de Quarel: 200 quarters wheat
  John Poter: 7 tuns woad

Ship called *la Maudelyn* (of Kingston-upon-Hull)
Master: John Russel of Hull
Cargo: 300 quarters wheat in addition to portage from which [*ccc quar' frumenti p't' port' unde*]:
  Robert de Alleslegh(?): 200 (quarters)
  William de Butoton(?): 100 quarters
Custom: no custom

Ship called *la cog Seint Nicholas* of Le Vivier
Master: Geoffrey Lukas
Cargo: Nicholas le Graunt: 20 quarters barley, 20 quarters oats, 6(?) quarters wheat

Ship called *la cogge Seint Jon* of Le Vivier
Master: Giles le Pycherer
Cargo: Ives le Britun: 40 quarters barley, 14 quarters oats, 1 C garlic, 3 bushels simnel flour [*sinelli*], 1 C canvas and 15 yards canvas
Custom: 4½d for garlic; [which] J. de Smalecumb received

Ship called *Benedicte* of Weymouth
Master: Gilbert(?) Petypas
Cargo: William de Cicestr': 40 quarters wheat

Ship called *la Margarete*(?) of Exmouth
Master: Walter de Ilfridecumb
Cargo: John de Smalecumb and other merchants of Exeter: 700 quarters salt

Ship called *Seinte Marie cog* of Poole
Master: Adam le Whyte
Cargo: Ralph le Degher: 82 pipes potash, 5 tons alum[115]
  Matthew le Peleter: 2 fardels skins [*peletr'*]
  Robert Rogemund: 1 fardel and 1 barrel skins
Custom: no custom

Ship called *la Blythe* of Hook [*Hamelehok*][116]
Master: Henry Wakelyn
Cargo: John le Perour: 1 fardel drapery
  Hugh ... and Ralph de Lostythyel: 1 fardel drapery and ..., customed
  Thomas le Furbur: 1 fardel drapery, 2 bales wax
  William Brewer: 2 C battery-ware

---

[115] *Almonds* crossed through and *alum* written in next.
[116] *Hamelhoke* or some variation is noted as a homeport on seventeen occasions; it almost certainly referred to the settlement of Hook on the Hamble river in the parish of Titchfield (Hampshire). Three times the homeport is simply given as Hook. The smaller port of Hamble (noted twice) was located on the opposite bank of the Hamble river in the parish of Hamble-le-Rice.

Ship called *la Wake* of Hook [*Hok*]
Master: Roger Walkelyn
Docked: 13 August [1313]
Cargo: John le Someter: 20 tuns woad, 3 millstones
Custom: Robert de Doune for the custom, 20s, to be paid on
    Thursday, the vigil of St[117] Bartholomew [23 August 1313]

Ship called *Seynt Jake* of Barfleur [*Barssflute*]
Master: Henry Cauwe
Cargo: 200 stones weld, 2 barrels pitch, ½ seam garlic for portage

Ship called *la Floryete* of Guernsey
Master: Robert de Geneys
Cargo: Robert de Geneys: 3 pieces linen cloth, 5 yards serge of Caen
    [*sarg' de caain*], 28 seams onion (and are customed 12d), 2 seams garlic

Ship called *Nostre Dame* of St Valéry-sur-Somme
Master: Walter le Picar'
Cargo: Peter le Monyer: 30 tuns woad, 700 stones weld
    The mariners: 60(?) M onions, 7 seams cockles [*cokayll*]
    Walter le Picar' shipmaster: 3 seams garlic, 1 piece cloth (4d in the pyx)
    The mariners: 2 C steel? [*cc de acrum*(?)], 5 seams garlic
Custom: Alured Aylward for the custom; 30s

{[Items] found for Taunton concerning custom in three locations
have this [mark, i.e., a drawing of a hand with finger pointed]}[118]

Roll of Customs in the sixth year of King Edward [II][119]

1315/16 (m. 22) EXETER–ROLL OF CUSTOMS OF WINE LAND-
        ED AT THE PORT OF EXMOUTH FROM THE FEAST OF
        ST MICHAEL IN THE NINTH YEAR OF THE PRESENT
        KING EDWARD [II]

Ship called *la Jouwanette* of Teignmouth
Master: Richard le Whyte
Docked: 13 November 1315
Cargo: 89 tuns 11 pipes wine of which:
    Martin le Keu: 10 tuns 4 pipes
    William le Keu: 1 tun
    Joan de Smalecombe: 3 tuns
    Thomas Thoraud: 2 tuns
    Richard le Keu: 19 tuns 1 pipe
    William le Skynner: 2 tuns
    Gilbert de Combe: 19 tuns 4 pipes, 7 M iron
    Thomas atte Burne: 3 tuns (customed)

[117] *Laur* crossed through.
[118] This is written in a much later hand and refers to the two entries containing
imports by three Taunton burgesses, both of which are marked in the margin with the
same drawing of a hand; see above, n. 110.
[119] Written in very large letters at the bottom of the membrane.

Robert Lome: 1 tun for portage
John Luverych: 9 tuns (customed)
Henry de Lufetone: 1 tun for portage
John de Bovy: 14 tuns 1 pipe
Michael de Bovy: 1 tun (paid [custom])
Thomas Lythenard: 1 tun (paid custom)
Richard le Whyte: 1 tun for portage
John Luverych:[120] 18 C iron, customed
John de Yeustetorre: 18 C iron, customed
Robert Rowe: 18 C iron, customed
Richard le Whyte: 1 tun, customed (paid)
The mariners have 2 tuns for portage
Custom: Martin le Keu of Bridford for the custom; 4s 7d for wine custom, ... received 12d; afterwards M. received all per the hand of Martin Cocus; iron custom, 18d

Ship called *la Seynte Marie cog* of Ilfracombe
Master: Benedict Clement
Docked: 13 November 1315
Cargo: 48 tuns 15 pipes wine of which:
Richard le Keu: 8 tuns 4 pipes
William le Keu: 3 tuns
Martin le Keu: 3 tuns
Adam de Smalecombe: 2 tuns
Thomas Thoraud: 1 tun
Walter de Hughetone: 18 tuns 4 pipes
Nicholas Busse: 12 tuns 3 pipes
Benedict Clement: 1 tun for portage
Thomas Lythenard: 2 pipes, customed
The mariners: 2 pipes
Custom: 8d, [which] Matthew received

Ship called *le cog Seynt Gile* of Sidmouth
Master: William Spede
Docked: 25 November 1315
Cargo: 96 tuns 7 pipes wine of which:
Gilbert in the Combe: 5 tuns
Thomas de Heantone: 10 tuns
John Somery: 10 tuns 6 pipes (customed)
John de Ercedekne: 8 tuns
Robert atte Rixen: 11 tuns
John de Fenton: 1 tun
William de Okampton: 6 tuns
John de Fenton: 3 tuns
Robert le Taverner: 1 tun
Joan de Smalecombe: 13 tuns
Adam Broun: 4 tuns
William le Skynner: 3 tuns
Ralph le Sanger: 7 tuns (customed) of which 1 tun for drink [*beverag'*] and 1 tun for portage

[120] *Henry de Lufetone, customed* is expunged.

William Spede shipmaster: 1 tun for portage
John Hake: 5 tuns (customed) of which 1 for portage
Richard Todewille: 4 tuns (cutomed) of which 1 for portage
John Chanoun: 3 tuns (customed) of which 1 tun for portage
William Turkeby: 1 pipe for portage
Nicholas atte Putte: 1 tun for portage
John atte Putte: 1 tun for portage
Robert Lode: 1 tun for portage
Robert Jan: 1 tun for portage
John Chanoun: 4 quintals iron
William Turkeby: 4 quintals iron
Richard de Todewille: 3 quintals iron
Hamelin Sanger: 3 quintals [iron]
Custom: Robert atte Ryxen for the custom; wine custom, sum[121] 10s;
    iron custom, 7d

Ship called *la Seynte Marie cog* of Exmouth
Master: Peter Golloc
Docked: 30 November 1315
Cargo: 112 tuns 9 pipes wine of which:
    William Austyn: 8 tuns 1 pipe
    Roger le Taillour: 8 tuns
    John Dyrkyn: 4 tuns
    Peter Soth: 2 tuns
    Elias de Hemmeston and Thomas Gerveys: 2 tuns
    John Austyn and John le Perour: 1 tun
    John Perour for himself [*per se*]: 1 pipe
    Philip Lovecok: 36 tuns 4 pipes
    Clement de Hamptone: 9 tuns
    Walter Lovecok: 7 tuns 1 pipe
    William Ralle: 6 tuns (quit of custom)
    Thomas Forbour: 18 tuns 1 pipe
    Thomas Thoraud: 1 tun
    Thomas Forbour: 11 quintals iron
    Peter Golloc shipmaster: 4 tuns of which 2 for portage
    Paye Hardy: 1 tun for portage
    Adam Slegh: 2 tuns (quit of custom)
    David Cofyn: 1 tun for portage
    Alexander de Clist: 1 tun for portage
    Adam Slegh: 5 quintals [iron] (quit of custom)
    Richard Janekyn: 1 tun for portage
Custom: wine custom, 6s 4d of which 2s 8d in the pyx; iron custom,
    2d, in the pyx

Ship called *la Alisceote* of Dartmouth
Master: Gilbert Do of Dartmouth
Docked: 23 December 1315
Cargo: Gilbert Do of Dartmouth: 16 tuns wine and 3 pipes (for portage)
Custom: Matthew Pellipar' for the custom; 5s 4d [which] Matthew received

---

[121] *8s* crossed through.

Ship called *la Margarete* of Exmouth
Master: Luverych
Docked: 1 January 1316
Cargo: 50 tuns 5 pipes wine of which 1 tun for drink [*beverach'*] and 1
tun empty [*de vac'*]; and of the remainder:
Walter de Hughetone: 15 tuns 2 pipes
Nicholas Busse: 3 tuns
Philip Lovecok: 10 tuns 1 pipe
Clement de Hamptone: 1 tun (customed)
William Ralle: 3 tuns (custom paid)
Walter Lovecok: 2 tuns
Robert de Stanbrigg: 2 tuns, customed[122] (free per Topsham)
Rychabella, widow of Robert Irlond: 4 tuns (free per Topsham)
Gilbert de Combe: 1 tun 1 pipe
John Averey: 2 tuns (free per Topsham)
Luverych the shipmaster: 3 tuns (free)
William Smyth: 1 tun for portage
Custom: 16d of which 12d in the pyx

Ship called *la Seynte Marie cog* of Exmouth
Docked: 4 May 1316
Cargo: 114 tuns 8 pipes wine of which:
Philip Lovecok: 20 tuns 4 pipes (free)
Clement de Hampton: 4 tuns (customed)
Walter Lovecok: 4 tuns (free)
William Ralle: 5 tuns (customed)
William Austyn: 3 tuns (free)
Martin le Keu: 9 tuns 1 pipe (free)
William le Keu: 4 tuns (free)
Richard le Keu: 7 tuns (free)
William Pellipar': 2 tuns (free)
William de Saundervyle: 5 tuns (customed, paid all)
John[123] de Bovy: 7 tuns (free)
Gilbert de Combe: 8 tuns
John Luverych: 2 tuns (customed, paid all)[124]
John Averey: 6 tuns (doubt concerning custom? [*dub' de cust'*])
Peter Golloc: 2 tuns (free)
Elias Slegh: 1 tun (customed, paid all)
Peter Golloc: 1 pipe (free)
John le Perour: 6 tuns 1 pipe (free)
Roger Leyz: 4 tuns (free)
Robert le Carpenter: 6 tuns 1 pipe (customed, paid all)
Michael de Bovy: 1 tun (paid all)
(Joan)[125] de Smalecombe: 5 tuns (free)[126]

---

[122] *Customed* crossed through.
[123] *Adam* crossed through.
[124] *Free* crossed through in superscript.
[125] *Adam* crossed through and *Joan* written above.
[126] *Customed* written in superscript and crossed through.

Adam de Smalecombe: 2 tuns (free)[127]
John Averey (free) and John Bovy (free): 1 tun [1] pipe
William Ralle: 2 quintals iron (customed)
Custom: wine, 8s 4d; iron, 1d

Ship called *la Rode cog* of Lyme
Master: Robert Sampsoun
Docked: 18 July 1316
Cargo: Guillaume de Aguilloun, a Gascon: 60 tuns 4 pipes wine, all
    customed
Custom: Richard le Seler for the custom; sum 21s 4d

Ship called *le Margarete* of Exmouth
Master: Adam Slegh
Docked: 14 August 1316
Cargo: 68 tuns 4 pipes wine of which:
    Philip Lovecok: 28 tuns 3 pipes (free)
    Clement de Hampton: 5 tuns (customed)
    William le Keu of Bridford: 2 tuns (free)
    John de Bayone: 10 tuns (free)
    Walter Lovecok and Thomas le Furbour: 2 tuns
    Roger de Clist: 1 tun for portage
    The widow of Robert de Irlond: 2 tuns
    Edith Gyrard: 1 tun
    Robert de Stanbrugg: 1 tun 1 pipe
    Adam Slegh shipmaster: 2 tuns
    Richard Harvest: 1 tun for portage
    Robert atte Rixen: 1 tun
    Richard de Gatepath: 12 tuns in his custody of which the same
        Richard has 4 tuns, customed (paid), which belong to John Dollyng
    Joan de Smalecumbe: 2 tuns
    Thomas le Barbour: 1 tun
    Richard de Gatepath: 4 tuns
    Robert le Taverner: 1 tun
    Richard Harvest: 7 quintals iron
    Geoffrey atte Wille: 2 quintals iron
    Potel le Passeger: 1 quintal [iron]
    William Slegh: 1 quintal [iron]
    Richard de Tavistok: 2 Carchil
    John de Bayone: 13 yards tarred rope? [*v'gat' t're*]
Custom: wine, 3s of which 16d in the pyx; iron, 2d; archil, 4d, in the pyx

Sum total both in and out of the pyx–£3 12d of which Lord Hugh de
Curtenay [has] for one-third part–20s 4d

John de Shyrborne queries Walter Parker on a plea of trespass for
which claim he assigns a pledge for the prosecution[128]

---

[127] *Customed* written in superscript and crossed through.
[128] Written in the bottom tail of the membrane; it probably represents a note made by
one of the clerks.

1315/16 (m. 21) ROLL OF CUSTOMS OF THINGS FOR SALE LANDED AT THE PORT OF EXMOUTH FROM THE NINTH REGNAL YEAR OF KING EDWARD SON OF EDWARD THE KING

Ship called *le Vertboys* of Le Vivier
Master: Reginald Bryant
Docked: 17 October 1315
Cargo: Nicholas le Gogeys: 31 pipes potash
Custom: no custom

{Scrutinized}[129]

Ship called *le Lacy* of Keyhaven
Master: William le Whyte
Docked: 15 October 1315
Cargo: William le Whyte: 42 quarters coal
Custom: no custom

Ship called *le neof Seynt Esperyt* of St Valéry
Master: William le Brewes
Docked: 20 October 1315
Cargo: 16 tuns and 1 barrel woad of which:
  John le Poter: 6 tuns
  Thomas Thoraud: 5 tuns
  John Petyt and Henry de Gatepath: 5 tuns 1 barrel (of which half is John's)[130]
  Thomas Thoraud: 8 barrels potash
  John le Petyt: 6 barrels potash
  John le Potter: 110[131] stones weld
  And 40 M onions for portage
Custom: 8s 6d [which] Matthew received

Ship called *le Passauaunt* of Guernsey
Master: Peter de Hady
Docked: 25 October 1315
Cargo: John le Perour: 1 fardel of cloth
  William le Breuwer: 1 fardel of cloth
  William le Breuwer and John Coc: 4½ C iron
  William Breuwer: 1 chest of merchandise [*cista mercimon'*]
  John Coc: 1 chest of merchandise
  Robert de Mountailles: 1 fardel of towels
Custom: 2d in the pyx

[129] This word is scribbled near the middle of the membrane in the same hand that made the notations concerning Taunton in the account for the previous year; see n. 17 above.

[130] *5 tuns 1 barrel* has a line drawn over it.

[131] The *ii* of *cii* is crossed out and *x* written above.

Ship called *la Sauve* of St Valéry
Master: Robert Bryant
Docked: 3 November 1315
Cargo: Peter le Moners: 36 [tuns] woad, 18 pipes potash, 300 stones
    weld
    And 120 M onions of which half for portage and half customed
        (7½d for custom)
    John de Ruwe: 108 M onions (10d for custom)
    And 12 harnesses [*de cordes heres*][132]
Custom: sum, 37s 8½d which Matthew received

Ship called *Seynte Mare bot* of Sandwich
Master: Nicholas Groward
Docked: 10 December 1315
Cargo: Ives Byrche: 62 pipes potash woad, 20 quarters coal, 1 bale
    alum, 2 M iron
    Robert Rogemound: 3 bales skins [*pell'*]
    Thomas de Moltone and Henry Lovecok: 7 bales alum
    Geoffrey atte Boghe: 1 bale almonds
    Richard Tuk: 1 bale almonds
    John in the Haye and Ralph de Thornbury: 5 fothers lead
    Hugh de Tuvertone: 1 bale almonds, customed
    Walter in the Toune: (2)[133] bales alum, customed
Custom: For Walter, Henry Lovecok; for Hugh, Robert Rogemound;
    custom 16½d of which 11d in the pyx; afterwards, all [put] into the
    pyx

Ship called *la Jouwanette* of Winchelsea
Master: Richard Havebok of Winchelsea
Docked: 14 January 1316
Cargo: Richard Havebok of Winchelsea: 50 copes figs and raisins
Custom: no custom because free through the Cinque Ports

Ship called *le Lacy* of Kyave [Keyhaven?]
Master: William Wolloner
Docked: 14 January 1316
Cargo: William Wolloner shipmaster: 40 quarters *garb'*[134]

Ship called *la Margerie* of Yarmouth[135]
Master: Peter de Orliesby
Docked: 13 January 1316
Cargo: 38 lasts, 10 mease and 8 cades [herring] of which:
    John Whytebrother: 3 lasts 1 M and 1 cade
    Philip Luvecok: 2 lasts 4 M

---

[132] *3 crossed through and 12 written in; *cordes* also crossed through.*
[133] *1 crossed through and 2 [due] written above.*
[134] Normally *garba* is a measure (used for such items as garlic, iron, or weld) or refers
to a sheaf of corn (or less frequently, a sheaf of arrows), but none of these translations
seem to fit with the measure in quarters.
[135] *Dartmouth* crossed through and *Yarmouth* written in.

William de Okampton and Robert [de Okampton] [*de eadem*]: 2 lasts 3 M

John de Fenton: 22 M

Robert le Taverner and Richard Gaudethoun: 10 M

Nicholas le Skynner of Lydford: 5 lasts 7 M and 1 cade

Philip Luvecok: 16 M

Gilbert in the Cumb: 15 M

Adam Perour: 3½ lasts, and 3 cades for his own food [*pro potura sua*]

Martin le Keu: 2 M

Richard Baret: 3 lasts 3 M and 1 cade

Ralph de Nyweton: 3 M

Thomas de Molton: 2 lasts

Thomas le Furbur: 1 last 3 M

Geoffrey atta Boghe: 1 last 9 M

John de Boltelston: 11 M

Thomas Fastol: 1 last

John Tybot: 1 last

Adam de Nyweton: 2 lasts 1 M

William Brywere: 3 M 1 cade

Peter de Ermesby: 2 lasts and ½ for portage

Roger de Gernemuth: 3 M for portage

And 2 cades for portage

Ship called *la Vertboys* of Le Vivier
Master: Reginald Bryaunt
Docked: 28 January 1316
Cargo: William de Viviers: 900 cords garlic[136]
    Richard de Cauntelo: 1 fardel drapery[137]
    William Barry of Lyme: 1 fardel drapery, 1 piece cloth
    John Bussoun: 1 piece canvas containing 30 yards
Custom: John de Sancto Nicholao for the custom; garlic, 23d [which] Matthew received

Ship called *la neof Seynt Esperit* of St Valéry
Master: William Bryaunt
Docked: 25 February 1316
Cargo: John le Poter: 19 tuns woad, 100 (and 60) stones weld
    And 30 (M) onions for portage
    The shipmaster: 12 quarters coal
Custom: Ralph le Degher for the custom; woad, 19s {Matthew received all}

Ship called *Seynt Marie bot* of Harwich
Master: William Laurenz
Docked: 4 March 1316
Cargo: Ralph le Degher: 24 barrels potash woad

---

[136] *Alle* crossed through before *cordes*.

[137] Before *Richard* is a *W* crosssed through. *2 bales drapery* crossed through and *1 fardel* written next.

Ship called *Le Nicholas* of Hook [*Hamelehoke*]
Master: William Scothard
Docked: 16 April 1316
Cargo: Peter le Moners: 16 tuns woad, 6 barrels potash
Custom: 16s; {Matthew received all}

Ship called *la Malekyn* of Hook [*Hamelehok]*
Master: Nicholas Waleys
Docked: 16 April 1316
Cargo: Peter le Moners: 13 tuns woad, 2 barrels potash
Custom: 13s; {Matthew received all}

Ship called *le Messager* of Orford
Master: Abraham Ode
Docked: 23 April 1316
Cargo: 16 tuns woad of which:
  John le Petit: 8 tuns
  Thomas Hamound: 8 tuns woad (paid), 100 stones weld
Custom: ...8s; ...16s {Matthew le Skynner received all by the hand of
  John Petit on Wednesday next after the feast of St Augustine,
  Apostle of the English [2 June 1316]

Ship called *le Ros* of Exmouth
Master: Harlewin Bolt
Docked: 24 May 1316
Cargo: Harlewyn Bolt: 60 quarters coal

Ship called *la Margarete* of Exmouth
Master: William Knyght
Docked: 26 May 1316
Cargo: William Knyght: 60 quarters coal, 100 horseshoes [*ferur'
  equorum*]

Ship called *le Messager* of Orford
Master: Abraham Ode
Docked: 12 June 1316
Cargo: Peter le Frere [and] Hamond le Engleys: 7 (tuns)[138] woad
  And 20 quarters coal
Custom: Thomas Hamound for the custom; woad, 7s; M. received
  all

Ship called *la Jouwanette* of Dartmouth
Master: John Luverych
Docked: 25 June 1316
Cargo: Geoffrey Flemmyng: 105 quarters salt
  (The shipmaster): ½ C canvas
Custom: canvas, 2d, in the pyx

---

[138] *Quarters* crossed through and *tuns* inserted above.

Ship called *la Seynt Johan* of [ ][139]
Master: Sampson Firans
Docked: 13 July 1316
Cargo: John [ ][140] : 10 tuns woad
Custom: Robert de Doune for the custom

Ship called *le cog Seynt John* of Cherbourg [*Shyreburgh*]
Master: Richard le Pelee
Docked: 27 August 1316
Cargo: William Iver: 1 M garlic (customed, paid 2s 1d)
   William Blakeman of Melcombe: 11 C garlic (no [custom] because
     in the freedom of Melcombe)
   Richard le Pelee shipmaster: 80 tresses garlic (paid 2s), 36 cords
     onions (paid ½d), 2 bushels woad (paid ½d)
   (Robert Martoil): 4 fardels merchandise (customed, 6d), 1 pipe
     archil (8d paid)
Custom: 3s 6d

Ship called *la Rose* of Exmouth
Master: Harlewin Bolt
Docked: 28 August 1316
Cargo: Henry de Gatepath and William Breuwer: 7 tuns 1 pipe woad,
   9 barrels potash woad, 20 M teasels, 1 fardel drapery and towels
   John Jullen: ½ dozen misericords [*di' (xii) de miserecord*], 5 lanterns
Custom: no custom because in the freedom of Exeter

Ship called *la Welyfare* of Orwell
Docked: 8 September 1316
Cargo: 42 tuns 1 pipe woad of which:
   Peter le Moner: 21 tuns (paid all)
   John le Poter: 16 tuns; 1 pipe[141] (barrel containing 1 quarter)
   John Petit: 5 tuns; John le Poter: 6 seams garlic
   And 3 seams garlic for portage
Custom: 42s

1316/17 (m. 20) ROLL OF CUSTOMS OF WINE LANDED IN THE
       PORT OF EXMOUTH FROM THE TENTH YEAR OF
       KING EDWARD [II]

Ship called *la Margarete* of Exmouth
Master: Walter Edmound
Cargo: 78 tuns wine of which:
   Walter de Hughetone: 27 tuns (2 pipes) (free)
   Philip Lovecok: 10 tuns (free)
   Nicholas Busse: 5 tuns (free)
   William Dyne: 9 tuns (W. de Hugh' is [pledge] for the custom) [*cust'*
     est pro W. de Hugh'])

[139] A blank space left in the manuscript for the homeport.
[140] A blank space left in the manuscript for the surname.
[141] *1 pipe* crossed through.

Elias de Hemmeston: 11 tuns 2 pipes (free)
William Mounteyn: 2 tuns (free)
John Averey: 4 tuns of which he has 1 for portage
Walter Edmound shipmaster: 2 tuns for portage
Richard Davy; 1 tun for portage
John Gorsy: 1 tun for portage
Henry Carpenter: 1 tun for portage
(Robert),[142] servant of Robert Tabernar' (paid custom): 1 tun
Elias de Hemmeston: 1 ton salt
Custom: Walter Hugheton for the custom; 40d

Ship called *la Blythe* of Yarmouth
Master: Henry de Lacy
Docked: the same day as above
Cargo: 39 tuns 6 pipes wine of which:
  John le Perour: 14 tuns 2 pipes
  Thomas le Furbour: 15 tuns 2 pipes
  Robert de Criditon carpenter: 9 tuns 2 pipes (paid custom)
  Adam Perour: 1 tun
Custom: John le Perour for the custom; 40d, also 4d; [which] {Michael received}[143]

Ship called *la nawe Seynt John* of Teignmouth
Master: Jordan Phelp
Docked: the same day as above
Cargo: 16 tuns wine of which:
  John le Perour: 5 tuns
  Thomas le Furbour: 5 tuns
  Adam le Perour: 1 tun
  Robert de Criditon: 5 tuns (paid)
  Simon de Monte Acuto: 1 pipe
Custom: John le Perour for the custom; 20d [which] {[Michael] also received}

Ship called *le Godyer* of Teignmouth
Master: Roger Bolt
Docked: same day as above
Cargo: 60 tuns 3 pipes wine of which:
  Philip Lovecok: 10 tuns
  Roger le Taillour: 7 tuns
  William Austyn: 3 tuns 2 pipes
  Thomas Gerveys: 1 tun
  Richard de Gatepath: 7 tuns
  John Gervey: 1 tun
  John Luverych: 13 tuns 1 pipe
  John de Bovy: 5 tuns
  John Row: 1 tun for portage

---

[142] *William* crossed through and *Robert* written above.

[143] The annotation here and below, *Michael received*, is written in a very rough hand that could be that of Michael Thoraud, the chief steward in 1316/17; see Appendix 2, below.

Roger Bolt shipmaster: 1 tun for portage
A certain [*quidam*] Cofyn: 1 tun for portage
Thomas le Barbour: 4 tuns
John Dyrkyn: 3 tuns
Michael Thoraud: 2 tuns
Thomas le Furbour: 1 tun
Custom: 5s 4d [which] {Michael received}

Ship called *la Seynte Croitz* of Teignmouth
Master: Henry Kech
Docked: 29 October 1316
Cargo: 91 tuns 17 pipes (wine) of which:
  Gilbert de Combe: 22 tuns 4 pipes
  Roger Beyvyn: 2 tuns
  Martin le Keu: 11 tuns 3 pipes
  William le Keu: 5 tuns 1 pipe
  Richard le Keu: 20 tuns 7 pipes
  William le Skynner: 6 tuns
  Adam Broun: 6 tuns
  John Beauforest: 4 tuns
  John de Bovy: 10 tuns 1 pipe
  Henry Kech: 3 tuns of which 2 for portage and 1 customed because
    he is the shipmaster
  Ralph de Porte: 1 tun
  Michael de Bovy: 1 tun (customed)
  William Gascoyng: 1 pipe for portage
Custom: 8d [which] {Michael received}

Ship called *le cog Nostre Dame* of (Exmouth)[144]
Master: Peter Golloc
Docked: 2 November 1316
Cargo: 105 tuns 16 pipes wine of which:
  Philip Lovecok: 30 tuns 6 pipes
  William Dyn: 17 tuns (customed)
  John de Bayone: 4 tuns 1 pipe
  Also 1 pipe, customed
  William Ralle: 3 tuns
  Michael Thoraud: 8 tuns
  Thomas Thoraud: 13 tuns 1 pipe
  Peter Golloc shipmaster: 3 tuns (2 pipes) of which 2 [tuns] for
    portage and the rest customed[145]
  John Grenehulle: 1 tun for portage
  Richard Jan: 1 tun (customed)[146]
  Robert Jenekyn: 1 tun, customed
  Roger atte See: 1 tun for portage
  Walter Coulesworthy: 1 pipe, customed
  Thomas Chaillewey: 1 pipe for portage
  William de Saundervyle: 5 tuns

[144] *Exewyk* crossed through and *Exmouth* inserted above.
[145] *And the rest customed* crossed through.
[146] *Portage* underlined and *customed* written above.

In the custody of Adam le Perour: 17 tuns (4) pipes of which 5 tuns
  1 pipe are customed
Custom: John de Bayonne for the custom; sum 9s [which] {Michael
  received}

Ship called *le cog Seynt Gile* of Sidmouth
Master: Richard de Todewille
Docked: 7 November 1316
Cargo: 93 tuns 10 pipes [wine] of which:
  John Somery: 31 tuns 10 pipes (in his custody) of which Lord W.
    bishop of Exeter and Thomas de Henton have 18 tuns 4 pipes
    and the rest, viz., 13 tuns 6 pipes [belong to] John and are cus-
    tomed
  John Ercedekene: 2 tuns
  Joan de Smalecombe: 14 tuns
  Thomas le Barbour: 4 tuns
  Robert atte Rixen: 6 tuns
  William de Okampton: 2 tuns
  Thomas Lythenard: 1 tun (customed)
  Thomas Thoraud: 14 tuns (of which Walter Kaulesworthy has 1
    tun and Michael Thoraud has 6 tuns)
  Richard de Todewille shipmaster: 19 tuns in his custody of which
    10 tuns for portage and 9 tuns customed, also 9 quintals iron
Custom: wine, 9s 8d; iron, 4½d; also 4d for 1 tun; [which] {Michael
  received}

Racked wines [*Rek*]

Ship called *la Margarete* of Exmouth
Master: Walter Edmound
Docked: 16 February 1317
Cargo: 86 tuns wine of which:
  William Dyne: 41 tuns (customed)
  Walter de Hugheton: 22 tuns 3 pipes
  Nicholas Busse: 4 tuns 1 pipe
  Gilbert de Combe: 5 tuns
  John Gyrard: 4 tuns 1 pipe
  Walter Edmound: 2 tuns (portage)
  John, son of John de Nymet: 2 tuns (customed,[147] quit because J.
    Nymet is in the freedom)
  Nicholas atte Putte: 1 tun for portage
  William Gorcy: 1 tun for portage
  John Dollyng: 1 tun (customed)
  Philip Lovecok: 1 pipe
  Nicholas Tykele: 3 C iron for portage
Custom: Walter de Hugheton for the custom; 14s 8d[148] (per J. Davy)
  of which 4d in the pyx

---

[147] *Customed* crossed through.
[148] *8d* crossed through and *per J. Davy* written above.

Ship called *la Margarete* called *Langbord* of Exmouth
Master: Adam Slegh
Docked: 27 March 1317
Cargo: 67 tuns 2 pipes [wine] of which:
  Philip Lovecok: 29 tuns 3 pipes
  Richard de Gatepath: 7 tuns
  John de Bayone: 3 tuns
  William Austyn [and] Roger Leyz tailor: 7 tuns
  Robert de Stanbrigg: 8 tuns
  Richard Harvest of Kenton: 3 tuns
  Adam Slegh shipmaster: 2 tuns for portage
  The same shipmaster (paid 4d) and Philip Lovecok: 1 tun
  Adam Top of Teignmouth: 2 tuns, customed
  Henry Carpenter: 1 tun
  William Ralle: 4 tuns
  Henry de Hugheton: 2 quintals iron
  William Jobbe: 17 quintals [iron]
  Richard de Gatepath: 3 quarters rye
  Philip Lovecok: 2 quintals iron
  William Ralle: 3 quintals iron
  Richard de Gatepath: 2 bales sugar [*zucre*]
  John de Bayon: 1 C wax
  Philip Lovecok: ½ C wax
  Adam Slegh: 60 pounds wax
Custom: wine, 12d; iron, 1d in the pyx

Ship called *la Margarete* of Exmouth
Master: Walter Edmound
Docked: 10 April 1317
Cargo: 83 tuns 13 pipes wine of which:
  Martin le Keu of Bridford: 10 tuns 2 pipes
  Richard le Keu: 9 tuns
  William le Keu: 2 tuns
  Gilbert de Combe: 10 tuns 1 pipe
  Joan de Smalecombe: 3 tuns
  Adam Broun: 3 tuns
  John de Bovy: 3 tuns
  John de Bayone: 1 tun
  John de Luverych: 5 tuns, customed
  Thomas le Furbour: 11 tuns 1 pipe
  John Treydeners: 3 tuns
  William le Skynner: 2 tuns
  Adam Perour: 6 tuns of which 2 tuns are customed (M. le Keu for
    the custom)
  Richard de Tavystok: 9 tuns 1 pipe, customed (M. le Keu for the
    custom)
  Thomas Thoraud: 1 tun
  William Dyne: 3 pipes
  Nicholas de la Pytte with two of his fellow mariners: 3 tuns for
    portage

Walter Edmond shipmaster: 4 pipes of which 2 for portage and 2 customed

Roger Serle: 1 pipe for portage

Michael de Bovy: 2 tuns (customed)[149]

William de Kerdewille and his fellows: 4 quintals iron

Custom: Martin le Keu of Bridford for the custom; wine, 7s 4d; iron, 2d in the pyx

Ship called *le cog Notre Dame* of Exmouth
Master: Peter Gollok
Docked: 3 May 1317[150]
Cargo: 107 tuns 13 pipes wine of which:

Philip Lovecok: 29 tuns 3 pipes

John le Perour: 17 tuns 5 pipes

Robert de Criditon: 4 tuns 1 pipe (customed, paid Thomas Toraud)

Clement de Hampton: 6 tuns 1 pipe (customed)

William Ralle: 1 tun

John de Bayone: 8 tuns

John de Ercedekene: 1 tun

Richard Hurt: 1 tun

Roger Leyz tailor: 3 tuns

William Austyn: 1 tun

William de Chageforde: 1 tun

Thomas Gerveys: 1 tun (customed, paid)

John Dyrkyn: 1 pipe

Michael Toraud: 9 tuns

Thomas Thoraud: 14 tuns 1 pipe

Richard de Tavystok: 2 tuns (customed, paid T. Toraud)

Thomas Lythenard: 2 tuns (customed, paid T. Toraud)

Adam Broun: 1 tun

Peter Gollok: 3 tuns 1 pipe (of which 2 [tuns] for portage)

Richard Janekyn: 1 tun for portage

Robert Janekyn: 1 tun for portage

Elias Slegh: 1 tun for portage

Robert le Carpenter: 1 C wax (customed)

Thomas Chaillewalle: 2 quintals iron (paid)

Richard Harvest: 1 quintal [iron]

John Canoun: 1 quintal [iron] (paid)

Elias Botswayn: ½ quintal [iron]

Robert Ware: 1 quintal [iron]

Richard Davy: 1 quintal [iron]

William Elis: 1 quintal [iron]

Henry de Hugheton: 2 quintals [iron]

Nicholas Lovecok: 2 pounds saffron

Custom: wine, 5s 8d; wax and iron, 6½d in the pyx; saffron, 2d in the pyx

---

[149] *For portage* crossed through and *customed* written above.
[150] *April* crossed through and *May* written in.

Ship called *le Nicholas* of Teignmouth
Master: Robert Peverel
Docked: 26 May 1317
Cargo: 18 tuns wine of which:
  Robert atte Ryxen: 5 tuns
  William de Okampton: 3 tuns
  John Trikot: 1 tun
  Onger atte Hole: 1 tun, and 8 tuns, customed
  Robert atte Rixen: 5 dozens cordwain
  Onger atte Hole: 5 dozens cordwain
  The same Robert: 9 pounds saffron
  The aforesaid Onger: 9 pounds saffron, 1 bale cumin, 1 C wax, ½ C
    pepper, 1 bale Spanish soap [*sop de Ispannia*]
  Geoffrey de Kenton: 1 pound saffron, 1 pound pepper
  Robert Peverel shipmaster: (18) pounds pepper[151]
  William Deneman: 4 pounds pepper
Custom: Robert atte Rixen for the custom of wine, 3s; sum of petty
  custom, 2s 1½d in the pyx

Look at the other side [*Respice in tergo*][152]

2 quintals iron of Henry Hugheton

(m. 20d) [**1316/17** wine account continued]

Ship called *le cog Nostre Dame* of Exmouth
Master: Peter Gollok
Docked: 4 June 1317
Cargo: 7 tuns 5 pipes wine of which:
  Philip Lovecok: 2 tuns 2 pipes
  Peter Gollok: 2 tuns 1 pipe
  John le Perour: 1 tun
  Richard de Gatepath: 2 tuns 2 pipes
  Peter Gollok: 7 quintals iron
  Richard Gille: 2 quintals iron
  Thomas Chaillewille: 1 quintal iron (customed)
  John Canoun: 1 quintal iron (customed)
  John Challe: 1 quintal iron
  Robert Walle:[153] 1 quintal iron
  Philip Lovecok: 5 quintals iron
  Richard de Gatepath:(5)[154] quintals [iron]
  The aforesaid Philip and Richard: 3 bales alum
  The aforesaid Richard: 8 pounds saffron, 20 pounds sugar, 4 dozens
    and 4 hides [*pell'*] of cordwain, 40 pounds pork grease [*unguent porc'*]
Custom: no custom on wine; iron custom, 1d in the pyx

[151] *12* crossed through and *18* written above; *saffron* crossed through and *pepper* written next.
[152] Written in large letters at the bottom of the membrane. The following note is written in small letters at the very bottom corner of membrane.
[153] *Bythe* crossed through and *Walle* written next.
[154] *1* crossed through and *5* written above.

Ship called *le cog Notre Dame* of Hythe [*Hethe*]
Master: Henry de Hethe
Docked: 5 June 1317
Cargo: John de Nywedenne of Winchelsea: 17 tuns 1 pipe wine
Custom: no custom because of the freedom of the Cinque Ports

Ship called *la Margarete* of Exmouth
Master: Walter Edmound
Docked: 7 June 1317
Cargo: 3 tuns (4 pipes)[155] wine, viz.,
   The shipmaster: 2 [tuns] for portage and 1 tun for drink
   [And] 1 pipe for portage[156]
   Roger Serle: 1 pipe for portage
   Nicholas atte Pytte: 1 pipe for portage
   John Averey: 1 pipe for portage
   Richard de (Tavistok):[157] 1 barrel archil
   Also 9 quintals iron in the place of 1 portage of the [ship]master
   John Averey: 2 quintals iron
   Nicholas Tykele and William Fabr': 2 quintals [iron] for portage
Custom: no custom

Ship called *la Margarete* of Exmouth
Master: Adam Slegh
Docked: 8 June 1317
Cargo: 3 tuns 1 pipe wine of which:
   Philip Lovecok: 1 tun
   The shipmaster: 1 tun (quit)
   Adam de Stanbrigg: 1 tun (quit)
   Also 1 pipe for drink
   Richard Harvest and the shipmaster: 3 quintals iron, not customed
   Robert de Stanbrigg: 4 quintals [iron]
   Philip Lovecok: 5 quintals [iron]
   Adam Slegh and others of the ship: 21 quarters wheat
   Geoffrey atte Wille: 2 quintals iron (customed 1d)
   Philip Lovecok: 80 yards canvas
   The shipmaster: 50[158] yards canvas and linen cloth
   Geoffrey atte Wille: 30 yards canvas
   Adam Grype: 20 yards canvas
   Robert Stanbrigg: 40 yards canvas
   Philip Lovecok: 10 pounds saffron
   The shipmaster and Richard Harvest: 4 barrels pitch, 50 boards for
      the ship [*bord' pro nav'*], also ½ M nails
Custom: iron, 1d in the pyx

---

[155] *1 pipe* in superscript crossed through and *4 pipes* written in.
[156] It is unclear whether the 2 tuns or 1 pipe (or both) represent the portage claimed by the shipmaster.
[157] *Gatepath* crossed through and *Tavistok* written above.
[158] *40 yards 45* crossed through and *50* written next.

Tenth regnal year of the present king

1316/17 (m. 19) ROLL OF CUSTOMS OF WOAD AND OTHER
MERCHANDISE FROM THE TENTH YEAR OF THE
PRESENT KING EDWARD [II]

Ship called *le Langbord* of Exmouth
Master: William Slegh
Docked: 4 October 1316
Cargo: Philip Lovecok: 100 quarters of salt
Custom: no custom

Michael Thoraud received 3s 10d from the custom of woad for carriage beyond the gate

Ship called *la Welyfar* of Ottermouth
Master: Robert Bowey
Docked: 6 December 1316
Cargo: William Breuwer: 100 stones weld, 3 pipes potash, 2 M onions
  Alured Horn: 1 M iron, 1 M onions, 2 pieces cloth
  Roger de Clist: 1 piece cloth
  Richard Dyrkyn: 1 M iron
  The same Richard and Roger: 5 M onions, 80 yards canvas
  William Hok: 5 quintals iron, 80 yards canvas
  Roger Clist: 2 seams garlic
Custom: William Breuwer for the remainder [of the custom?]; ... 7½d;
  ... 3½d in the pyx

Ship called *la Alizote* of Dartmouth
Master: John Breuwer of Dartmouth
Docked: 10 December 1316
Cargo: 4 lasts 6 M herring of which:
  Richard Baret: 2 lasts
  Ralph de Nyweton mercer: 3 M
  John de Botelston: 3 M
  John Tybaud of Yarmouth: 2 lasts
Custom: no custom

Ship called *la Ros* of Exmouth
Master: Harlewin Bolt
Docked: 10 December 1316
Cargo: 3 lasts 11 M herring of which:
  John Wytebrother: 1 last 3 M and 1 cade
  Philip Lovecok: 4 M
  Nicholas de Lydeford: 3 M
  Robert Taverner: 3 M
  Richard Gaudethoun: 3 M
  Adam de Nyweton: 1 last
  Thomas de Molton: ½ last
Custom: no custom

Ship called *le cog* of Hook [*Hamelehok*]
Master: William Oslak
Docked: 11 December 1316
Cargo: 5 packs drapery of which:
    John Gregory of Lyme: 1 pack
    Thomas atte Hapst: 2 packs (paid)
    Francis de Outrelot: 1 pack (paid)
    Robert Russel of Taunton: 1 pack
Custom: sum, 12d [which] {Michael received}

Ship called *la neof Notre Dame* of Hook [*Hamelehok*]
Master: John le Duc
Docked: 16 December 1316
Cargo: Edmund Brytoun and Thomas Jacob: 42½ quarters salt
    And 3 quarters for portage
    William de Herdewyne: 1 bale cumin and 1 bale tar [*tarre*]
Custom: no custom

Ship called *le Welyfar* of Dover
Master: William Sandercok of Dover
Docked: 20 December 1316
Cargo: Ives Byrch and Hugh Sampson: 4 fothers lead, 50 pipes
    potash, 10 bales alum, 1 M[159] copper [*coper*]
    Hugh Sampson: 3 trendles wax weighing 3 C
    Walter Ladde: 1 bale alum, 1 bale rice
    Robert Rogemound: ½ quarter salt
Custom: no custom because in the freedom of Exeter

Ship called *le Symenel* of Sidmouth
Master: Richard Bodde
Docked: 30 December 1316
Cargo: 6½ lasts 2 M and 4 cades [herring] of which:
    Thomas de Molton: 1 last 4 M
    John Tybaud of Yarmouth: 2 lasts
    Adam de Neweton:[160] 1 last 2 M and 1 cade
    John de Whytebrother: 1 last 1 M and 1 cade
    Nicholas de Lydeford: 3 M
    Richard Gaudethoun: 3 M
    Adam Vode of Lyme: 1 last
Custom: no custom

Ship called *la Margarete* of Exmouth
Master: Roger le Sangere
Docked: 12 January 1317
Cargo: Roger le Sangere: 60 quarters coal

---

[159] *CC de C* crossed through and *1 M of copper* written in.
[160] *Sma* crossed through and *Neweton* written in.

Ship called *la neof Seynt Johan* of St Valéry
Master: John le Voil
Docked: 15 January 1317
Cargo: Peter Moner: 20 tuns woad, 400 stones weld {(paid)}
Custom: Thomas Petit for the custom; 20s

Ship called *la neof Seynt Johan* of Dartmouth
Master: Gilbert Doo
Docked: 16 January 1317
Cargo: Gilbert Doo: 60 quarters barley and Caen stone [*petris de Caan*]
   Richard le Seler: 1 ton salt, 2 tons barley, 3 tuns wine
Custom: no custom

Ship called *la Blythe* of Weymouth
Master: Walter Warman
Docked: 28 January 1317
Cargo: Francis de Maze: 130 quarters salt
Custom: no custom

Ship called *le Seynt Nicholas* of Le Vivier
Master: Ralph Bertram
Cargo: Peter de Carre: 1300 cords garlic, 1 seam onions, 2 tons salt, 2 quarters vetches [*vesces*]
Custom: 7d in the pyx

Ship called *la Jowhanette* of Dartmouth
Master: Thomas Cok
Docked: 21 January 1317
Cargo: Lawrence de Spaynge: 60 quarters salt
Custom: no custom

Ship called *la Charytee* of St Valéry
Master: Peter Sampson
Docked: 8 February 1317
Cargo: 39 tuns woad of which:
   John Petit: 15 tuns [woad], 100 stones weld
   John Poter: 12 tuns [woad], 100 stones weld
   Michael Poter: 12 tuns [woad]
Custom: 39s

Ship called *la Shalwe* of Winchelsea
Docked: 6 February 1317
Master: Thomas Codelowe
Cargo: Thomas Codelowe: 3 lasts containing 32 M herring
Custom: no custom because free of the Cinque Ports

Ship called *le Mesager* of Dartmouth
Master: John Cocus
Docked: 16 February 1317[161]

---

[161] *The same day* crossed through before date.

Cargo: Franciscus Mace: 25[162] copes and 1 frail figs and raisins, and 2[163] quarters, and 4 cow and ox hides, 4 jars oil not for sale [*non vendibil'*] Germeyn, valet of the same Franciscus: 1 frail raisins

Ship called *la neof Seynt John* of Guernsey
Master: John Dyram
Docked: 1 April 1317
Cargo: John la Cornaille: 14 quarters wheat, 34 quarters barley, 3 quarters peas, 3 quarters oats, 5 bacons, ½ seam garlic, 3 pieces linen cloth
Custom: 5d in the pyx

Ship called *le cog Notre Dame* of St Sampson
Master: William de la Ruwe
Docked: 29 April 1317
Cargo: William de la Ruwe shipmaster: (50 quarters)[164] wheat, 1½ quarters beans and peas, ½ quarter barley, 13 bacons
Custom: 3¼d in the pyx

Ship called *le Michel* of Teignmouth
Master: William atte Wode
Docked: 17 April 1317
Cargo: Andrew Roberd: 100 quarters salt

Ship called *le Lyon* of Lymington
Master: John le Whyte
Docked: 3 June 1317
Cargo: John le Whyte: 6 quarters salt

Ship called *le cog Seynt John* of Dartmouth
Master: John Pykard
Docked: 28 June 1317
Cargo: John le Baker of Dartmouth: 60 quarters wheat, 16 C rabbit skins

Boat called *Seynt Marie bot* of Lyme
Master: William Chepe
Docked: 29 June 1317
Cargo: Geoffrey Artour of King's Lynn [*Lynn*], William Fabr', Adam Vode: 21 quarters salt

Boat called *le Genger* of Polruan
Master: John Mark of Polruan
Docked: 1 July 1317
Cargo: Ives Byrch: 5 bales alum, 10 barrels potash woad, 2 M iron, ½ quarter [of] 1 C wax,[165] 2 bales almonds
Custom: no custom

---

[162] *Frails* crossed through.

[163] The first two strokes of the *iiii* are expunctuated, indicating it should read *ii*. The commodity also appears to be missing since neither fruit nor hides were measured in quarters, although it is possible that *2 quarters* of one cope or one frail of figs and raisins was meant.

[164] *30 quarters* crossed through and *50 quarters* written above.

[165] It is unclear whether the ½ quarter goes with the iron or wax since the phrase reads *ii^m ferr' di' quart' C cere.*

Ship called *la cog Seint Johan* of Weymouth
Master: Hugh de la Hope
Docked: 20 August 1317
Cargo: William de Serur' of Bayonne: 45 quarters wheat

(m. 19d) [**1316/17** merchandise account continued]

Ship called *la Margaret* of Hamble [*Hamele*]
Master: Roger Olak
Docked: 4 July 1317
Cargo: Peter le Monoyer: 14 tuns woad
Custom: 14s [which] {Michael received}

Ship called *la Rodecog* of Teignmouth
Master: Philip Sparke
Docked: 5 July 1317
Cargo: Peter le Monyers: 35 tuns woad, 300 stones weld
Custom: Ralph le Degher for the custom; 35s [which] {Michael
    received}

Ship called *la Johannette* of Teignmouth
Master: Gilbert Whetepain
Docked: 7 July 1317
Cargo: John de Beauforest: 30 quarters wheat, 10 quarters rye, 14
    dickers and 4 hides
Custom: no custom because in the freedom

Ship *Beate Marie Magdalene* of Bayonne
Master: John de Quirera
Docked: 18 July 1317
Cargo: William de Vingneau of Bayonne: 210 quarters salt, 4 bales
    cumin, 3 M cork [*Cork*]
Custom: Richard le Seler for the custom; 5d

Ship called *la cog Seint Sampson* of Guernsey
Master: John de Beauner
Docked: 7 September 1317
Cargo: John de Beauner and Richard Peryn: 18 seams garlic, 3 seams
    onions, 1 piece linen cloth containing 60 ells
Custom: 20d; all paid into the pyx in the presence of the Mayor

Ship called *la Johannette* of Guernsey
Master: Richard la Cornaild
Docked: 7 September 1317
Cargo: Richard la Cornaild and John de Rocher: 2½ seams garlic, 1
    frail and 2 seams onions, 2 pieces canvas
Custom: 19½d; all paid into the pyx in the presence of the Mayor

Roll of customs of wine and other merchandise landed at the port of the city of Exeter for diverse years in the time of Edward I and Edward II[166]

Roll of diverse accounts of Receivers of the city of Exeter in diverse years in the time of King Edward I

1317/18 (m. 18) ROLL OF CUSTOMS OF WINES LANDED AT THE PORT OF EXMOUTH FROM THE ELEVENTH YEAR OF KING EDWARD [II]

Ship called *le Godyer* of Teignmouth
Master: John Henri
Docked: 20 October 1317
Cargo: 62 tuns 5 pipes wine of which:
   Philip Lovecok: 28 tuns (free)
   Clement de Hamptone: 7 tuns 1 pipe (customed)
   William Dyne: 7 tuns (customed)
   John de Bayone: 7 tuns 1 pipe (free)
   Richard de Gatepath: 2 tuns (free)
   John Trikot: 2 tuns (free)
   Henry de Hugheton: 1 tun 1 pipe (customed)
   Thomas de Tetteborne: 1 tun (free)
   Gilbert in the Combe: 2 tuns (free)
   Nicholas Busse: 1 tun (free)
   John Row: 1 tun for portage (free)
   Lambert Ryhorn: 1 tun for portage
   A certain David: 1 pipe for portage
   A mariner: 1 pipe (customed)
   Joan de Smalecombe: 1 tun (free)
   John de Ercedekene: 1 tun (free)
Custom: John de Bayone for the custom: 6s of which 4½d in the pyx

Ship called *le Godyer* of Teignmouth
Master: Stephen Stok
Docked: 24 October 1317
Cargo: 85 tuns 8 pipes wine of which:
   Roger Leyz tailor: 8 tuns (free)
   Thomas le Barbour: 3 tuns (free)
   John Dyrkyn: 2 tuns (free)
   William Austyn: 5 tuns (free)
   Thomas Gerveis: 2 tuns (customed)[167]
   Thomas le Furbour: 20 tuns (free)
   Adam le Perour: 1 tun (free)
   William de Okampton: 4 tuns (free)
   Ives de Halghewille: 2 tuns (free)

---

[166] Written in a fifteenth- or early sixteenth-century hand on an attached membrane that serves as the cover of Customs Roll 1 when rolled up. The note that follows is written in an even later hand (probably mid to late sixteenth century).

[167] *Free* crossed through before *customed*.

Gilbert de Combe: 7 tuns 4 pipes (free)
John le Perour: 15 tuns (free)
Walter le Furbour: 5 tuns (1 pipe) wine (customed)
Robert le Carpenter: 11 tuns (customed)
The shipmaster: 2 pipes (customed)
Custom: Robert de Criditon carpenter for the custom; 7s, all in the pyx

Ship called *la Margarete* of Exmouth
Master: Walter Parys
Docked: 6 December 1317
Cargo: 81 tuns 15 pipes [wine] of which:
  Thomas Thoraud: 18 tuns 2 pipes (free)
  Nicholas Busse: 12 tuns 4 pipes (free)
  John Ercedekene: 3 tuns (free)
  Joan de Smalecombe: 6 tuns 1 pipe (free)
  Walter Parys shipmaster: 3 tuns [and] 1 pipe for portage (free)
  Ives Byrch: 1 tun (free)
  Walter de Hughetone: 19 tuns 4 pipes (free)
  John Somery: 5 tuns (customed)
  Master John de Stokes: 2 tuns 1 pipe (free)
  Thomas le Barbour: 1 tun (free)
  Robert de Stanbrugg: 1 tun for portage (free)
  John Averey: 2½ tuns 1 pipe (free)
  Edith de Toppysham: 4½ tuns 1 pipe (free)
  Walter atte Hole of Exminster: 4 tuns (customed)
  Walter de Kerdewille: 4 quintals iron
  Thomas Lythenard: 2 quintals iron
Custom: wine, 3s, all in the pyx; iron, 3d in the pyx

Ship called *le cog Nostre Dame* of Exmouth
Master: Peter Golloc
Docked: 6 December 1317
Cargo: 107 tuns 12 pipes [wine] of which:
  Philip Lovecok: 39 tuns 4 pipes (free)
  Thomas Thoraud: 22 tuns 2 pipes (free)
  William Ralle: 3 tuns (free)
  Thomas[168] de Tetteborne: 2 tuns 4 pipes (free)
  Ives Byrch: 12 tuns (free)
  Robert de Okamptone: 2 tuns (free)
  Peter Golloc shipmaster: 4 tuns (free)
  Elias de Hemmestone: 3 tuns (free)
  John Challe: 1 tun portage (free)
  Geoffrey Yvon: 1 tun for portage (free)
  John le Perour: 3 tuns 2 pipes (free)
  Thomas le Furbour: 3 tuns (free)
  Richard Dyrkyn: 3 tuns (free)
  John de Bayone: 2 tuns (free)
  Clement de Hampton: 1 tun (customed)

---

[168] *Thoraud* crossed through.

Roger le Yung: 2 tuns (customed)
Richard de Gatepath: 4 tuns (free)
Custom: 12d, of which 8d in the pyx

Ship called *la Jowanette* of Teignmouth
Master: Luverych in the Combe
Docked: 19 November 1317
Cargo: 97 tuns 10 pipes wine of which:
  Gilbert de Combe: 29 tuns 2 pipes (free)
  William Cocus of Bridford: 5 tuns (free)
  Martin le Keu of Bridford: 10 tuns 2 pipes (free)
  Richard le Keu of Bridford: 24 tuns 4 pipes (free)
  John de Bovy: 1 tun (free)
  Michael de Bovy: 2 tuns (customed)
  John de la Mare: 1 tun (customed)
  Thomas le Spicere: 2 tuns (free)
  William le Skynnere: 2 tuns (free)
  John Ercedekene: 1 tun (free)
  Joan de Smalecombe: 3 tuns (free)
  John Luverych: 8 tuns 1 pipe (customed)
  Henry Sprot: 1 tun for portage
  Luverych in the Combe: 5 tuns of which 2 tuns for portage (3 tuns customed)
  Nicholas Busse: 1 pipe (free)
  Jordan Lom: 3 tuns of which 2 tuns customed, 1 tun for portage (customed)
  Henry Luneton: 1 tun for portage
  John de Bovy: 2 bales almonds
Custom: 5s 8d of which 4s 8d in the pyx

Ship called *la Seynt Jake* of Teignmouth
Master: Adam de la Clyve
Docked: 20 November 1317
Cargo: 38[169] tuns 2 pipes wine of which:
  Gilbert in the Combe: 15½ tuns 1 pipe (free)
  John Beauforest: 15½ tuns 1 pipe (free)
  Henry Kech: 4 tuns (customed)
  Adam atte Clyve shipmaster: 2 tuns portage
  Thomas atte Burne: 1 tun portage
  Wymond de Wyght: 1 tun portage
  Gilbert in the Combe and John Beauforest: 10 tons iron, 5 C wax
  Henry Kech: 17 quintals iron
  Thomas atte Burne and Wymond de Wyght: 17 quintals iron
  Lawrence de Pouderham: 3 quintals iron
Custom: wine, 16d, all in the pyx; iron, 18½d, all in the pyx

Ship called *la Margarete* of Exmouth called *Langbord*
Master: William Slegh
Docked: 21 November 1317

---

[169] *Pipes* crossed through.

Cargo: 71 tuns 4 pipes wine:
  Thomas de Hentone, Treasurer of [the Cathedral of] Exeter:
    for his drink [*ad potum suum*] 5 tuns 2 pipes (free)
  Walter de Hugheton: 3 tuns (free)
  Robert de Okampton: 7 tuns (free)
  John de Fenton: 5 tuns (free)
  William de Okampton: 2 tuns (free)
  Walter de Sweyngtill: 5 tuns (free)
  John Ercedekene: 6 tuns (free)
  Henry de Gatepath: 5 tuns (free)
  Michael Thoraud: 8 tuns (free)
  Thomas Thoraud: 3 tuns (free)
  Clement de Hamptone: 3 tuns (customed)
  John de Bayone: 1 tun (free)
  William Dyne: 2 tuns (customed)
  Robert de Wotton: 2 tuns (free)
  Richard de Gatepath: 1 tun (free)
  Thomas Codelep: 1 tun (free)
  Adam Broun: 4 tuns (free)
  Geoffrey atte Wille: 1 tun for portage (free)
  William Slegh: 1 tun (customed)
  Robert de Stanbrigge: 4 tuns (free)
  Avicia Perour: 1 tun (free)
  Thomas Challewille: 1 pipe (customed)[170]
  The mariners: 1 pipe for drink (quit)
  John de Fenton: 1 bale almonds
  William Golloc: 1 quintal iron
  Thomas Challewille: 1 quintal iron
  John Eliot: ½(?) quintal iron
  Walter Furbour: 20 pounds iron
  John Somery: 1 pipe wine (customed)
Custom: wine, 2s 8d of which 8d in the pyx; iron, 1½d [and] ¼d of
  which ¼d in the pyx

Ship called *le cog Notre Dame* of Teignmouth
Master: Richard Mugge
Docked: 3 December 1317
Cargo: 74 tuns 6 pipes wine of which:
  John de Bovy: 21 tuns 4 pipes (free)
  Richard de Tavistok: 1 tun (customed)
  John de Nyweton: 23 tuns 1 pipe (free)
  Onger de la Hole: 15 tuns (customed)
  Henry de Rocombe: 10 tuns of which 1 tun for portage (customed)
  Richard Mugge shipmaster: 2 tuns for portage
  John Mugge: 1 tun for portage
  The mariners: 1 tun for drink
  John de Bovy: 4 dozens cordwain
  John de Nyweton: 1 dozen cordwain

---

[170] *Free* crossed through.

Onger de la Hole: 8 dozens cordwain of which 1 dozen belongs to
  Ralph de Thornbury
Custom: wine, 8s 4d; cordwain, 3½d

Racked wines [*Rek*][171]

Ship called *le cog Notre Dame* of Exmouth
Master: Peter Golloc
Docked: 16 April 1318
Cargo: 112 tuns 12 pipes wine of which:
  Philip Lovecok: 28 tuns 4 pipes (free)
  Richard Cocus of Bridford: 6 tuns (free)
  Martin ...: 5 tuns 2 pipes (free)
  Gilbert de Combe: 3 tuns 1 pipe (free)
  Michael de Bovy: 3 tuns (customed)
  Thomas de Tetteborne: 3 tuns 1 pipe (free)
  William Ralle: 2 tuns (free)
  The same Thomas and William: 1 tun (free)
  Nicholas Lovecok: 1 tun (customed)
  John le Perour: 10 tuns 2 pipes (free)
  Elias de Hemmestone: 3½ tuns (free)
  Thomas le Barbour: 2 tuns (free)
  Peter Golloc: 6 tuns (free)
  John Cha... and Robert Janekyn: 2 tuns portage
  William Dyne: 12 tuns (customed)
  Clement de Hampton: 4 tuns (customed)
  Thomas Lythenard: 2 tuns (customed)
  Richard de Tavistok: 1 tun (customed)
  Thomas Thoraud: 17 tuns 2 pipes (free)
Custom: 7s 8d of which 16d in the pyx

Ship called *la Langbord* of Exmouth
Master: William Slegh
Docked: 16 April 1318
Cargo: 72 tuns 5 pipes wine of which:
  Philip Lovecok: 38 tuns 3 pipes (free)
  Thomas de Tetteborne: 1 tun (free)
  Henry de Hugheton: 1 tun (customed)
  Clement de Hampton: 7 tuns (customed)
  William Dyne: 7 tuns (customed)
  The shipmaster: 2 tuns for portage
  Robert de Stanbrigg: 4 tuns 1 pipe (free)
  Thomas le Barbour: 2 tuns (free)
  Richald' de Toppysham: 1 tun (free)
  William de Criditon and William Edmound: 1 tun (free)
  Walter de Hugheton: 7 tuns 1 pipe (free)
  Edith Gyrard: 1 tun (free)
  Henry de Hugheton: 4 quintals iron

---

[171] *Rek* repeated six times in very large letters across the membrane.

William Golloc: 2 quintals iron
Thomas Challewille: 2 quintals iron
Philip Lovecok: 2 quintals iron
Custom: wine, 5s of which 2s 8d in the pyx; iron, 2d

Ship called *la Margarete* of Exmouth
Master: Edmund Parys
Docked: 25 April 1318
Cargo: 80 tuns 18 pipes wine of which:
  William Dyne: 20 tuns 4 pipes (customed)
  Walter de Hughetone: 14 tuns 4 pipes (free)
  Richard le Seler: 2 tuns (free)
  T... ... : ...½ tuns 1 pipe
  Martin Belebuche: 1½ tuns (free)
  John de Nymet senior: 3 tuns (free)
  William Bakoun: 8 tuns 2 pipes (free, of the Cinque Ports)
  ... Bolle mercer: 1 pipe
  Edmund Parys shipmaster: 6 tuns 1 pipe (free)
  Walter de Swengtill: 1 tun (free)
  Richard de Tavistok: ... ... (customed)
  Henry le Carpenter: 1 tun for portage
  Edith de Toppysham: 2 tuns 1 pipe (free)
  Thomas le Barbour and John Averey: 6 tuns 3 [pipes] (free)
  Nicholas Busse: 1 pipe (free)
  William le Skynnere: 2 tuns (free)
  Richard le Keu and Martin, his brother: 1 tun (free)
  John de la Mare: 1 tun (customed)
Custom: 4s 8d

Ship called *le Peres* of Sidmouth
Master: Roger le Sangere
Docked: 8 May 1318
Cargo: 48 tuns 10 pipes wine of which:
  Ives Byrch: 12 tuns 1 pipe (free)
  Elias de Hemmeston: 2 tuns (free)
  Richard Tuk: 9 tuns 2 pipes (customed)
  Pagan Breuwer: 7 tuns 2 pipes (free)
  William de Forde: 2 tuns (free)
  Walter de Morcestre: 1 tun (customed)
  Thomas Golde: 6 tuns (free)
  Ralph le Sangere: 5 tuns (customed)
  Henry Lange: 2 tuns (customed)
  Roger le Sangere: 2 tuns for portage
  William de Morcestre:[172]
  Hamelyn le Sangere: 2 pipes (customed)
  Richard Rubes and Geoffrey Michel: 3 pipes for portage
  John de Shyrborne junior: 1 C diverse spices
  Martin Belebuch: ½ C iron
Custom: 7s

[172] *William de Morcestre* crossed through.

Ship called *le Michel* of Exmouth
Master: Adam Slegh
Docked: 8 May 1318
Cargo: 48 tuns 4 pipes wine of which:
　　Thomas le Furbour: 18 tuns 1 pipe (free)
　　Roger Leyz tailor: 7 tuns (free)
　　William Austyn: 3 tuns
　　Thomas Gerveis: 2 tuns (free)[173]
　　John Ercedekene: 1 tun 1 pipe (free)
　　John le Perour: 7 tuns (free)
　　Robert le Carpenter: 3 tuns 1 pipe (customed)
　　Roger le Yung: 1 tun (customed)
　　Walter de Swengtill: 5 tuns (free)
Custom: 20d, all in the pyx

Sum total of wine custom this year–61s of which Lord Hugh de Courtenay [has] for the third part of wine–20s 4d.

1317/18 　(m. 17) EXETER–ROLL OF CUSTOMS OF SHIPS LANDING WITH WOAD AND OTHER MERCHANDISE FROM THE ELEVENTH YEAR OF THE PRESENT KING EDWARD [II]

Ship called *le cog Notre Dame* of Saltash
Master: John Caperoun
Docked: 1 November 1317
Cargo: William Breuwer and Pagan Breuwer: 6 bales alum, 2 M iron, 12 barrels potash woad, 30 M onions, 1 barrel oil, 16 mortars, 4 brass cooking-pots [*cacab' enee*], 23 pounds of brass in pans [*enee in patell*]
Custom: no custom because in the freedom of Exeter

Ship called *le Distr'* of Polruan
Master: Robert Brydewar'
Cargo: Robert Brydewar': 19 quarters salt and timber and wood [*salis & maer' Et boscum*]
Custom: no custom

Boat called *le Lyon* of Lymington
Master: John le Whyte
Docked: 12 December 1317
Cargo: John le Whyte: 10 quarters salt, 50 iron spurs [*di' C spord' ferri*]
Custom: iron, 1½d in the pyx

Ship called *le cog Seynt John* of[174] Weymouth
Master: Thomas le Lang
Docked: 13 December 1317
Cargo: William Baret of Weymouth: 32 barrels potash woad, 3 quarters woad, 12 garbs weld
Custom: 7½d, quit through the freedom of Weymouth

---

[173] *Customed* crossed through.
[174] *Teignmouth* crossed through.

Ship called *le cog Notre Dame* of Lymington
Master: John Caperoun
Docked: 14 December 1317
Cargo: John de Cantuar': 20 quarters salt
Custom: no custom

Ship called *la Margar'* of Hook [*Hok*]
Master: Roger de Houslake
Docked: 21 December 1317
Cargo: (John Fareford of Southampton): 36 pipes potash woad, 1
　　cope figs and raisins, 1½ M herring, 1 bale rice, 1 bale alum
　　Robert Hogheles of Chard: 2 sacks wool of Spain
Custom: no custom because of the freedom of Southampton

Ship called *le Seynt Cler* of Gosforth [*Goseford*]
Master: Robert Bast of Gosforth [*Goseford*]
Docked: 21 December 1317
Cargo: 23 lasts herring of which:
　　Richard Baret: 2 lasts
　　John Tybot: 1 last
　　Philip Lovecok: 1(½) lasts
　　Thomas de Molton: ½ last
　　Nicholas de Lideford: 4 lasts
　　John de Whytebrother: 2 lasts 1 M and 1 cade
　　Richard Reymound of Yarmouth: 1½ lasts
　　Thomas Oxton: 5 M 1 cade
　　Adam Perour: 1 last
　　William le Skynner: 1 last
　　Thomas Forbour: 11 M
　　William de Okampton: 8 M
　　Robert de Okampton: 5 M
　　(Adam)[175] de Nyweton mercer: 2 lasts
　　John Tybot of Yarmouth: 2 lasts
　　John de Fenton: 1½ lasts
　　Thomas Furbour: ½ last
　　Ralph de Thornbury: 1½ fothers lead
　　Adam de Nyweton mercer: tents [*tentes*]
Custom: no custom

Ship called *le cog Seynt Johani* of Teignmouth
Master: Richard Meynge
Docked: 27 December 1317
Cargo: John Petit: 14 tuns woad, 9 barrels potash, 300 stones weld
　　Richard Mugge: 5 M onions
Custom: woad, 14s paid to Martin; onions, ½d in the pyx

Ship called *le cog Seynt Jake* of Dartmouth
Master: Richard Gillot
Docked: 18 January 1318

---

[175] *Ralph* crossed through and *Adam* inserted above.

Cargo: Elias Mercer: 2 C salt
  William Edward: 7 copes figs and raisins, 8 jars oil
Custom: no custom because of the Cinque Ports

Ship called *le cog Seynt Nicholas* of Le Vivier
Master: Nicholas Rydel
Docked: 23 February 1318
Cargo: Roland de Mictoun: 17 C garlic
Custom: 2s 4d

Ship called *la Margarete* of Ottermouth
Master: Stephen Crabbe
Docked: 4 March 1318
Cargo: William Breuwer and John Lukeys: 40 quarters wheat, 2
    seams garlic
  John Lukeys: 2½ bales alum, 7 copes figs and raisins, 2 barrels
    potash woad, 5 M onions
  William Breuwer: 3 M onions, 1 barrel oil, 1 piece cloth, 12 lanterns
Custom: William Breuwer for the custom; 16d ... in the pyx

Ship called *le Benedicite* of Yarmouth
Master: John Robyn
Docked: 8 March 1318
Cargo: 16 lasts herring of which:
  John Robyn: 3 lasts 1 M
  Adam de la March: 1½ lasts 3 M
  William Foloflove: 2 lasts 8 cades
  Adam de Chestr': (7 lasts)
  The shipmaster: 1 ton wheat
  Geoffrey Stonyng: 1½ lasts
Custom: no custom because of the freedom of Yarmouth

Ship called *la Belecote* of London
Master: John de Bredstrete
Docked: 30 March 1318
Cargo: 17 tuns 1 pipe woad of which:
  Nicholas le Veyl: 9 tuns
  William Tornecoyse: 5 tuns
  Engeran de Bom: 3 tuns 1 pipe
Custom: 18s

Ship called *le Welyfare* of Lyme
Master: William Medrigg
Docked: 30 March 1318
Cargo: Peter le Moner: 16 tuns woad, 100 quarters mixed rye and
  wheat, 10 quarters barley, 50 M onions
  Simon Fode: 15 quarters barley, 10 quarters wheat
  John de Bayone and John Doddyng: 6 quarters wheat and rye
  The shipmaster: 2 quarters wheat and rye
Custom: woad, 16s

Ship called *la Cristofere*
Master: John Kempe
Docked: 5 April 1318
Cargo: John Kempe: 20 quarters barley

Ship called *la Jowanette* of St Valéry
Master: John le Gros
Docked: 8 April 1318
Cargo: Nicholas[176] le Webbe of Taunton: 7 tuns woad, 30 stones weld
Custom: quit because in the freedom of Taunton[177]

Ship *Sancti Johannis* of Lyme
Master: Robert Patrich
Docked: 17 May 1318
Cargo: Robert Patrich: 100 quarters salt

Ship called *le Alicote* of Dartmouth
Master: Robert atte Knolle
Docked: 17 May 1318
Cargo: Robert atte Knolle, John Skounz, Richard le Baker: 100 quarters wheat, also 100 pounds copper [*coper*]
Custom: ...

Ship called *le Vertbois* of Le Vivier
Master: John Brian
Docked: 14 May 1318
Cargo: John de Gardyn: 6 pipes salt of Normandy
Robert Colas: 12 C garlic, 3 pots grease [*ollis unguent'*]
And 20 yards canvas for portage
Custom: ...

Ship called *le cog Notre Dame* of Abbeville
Master:[178] Peter Daniel
Docked: 18 May 1318
Cargo: Lawrence de Lysshebon: 120 quarters wheat
Custom: ...

Ship called *le Jouwanette* of Caen
Master: John Erman
Docked: 21 May 1318
Cargo: Geoffrey de Bailloul: 300 quarters wheat and barley, 1 quarter peas
Custom: ...

Ship called *la Margarete* of Ottermouth
Master: Crabbe of Ottermouth
Docked: 27 April 1318

---

[176] *De* crossed through.
[177] Another hand is drawn in the margin with a finger pointing to this entry because of its reference to Taunton (see above, n. 110).
[178] *Davy* crossed through.

Cargo: 80 quarters wheat, 4 C canvas, 6 stones woad [*wayde*], 2 pieces cloth of Rouen, long cloths containing 40 ells with one [ell] remaining [*ii peciis panni de rotomago Long' panni cont' xl uln' cum uno rem'*],[179] 20 ells tiersain cloth [*xx uln' de terceyne*]
Custom: …

Ship called *le Michel* of Hook [*Hameleok*]
Master: John Michel
Docked: 13 May 1318
Cargo: Michael Poter: 17 tuns woad, … 3 barrels potash, 180 stones weld [*iiii^{xx}. C. petr' Walde*][180]
Custom: …

Ship called *le Katerine* of Dover
Master: William Godyn
Docked: 26 May 1318
Cargo: William Fachours and Elias Gobert: 122 quarters wheat, 80 [quarters] oats, 20 quarters beans, 8 sheep [*multon*], 17 bacons, 1 C grease [*ungenti*]
Henry Brytoun: 4 pieces cloth, 33 pairs hose
Custom: …

Ship called *le Lion* of Southampton
Master: John le Whyte
Docked: 12 June 1318
Cargo: John le Whyte: 12 quarters salt
Custom: …

Ship called *la Jowanette* of Guernsey
Master: John Pilet
Docked: 25 June 1318
Cargo: (Nicholas)[181] de Chegny: 34 quarters wheat, 4½ quarters barley
Richard le Cornaille, valet of the ship: 20 yards canvas
Custom: …

Boat called *le cog* of Poole
Master: John le Ros
Docked: 25 June 1318
Cargo: John le Ros: 8 quarters salt, 2 stones [*petr'*] 5 bushels wheat

Ship called *le Seynt Johan* of St Valéry-sur-Somme [*Summe*][182]
Master: Robert Folie
Docked: 26 June 1318
Cargo: Richard de Gysye: 300 quarters wheat

---

[179] It is unclear whether the phrase starting with *long cloths* was a separate import or meant to describe the 2 pieces of Rouen cloth.

[180] The multiplication (4 x 20 x 100) actually yields 8,000, an amount substantially above the next largest cargo of weld (400 stones). The scribe must have meant 180 (4 x 20 + 100).

[181] *Richard* crossed through and *Nicholas* inserted above.

[182] See n. 13, above.

Ship called *la Seynt Johan* of Barfleur
Master: Godefrus' Benhaut
Docked: 28 June 1318
Cargo: Master Nicholas de Fovyle of Rouen: ... [stone][183]

Ship called *la Alicote* of Dartmouth
Master: Martin Seger
Docked: 15 July 1318
Cargo: ... de Lenne and Sensu de Castre: 100 quarters [salt][184]
   Sensu de Castre: 43 jars oil
Custom: ...

A boat of Poole
Master: Richard Mone
Docked: 17 July 1318
Cargo: Richard Mone: 6 quarters salt

A boat of Lymington
Master: William de Nywbury
Docked: 18 July 1318
Cargo: William de Nywbury shipmaster: 12 quarters salt

Ship called *le hollok Seynt Sampson*
Master: John de Beaner
Docked: 20 August 1318
Cargo: 9 seams onions, 12 seams garlic, 3 pieces linen cloth, 2 pieces canvas
Custom: 19d in the pyx

Ship called *la Margarete* of Exmouth called *Langbord*
Master: Geoffrey atte Wille
Docked: 22 August 1318
Cargo: Philip Lovecok (and Robert Stanbrigge): 300 quarters salt

Ship called *le Godyer* of Ottermouth
Master: Nicholas Ok
Docked: 28 August 1318
Cargo: Nicholas Ok shipmaster: 120 quarters coal
   Thomas Codelep: 1 bale licorice [*lykoryz*], 1 bale almonds
Custom: ...

Ship called *le Michel* of Yarmouth
Master: Ralph Crestian
Docked: 1 September 1318
Cargo: William Mounteyn: 300 quarters salt

Ship called *le cog Notre Dame* of Poole
Master: Adam le Whyte
Docked: 16 September 1318
Cargo: John le Poter: 16 tuns woad, 5 barrels potash woad, 40 stones weld
   The shipmaster: 20 M onions
Custom: 16s ...

---

[183] *Stone [Petr']* appears in the margin where the imported commodity is usually noted; the cargo was probably Caen stone.
[184] *Salt* written in the margin.

(m. 17d) [**1317/18**]

Taunton[185]

The 11th year

1318/19 (m. 16) EXETER–ROLL OF CUSTOMS ON WINE LAND-
ED AT THE PORT OF EXMOUTH FROM THE FEAST
OF ST MICHAEL IN THE TWELFTH YEAR OF KING
EDWARD [II] TO THE SAME FEAST FOLLOWING

Ship called *la Margarete* of Exmouth called *Langbord*
Master: Parys Edmound
Docked: 25 October 1318
Cargo: 65 tuns 8 pipes wine of which:
   Philip Lovecok: 41 tuns 4 pipes
   Walter de Hugheton: 10 tuns
   Thomas de Tetteburne: 1 tun 3 pipes
   Henry de Hugheton: 1 tun (customed)
   Nicholas Lovecok: 1 tun (customed)
   Parys Edmound shipmaster: 3 tuns
   Robert de Stanbrigge: 6 tuns 1 pipe
   William Slegh: 1 tun for portage
   John Vele: 1 tun for portage
   Philip Lovecok: 10 quintals iron
   Geoffrey atte Wille: 14 quintals [iron]
Custom: 8d, in the pyx

Ship called *le Peter* of Sidmouth
Docked: 26 October 1318
Cargo: 45 tuns 6 pipes wine of which:
   Thomas Thoraud: 20 tuns 3 pipes
   Thomas de Heantone: 1 tun
   Oliver Mathu: 1 tun
   John de Bayone: 9 tuns
   Clement de Hamptone: 6 tuns
   Walter de Caulesworthy: 2 tuns
   Walter de Hugheton: 4 tuns 1 pipe
   Geoffrey Michel: 1 tun for portage
   John Pyttyng: 1 tun for portage
   The shipmaster: 2 pipes of which 1 customed
   Walter de Coulesworthy: 6 pounds saffron, 4 pounds pepper
Custom: For the custom is John Bayone {Thomas Thoraud}; 16d

Ship called *le Godyer* of Teignmouth[186]
Master: Julian Bolt
Docked: 22 November 1318

---

[185] Written in the same late hand as the notations on previous membranes concerning
Taunton (see above, n. 17).
[186] There is an X next to this entry in the left-hand margin; see above, pp 42–3.

Cargo: 56 tuns 3 pipes wine of which:
  Thomas le Furbour: 23 tuns 2 pipes
  Adam Perour: 1 tun
  Roger Leyz: 10 tuns
  William Austyn: 5 tuns 1 pipe
  Thomas Gerveis: 2 tuns, customed
  Julian Bolt: 1 tun for portage
  Richard Cokgere: 1 tun, customed
  John Bolt: 1 tun for portage
  John Row: 1 tun for portage
  John Hystorre: 1 tun for portage
  John Row: 17 quintals iron
  Thomas le Forbour and Roger Leyz tailor: the rest of the iron
  John le Perour: 5 tuns
  Robert de Criditone carpenter: 5 tuns {paid}
Custom: William Austyn and Thomas Furbour for the custom; wine,
  2s 8d; iron, 8½d

Ship called *le Godyer* of Sidmouth
Master: Robert Codeman
Docked: 22 November 1318
Cargo: 44 tuns 2 pipes [wine] of which:
  Jordan Ilbard: 11 tuns (paid custom)
  The Archdeacon of Wells: 2 tuns for drink
  Richard le Forester: 15 tuns, customed (paid)
  Henry de Rocombe: 15 tuns (1 pipe), customed (paid)
  William de Hok: 1 tun for portage
  The shipmaster: 1 pipe
  Henry Rocombe and Richard Forester: 2 bales cumin
Custom: wine custom, 15s [which] {M. Cocus received}; {then 2 tuns
  allowed for the Archdeacon of Wells}; cumin, 3d in the pyx

Ship called *la Margarete* of Exmouth
Master: John Averey
Docked: 22 November 1318
Cargo: 81 tuns 12 pipes wine of which:
  Walter de Hugheton ({quit}) and Nicholas Busse ({quit}): 28 tuns
  Richard de Chyssebych: 1 tun, customed ({error})
  The same Walter: 3 pipes
  Elias de Hemmeston: 9 tuns 3 pipes
  Thomas Golde: 4 tuns
  William Dyne: 13 tuns, customed ({Receiver received})
  John le Yung: 9 tuns
  Thomas le Barbour: 1 tun
  John Averey shipmaster: 2 tuns
  Thomas Jacop: 3 tuns
  Nicholas de Pytte [and] Hamelin Passemer: 2 tuns for portage
  Nicholas atte Pytte: 1 tun 1 pipe, customed ({Receiver received})
  Walter Papeiay: 1 tun 1 pipe, customed ({Receiver received})
  Walter Hardy: 7 tuns 1 pipe of which 1 tun for portage ({custom paid})

Elias Hardy: 1 pipe portage
Robert de Stanbrigg: 1 pipe
Nicholas Busse: 1 pipe
Custom: {5s 8d; [to be paid on?] Monday [*Lun'*]}

Ship called *le cog Notre Dame* of Exmouth
Master: Peter Golloc
Docked: 23 November 1318
Cargo: 95 tuns 25 pipes of wine of which:
    Philip Lovecok: 37 tuns 8 pipes
    Thomas de Tetteborne: 1 tun 3 pipes
    William Ralle: 3 tuns 1 pipe
    John le Perour: 15 tuns 2 pipes
    Robert le Carpenter: 10 tuns 2 pipes ({paid})
    Walter le Furbour: 2 tuns ({paid})
    Thomas Thoraud: 7 tuns 1 pipe
    Thomas Lythenard: 3 tuns ({paid})
    Richard de Tavistok: 1 pipe ({paid})
    Martin Belebuch: 2 pipes
    Michael de Oxton: 9 tuns
    Thomas Tokere of Kenton: 1 pipe (for portage)
    John Challe: 1 pipe portage
    Peter Golloc: 3 tuns
    Thomas le Barbour: 5 tuns
    Nicholas Lovecok: 1 pipe ({paid})
    Geoffrey Botour: 1 pipe
    Philip Lovecok and John le Perour: 2 bales almonds
Custom: 6s 4d; Robert le Carpenter for the custom

Ship called *le Godyer* of Teignmouth
Master: Stephen de Stok
Docked: 30 November 1318
Cargo: 69 tuns 23 pipes [wine] of which:
    Gilbert de Combe: 23 tuns 5 pipes
    John de Bovy and Hugh Sampson: 7 tuns (2 pipes)
    The Bishop of Exeter: 4 tuns
    Thomas de Heanton: 1 tun
    Alice, daughter of Gilbert de Come: 2 tuns
    John Luverych: 2 pipes
    John Beauforest: 2 pipes
    Richard Cocus: 15 tuns 7 pipes
    William le Keu: 1 tun
    Thomas Spicere: 2 tuns
    John de la Mare: 2 tuns
    Walter Prodhomme: 6 tuns
    John Eustaz: 3 tuns 3 pipes (of which 1 for portage)
    Michael Bovy: 3 tuns
Custom: wine custom paid to the Receiver, sum ½ mark

Ship called *le Michel* of Exmouth
Master: Adam Slegh
Docked: 29 November 1318
Cargo: 52 tuns 6 pipes [wine] of which:
  Thomas Jacop: 10 tuns 2 pipes
  Henry de Gatepath: 10 tuns 1 pipe
  Walter de Sweyngtill: 8 tuns
  John le Archedekene: 4 tuns 1 pipe
  Cecilia de Smalecombe: 4 tuns 1 pipe
  John de Fenton: 6 tuns
  Robert atte Rixen: 6 tuns 1 pipe
  Adam Parys: 2 tuns
  Adam Slegh shipmaster: 1 tun for portage
  William de Chaggeford: 1 tun
  Thomas Jacop: 8 quintals iron, 1 bale almonds
  Richard Hardy: 1 quintal iron
Custom: no custom because all [are] in the freedom of Exeter

Ship called *la Margarete* of Sandwich
Master: John Condy
Docked: 9 April 1319
Cargo: 43 tuns wine of which:
  Stephen de Uppeton: 10 tuns
  John Condy shipmaster: 10 tuns
  John Reyner: 10 tuns
  Peter Daulard: 13 tuns wine
Custom: no custom because in the freedom of the Cinque Ports

Ship called *la Margarete* of Exmouth
Master: John Averey
Docked: 19 April 1319
Cargo: 87 tuns 9 pipes wine of which:
  William Tailleder of *Pene*: 62 tuns 4 pipes
  Walter de Hughetone: 10 tuns 4 pipes
  John le Yung: 3 tuns
  Nicholas Tykele: 1 tun for portage
  John Averey: 3 tuns
  Henry le Carpenter: 1 tun for portage
  John Dollyng: 2 tuns (customed)
  Nicholas de la Pitte: 1 tun for portage
  Hamelin Passemer: 1 tun for portage
  Nicholas Busse: 1 tun
  Adam Parys: 1 tun for portage
  Nicholas de la Pitte: 1 tun 2 pipes (customed)
Custom: Walter de Hugheton for the custom; 23s 8d of which 12d in
  the pyx

Ship called *la Margarete* of Teignmouth
Master: Thomas Colepol
Docked: 17 May 1319
Cargo: 19 tuns wine of which:

Thomas Thoraud: 12 tuns
Thomas Lythenard: 2 tuns (customed)
Richard de Tavistok: 2 tuns (customed)
Robert le Taverner: 1 tun
Cecilia de Smalecombe: 1 tun
Thomas Colepol: 1 tun portage
Reginald de Honeton: 2 dozens cordwain
Thomas Thoraud: 2 pounds saffron
Reginald de Honeton: ¼ pound [*iiii de tot libr'*] saffron
Custom: 16d in the pyx and 2d owing

Ship called *Langbord* of Exmouth
Master: Walter Edmound
Docked: 23 May 1319
Cargo: 71 tuns 6 pipes wine of which:
　　William Ralle: 42 tuns
　　Robert Stanbrigg: 6 tuns
　　Walter de Hugheton: 10 tuns
　　Clement de Hamptone: 1 tun
　　John Dich': 1 tun
　　Gilbert de Combe: 2 tuns
　　The shipmaster: 2 tuns for portage
　　Elias Slegh: 1 tun for portage
　　William Slegh: 1 tun for portage
　　Geoffrey atte Wille: 1 tun for portage
　　John Veel: 1 tun for portage
　　Walter Tauntefer: 1 pipe
　　Philip Lovecok: 5 pipes
　　Thomas de Tetteborne: 2 tuns
　　Philip Lovecok: 12 quintals iron
　　Henry de Hugheton: 1 tun
Custom: 12d

Sum total of wine custom this year–63s 8d of which the third part for
Lord Hugh de Cortenay–21s 2½d

1318/19 (m. 15) EXETER–ROLL OF CUSTOMS OF WOAD AND
　　　　OTHER MERCHANDISE LANDED AT THE PORT OF
　　　　EXMOUTH FROM THE FEAST OF ST MICHAEL IN
　　　　THE 12TH YEAR TO THE SAME FEAST FOLLOWING

Ship called *le cog George* of Dartmouth
Master: Edward Adam
Docked: 16 November 1318
Cargo: John de Kerdyf: 100 quarters salt

Ship called *le Peter* of Brightlingsea [*Bryght Lyndesie*]
Master: Richard Godrych
Docked: 10 October 1318
Cargo: Peter le Moner: 20 tuns woad, 100 stones weld, 60 M onions
Custom: woad, 20s; onions, 9d; J. Treideners received all

Ship called *le hollok Seynt Sampson*
Master: John Beauner
Docked: 20 November 1318
Cargo: John Beauner shipmaster: 12 seams garlic, 10 seams onions, 3
    pieces linen cloth, 2 stones pork grease [*unguenti porcini*]
Custom: 20½d {in the pyx}

Ship called *le Michel* of Teignmouth
Master: Richard Langberd
Docked: 4 December 1318
Cargo: 10 lasts herring of which:
    Philip Lovecok: 1 last
    John de Fenton and Adam de Nyweton: 2 lasts
    Ralph Lovet: ½ last
    Martin le Keu of Bridford and Thomas de Molton: ½ last
    Richard Baret: 1 last
    John Whytebrother: 1½ lasts
    Thomas Furbour: 1 last
    Nicholas de Lydeford and Nicholas Waleys: 2½ lasts
Custom: no custom because of the freedom of Exeter

Ship called *la Sauvee* of Yarmouth
Master: John de Catfeld
Docked: 10 December 1318
Cargo: 34½ lasts herring of which:
    John Whytebrother: 3½ lasts
    William le Skynner: 2 lasts
    Thomas Furbour: 1½ lasts
    Richard Reymound (of Yarmouth): 1½ lasts
    Nicholas Waleys: 4 lasts 3 M
    Nicholas de Lydeforde: 2½ lasts 4 M
    Michael le Candeler: ½ last
    John le Perour: 5 M
    Philip Lovecok: 1 last
    Ives Byrch: 2½ lasts
    John de Fenton: 1(½) lasts
    Adam de Nyweton: 2½ lasts
    Thomas Fastel of Yarmouth: 5 lasts
    Richard Baret: 2½ lasts
    John Tibot: 2½ lasts
    John Whytebrother: 1 cade[187]
    Adam de Nyweton: 1 cade[188]
    Geoffrey le Degher: 1 last

Ship called *la Johanette* of Caen [*Caan*]
Master: William Mathu
Docked: 10 February 1319

---

[187] *M* crossed through.
[188] *M* crossed through.

Cargo: Bartholomew le Cras of Southampton: 10 tuns woad, 26 barrels
  potash, 2 tons peas [*pis*], 200 stones weld
  The valets of the ship: 20 M onions
Custom: 10s

Ship called *la nef de Seynt Johan* of Caen
Master: John Herman
Docked: 7 April 1319
Cargo: Robert Botery: 140 quarters barley, 1 quarter wheat, 80 yards
  canvas

Ship called *le Plente* of Hook [*Hamelehok*]
Master: William Holak
Docked: 9 April 1319
Cargo: John Lukeys: 2 tuns woad, 20 stones weld, (1)[189] fardel cloth, 1
  fardel canvas, 7 barrels potash weld [*cinerum walde*], 1½ C iron which
  contains 8 quintals
Custom: J. Ercedeken for the custom; 2s 6d

Ship called *le Seynt Nicholas* of Abbeville
Master: John de Bolyng
Docked: 12 April 1319
Cargo: John le Poter: 6 tuns woad, 8 barrels potash, 80 quarters
  wheat
Custom: 6s [which] the Receiver received

Ship called *la Johenette* of Harfleur
Master: Henry Marescot
Docked: 15 April 1319
Cargo: Robert de Tyngm': 6 tuns woad, 2 barrels potash, 50 quarters
  corn
Custom: 6s

Ship called *la neof de la Hope*
Master: Ralph[190] Gillard
Docked: 26 April 1319
Cargo: Luke de Pesses: 120 quarters barley, 10 C canvas
Custom: canvas, 10d in the pyx

Ship called *le cog Seynte Marie* of Teignmouth
Master: Richard Mogge
Docked: 1 May 1319
Cargo: Peter le Moner: 15 tuns woad, 100 quarters wheat, 200 stones
  weld [*walde*]
  The shipmaster: 6 quarters wheat
  And 6 tuns wine for portage
Custom: 15s {paid to the Receiver}

---

[189] *2 crossed through and 1 written above.*
[190] *Robert crossed through before Ralph.*

Ship called *la Rose* of Exmouth
Master: Harlewin Bolt
Docked: 2 May 1319
Cargo: Harlewin[191] Bolt: 30 quarters coal, ½ C boards [*bord'*]

Ship called *le Godyer* of Teignmouth
Master: Richard Hobel
Docked: 20 May 1319
Cargo: Peter le Moner: 15 tuns woad, 200 quarters wheat, 50 stones
    weld
Custom: 15s {paid to the Receiver}

Ship called *le Michel* of Dartmouth
Master: Thomas Gorwet
Docked: 1 June 1319
Cargo: Peter de Seynt Fyzycien: 9 tuns woad, 20 stones weld
Custom: 9s [which] {J. Treideners received}

Ship called *la Rode cog* of Poole
Master: Richard Mone
Docked: 11 June 1319
Cargo: Richard Mone: 16 quarters salt
    John Wade: 1 cope figs
Custom: 3d in the pyx

Ship called *la Messager* of Teignmouth
Master: Richard Tolle
Docked: 17 June 1319
Cargo: Ives Byrch and Thomas Codelep: 17 barrels potash
    John de Nyweton: 2 fardels canvas, 200 stones weld
    Ives Byrch: 200 iron spurs [*CC spordouns ferri*], 4 quintals iron
    William atte Forde of Tavistock: 400 yards canvas
    Ives Byrch: 5 fardels canvas
Custom: 3d in the pyx

Ship called *la Blyze* of Poole
Master: William Goderigge
Docked: 19 July 1319
Cargo: William Goderigge shipmaster: 6 quarters salt

Boat called *la Rode cog* of Poole
Master: Richard Mone
Docked: 23 July 1319
Cargo: Richard Mone shipmaster: 7 quarters salt

Boat called *le Jenynet* of Lymington
Master: William Boksy
Docked: 30 July 1319
Cargo: William Boksy shipmaster: 40 quarters salt

---

[191] *Henry* crossed through before *Harlewin*.

Boat called *la Blyze* of Poole
Master: William Godrigge
Docked: 30 July 1319
Cargo: William Godrigge: 5 quarters salt

Ship called *le Sauvee* of St Valéry
Docked: 1 August 1319
Cargo: Peter le Moner: 26 tuns woad, 13 pipes potash, 300 stones weld
   Gilbert Mote: 24 quarters corn, 3 tons flour, 4 dozens cordwain, 1
      piece cloth
Custom: Martin le Keu of Bridford for the custom; 26s, paid by
   Martin? [*s' Martins*]

Ship called *la Johanette* of St Valéry
Master: Robert Foly
Docked: 1 August 1319
Cargo: Michael Poter: 8 tuns woad, 200 stones weld
   Henry de Teyngm': 20 quarters corn, [ ] iron,[192] 2 pipes potash
Custom: 8s; {paid all to the Receiver}

Ship called *la Seynt Martyn* of *Vileter*
Master: Luke le Bocher
Docked: 1 August 1319
Cargo: John Hangard: 12 tuns woad, 40 stones weld
Custom: 12s; paid to the Receiver

Ship called *le Langbord*
Master: Walter Parys
Docked: 8 August 1319
Cargo: Thomas de Tetteburne and Robert de Stanbrigge: 80 quarters salt

Ship called *le Margarete* of Exmouth
Master: John Averey
Docked: 10 August 1319
Cargo: Walter de Hugheton and John le Yung: 500 quarters salt

Ship called *le hollow Seynt Sampson*
Master: John Beauner
Docked: 29 August 1319
Cargo: John de Beauner shipmaster: 19 seams garlic, 6[193] seams
   onions, 7 pieces linen cloth
Custom: 23d; paid to the Receiver

Ship called *le cog Notre Dame* of Guernsey
Master: John Pycard
Docked: 14[194] September 1319
Cargo: John Pycard shipmaster: 24 seams onions, 1 piece linen cloth,
   1 seam garlic
Custom: 13d; paid5

---

[192] A blank space was left in front of the iron entry where the amount and measure
should be.
[193] 7 crossed through before the 6.
[194] *February* crossed through.

1319/20 (m. 14) EXETER–ROLL OF CUSTOMS OF WINE FROM FEAST OF ST MICHAEL IN THE THIRTEENTH YEAR OF KING EDWARD [II] UNTIL THE SAME FEAST FOLLOWING

Ship called *la Rode cog* of Teignmouth[195]
Master: Henry Kech
Docked: 19 October 1319
Cargo: 91 tuns 3 pipes wine of which:
  Bernard Andru: 45 tuns 1 pipe
  Brun Carpenter: 45 tuns 2 pipes
  Henry Kech, shipmaster: 1 tun for portage
Custom: Richard le Seler for the custom; 30s [which] {the Receiver received}

Ship called *la Margarete* of Topsham
Master: John Averey
Docked: 31 December 1319
Cargo: 81 tuns 9 pipes wine of which:
  Walter de Hughetone and Nicholas Busse: 40 tuns 4 pipes
  Elias de Hemmestone: 11 tuns
  Richard le Forester: 12 tuns 2 pipes (customed)
  Hamelin Passemer: 1 tun for portage
  Dollyng Passemer: 1 tun for portage
  Adam Parys: 1 tun for portage
  Richard Davy: 1 tun for portage
  Simon Scot: 1 tun
  John Palmer: 1 tun 1 pipe
  The shipmaster: 4 tuns 1 pipe
  Nicholas Busse: 1 pipe
  Margaret Dyneham: 1 tun
  John de Fenton: 5 tuns
  William de Staverton: 2 tuns (customed)
  Elias de Hemmestone and Richard Forester: 1 bale almonds
Custom: Elias de Hemmeston for the custom; wine custom, 6s 4d; almonds custom, 4d

Ship called *Seynte Marie cog* of Exmouth
Master: Walter Edmound
Docked: 31 December 1319
Cargo: 108 tuns 14 pipes [wine] of which:
  Philip Lovecok: 28 tuns 4 pipes
  Thomas de Tetteburne: 4 tuns 4 pipes
  Walter de Hughetone: 4 tuns
  William Ralle: 3 tuns
  John Eustach: 2 tuns (custom paid)
  Adam de Burgoynge of London: 10 tuns 2 pipes (quit)[196]

---

[195] This entry also appears in the MCR; see above, p 68.
[196] *Customed* crossed through and *quit* written in.

Richard Cocus of Bridford: 20 tuns 2 pipes
John de la Mare: 2 tuns (custom paid)
Thomas Thoraud: 12 tuns 2 pipes
Robert de Okampton: 1 tun
William Gyrard of Bordeaux: 6 tuns 1 pipe (custom paid)
Alured Horn: 3 tuns
Walter Edmound: 3 tuns of which 2 tuns for portage (customed
John le Toker: 1 tun for portage
Robert Jan: 1 [tun] for portage
John Challe: 1 [tun] for portage
Thomas Jesse: 1 [tun] for portage
William Elys: 1 (pipe) for portage
John le Perour: 2 tuns
William Austyn[197]
Thomas le Furbour: 2 tuns
Thomas le Barbour: 2 tuns
Custom: 3s 8d [which] {the Receiver received}

Ship called *le Langbord* of Exmouth
Master: Adam Slegh
Docked: 10 January 1320
Cargo: 70 tuns 5 pipes [wine] of which:
Philip Lovecok: 36 tuns 5 pipes
Walter de Hugheton: 7 tuns
Thomas Thoraud: 5 tuns
Henry de Hugheton: 5 tuns
William Ralle: 1 tun
Thomas de Tetteburne: 1 tun
Thomas Furbour: 2 tuns
Thomas Lythenard: 1 tun (customed)
Kyngman Yedrych of Lyme: 2 tuns
Robert Stanbrigge: 3 tuns (customed, of which 1 tun for portage)
Richard Saundre: 2 tuns of which 1 tun for portage (customed)
Geoffrey atte Will: 1 tun for portage
John Vele: 1 tun for portage
Nicholas de Godescote: 1 tun (custom paid)
Adam Slegh: 2 tuns for portage because [he is] master
Custom: 20d

Ship called *la neof Seynte Marie* of Bermeo [*Vermuth*]
Master: John Dyes
Docked: 9 April 1320
Cargo: Henry Flynt of Bodmin: 13 tuns 7 pipes wine, 40 quarters
salt, 60 quarters wheat, 10 quarters mixed wheat and rye
Custom: ½ mark

Racked Wines [*Rek*]

---

[197] *William Austyn* crossed through.

Ship called *le Michel* of Teignmouth
Master: Walter Tolle
Docked: 7 (May) 1320[198]
Cargo: 71 tuns 3 pipes [wine] of which:
  Philip Lovecok: 21 tuns
  Richard le Keu of Bridford: 5 tuns
  William Ralle: 4 tuns
  Robert de Wotton: 10 tuns
  Thomas le Barbour: 7 tuns
  Thomas le Furbour: 3 tuns
  William Austyn: 3 tuns
  Richard de Tavistok: 3 tuns (customed)
  John de Bovy: 3 tuns
  Gilbert de Combe: 1 tun
  Thomas Toker [and] Cofyn David: 2 tuns for portage
  The shipmaster: 2 tuns of which 1 for portage and 1 customed
    (customed)
  John le Perour: 4 tuns
  Walter de Hugheton: 3 tuns
  Philip Lovecok and William Austyn: 3 pipes
Custom: 16d of which 4d received by the Receiver

Ship called *la Makehayt* of Lymington
Master: Walter Welyned
Docked: 7 May 1320
Cargo: (65 tuns)[199] 5 pipes [wine] of which:
  William Gyrard: 20 tuns 3 pipes (of which 1 tun damaged and 1
    tun [for] Adam Smalecomb)
  Bernard Andru: 43 tuns 2 pipes
  The shipmaster: 1 [tun] for portage
  Robert Shutere: 1 tun for portage
Custom: 22s; 15s paid to the Receiver

Ship called *le James* of Teignmouth
Master: William Payn
Docked: 7 May 1320
Cargo: 42 tuns 6 pipes [wine] of which:
  Ives Byrch: 10 tuns
  John de Nyweton: 4 tuns
  Thomas Golde: 2 tuns
  John Beauforest: 1 pipe
  Gilbert in the Combe: 10 tuns 1 pipe
  Michael Bovy: 2 tuns 1 pipe
  Martin Cocus: 1 pipe
  Thomas de Oxton: 9 tuns (2 pipes)
  Thomas Lythenard: 1 tun
  Alexander de la Grave: 1 tun, also 2 tuns for portage
  Thomas atte Bourne: 1 tun (customed)

[198] *April* crossed through and *May* inserted above.
[199] *64 tuns* crossed through and *65 tuns* written above.

Michael Bovy: 16 quintals iron
Ives Byrch: 2 tons iron
Robert Beauforest: 3 dozens cordwain
Custom: wine custom, 2s [which] the Receiver received; iron custom,
8d; the Receiver received all

Ship called *le Berthelemew* of Weymouth
Master: Edward Nichol
Docked: 9 May 1320
Cargo: 40 tuns 7 pipes wine of which:
   Bernard le Lestres: 34 tuns 7 pipes
   The shipmaster: 2 tuns of which 1 tun for portage
   Henry Vreke: 1 tun for portage
   William Kepe: 1 tun for portage
   John Barre: 1 tun for portage
   Robert Henry: 1 tun for portage
   The same Bernard: 210 quarters corn
Custom: 13s 8d; the Receiver received all

Ship called *le cog Seynt Giles* of Winchelsea
Master: William Saundre of Winchelsea
Docked: 13 May 1320
Cargo: 50 tuns 5 pipes wine of which:
   William Simon: 22 tuns 3 pipes
   William de Prestlong: 22 tuns 1 pipe
   Also 7 tuns wine for portage
Custom: 15s 8d; the Receiver received all

Ship called *le cog Notre Dame*
Master: Walter Edmound
Docked: 22 May 1320
Cargo: 17 tuns 1 pipe wine of which:
   Philip Lovecok: 3 tuns
   John le Perour: 2 tuns
   Alured Horn: 4 tuns
   Thomas Thoraud: 1 tun
   The shipmaster: 1 tun 1 pipe for portage
   Peter Golloc: 3 tuns
   William Slegh: 2 tuns, customed, of which 1 tun for portage
   Alured Horn: 40 quintals iron
   (Philip Lovecok):[200] 40 quintals iron
   Adam Wagge: 1 tun for portage
   Richard Whyte of Teignmouth: 10 quintals iron for portage
   The shipmaster: 11 quintals iron
   Peter Golloc: 11 quintals iron
   William Slegh: 7 quintals iron, customed
   Philip Lovecok, John le Perour [and] Michael Thoraud: 400 quar-
      ters salt
   John Challe: 2 quintals iron
Custom: wine, 4d in the pyx; iron, 3½d in the pyx

[200] *Alured Horn* crossed through and *Philip Lovecok* written above.

Ship called *le cog Notre Dame* of Teignmouth
Master: John Hardy
Docked: 26 May 1320
Cargo: 17 tuns 1 pipe wine [of which]:
    Henry de Rocombe: 4 tuns
    Jordan Elbard: 4 tuns
    Richard Forester: 4 tuns
    Richard Mugge: 4 tuns
    [Richard Forester and Richard Mugge]: 1 tun 1 pipe in common
    The aforesaid Henry and aforesaid other merchants: 30 quarters
        salt, 120 quintals iron, 2 bales almonds, 1 bale rice, 1 bale cumin
Custom: wine, 6s; iron, 5s; ... 12d

Ship called *la nau Sancti Michaelis* of Bayonne
Docked: 23 August 1320
Cargo: Peter de Marini: 6 tuns wine
    Peter de Marini and Michael Poter: 440 quarters wheat and maslin
Custom: 2s

Ship called *la neof Seynt Lowes* of[201] *Baydevyle*
Master: Nicholas le Praz
Docked: 20 September 1320
Cargo: Richard le Northerne: 15 tuns wine (of which 1 customed?
    [*unde 1 cussag'*]), 20 dozens cordwain, 12 dozens basan
Custom: wine, 4s 8d; cordwain, 12d

(m. 14d) [**1319/20** wine account continued]

Ship called *la neof Notre Dame* of Bayonne
Master: Andrew de Salers
Docked: 1 September 1320
Cargo: Girard de Caverepynes: 556 quarters corn
    Also 10 quintals iron for portage
    Also 2 bales almonds, 2 bales alum for portage, 1½ tons salt

Ship called *la cog Seynt Johan* of Jersey [*Gerresy*]
Master: John Goaz
Docked: 3 September 1320
Cargo: Geoffrey Pygaz [and] Walter Michel of Hareston: 2 C garlic, 6
    (M) onions
    Also 2 C and 1 quarter of onions for portage
Custom: 2s 8d of which 2s paid

---

[201] *Caen* crossed through.

1319/20 (m. 13) EXETER–ROLL OF CUSTOMS OF WOAD, GAR-
LIC AND OTHER MERCHANDISE FROM THE FEAST
OF ST MICHAEL IN THE 13TH YEAR OF KING
EDWARD [II] TO THE SAME FEAST ETC...

Ship called *le Barge* of Totnes [*Totton'*]
Master: Ralph Foliot
Docked: 13 October 1319
Cargo: Ralph Foliot shipmaster: 4 seams onions, 8 seams garlic, 1
  piece linen cloth
Custom: garlic, 11d [which] the Receiver received

Ship called *le Rode cog* of Teignmouth
Master: Richard Mone
Docked: 30 October 1319
Cargo: Richard Mone shipmaster: 8 quarters wheat

Ship called *le Long Batel* of Southampton
Master: Robert Deveneys
Docked: 5 November 1319
Cargo: Nicholas le Webbe of Taunton: 5 tuns woad, 4 barrels potash,
  20 garbs weld
  Nicholas le Taillour: 1 seam garlic
Custom: woad, 5s paid; garlic, 1d paid; [all] received

Ship called *le Michel* of Exmouth
Master: Richard Harvest
Docked: 6 November 1319
Cargo: 320[202] quarters wheat
  Philip Lovecok: 120 quarters
  Thomas le Barbour: 15 quarters
  John le Perour: 6 quarters
  The shipmaster: 20 quarters
  Robert de Criditone carpenter: the remainder

Ship called *la neof Seynt John* of Abbeville
Master: John le Beloyng
Docked: 7 November 1319
Cargo: Peter le Souton: 165 seams onions, 6 seams garlic, and 5
  seams cockles [*cokail*]
Custom: 7s 7d, [which] the Receiver received

Ship called *le cog Notre Dame* of Teignmouth
Master: Richard Mugge
Docked: 10 November 1319
Cargo: Henry de Rocombe, Jullain Illeberd, Richard Mugge, Gilbert
  in the Combe: 300 quarters wheat

---

[202] Written as *CCC xvi* but the *xvi* crossed through and *xx* written above.

Ship called *le cog Seynt Gile* of Sidmouth
Master: Ralph le Sanger
Docked: 11 November 1319
Cargo: The shipmaster: 300 quarters coal

Ship called *le Lang bot* of Dartmouth
Docked: 13 November 1319
Cargo: Thomas Thoraud: 50 quarters salt
    Henry de Gatepath: 2 tuns wine
    William de Criditon: 1 tun wine

Ship called *la neof Seynt Johan* of Guernsey[203]
Master: Ralph Fulloc
Docked: 14 November 1319
Cargo: Thomas Petit: 10 tuns woad
    Thomas Thoraud: ½ M dried fish
    Richard le Seler: 1 pipe wine
    Richard Whyot: 16 skins of cordwain for portage
Custom: 10s [which] the Receiver received

Ship called *la Sauve* of Great Yarmouth
Master: John Catfeld
Docked: 6 December 1319
Cargo: 37 lasts 4 cades herring of which:
    John Whytebrother: 3 lasts 3 M and 1 cade
    Thomas le Furbour: 2 lasts 9 M
    John le Perour: ½ last
    Nicholas Waleys: 2 lasts 9 M
    Robert de Silferton: 1 last
    Matilda Prout: ½ last 5 M
    Geoffrey le Deghere: ½ last 5 M
    Nicholas Waleys: 2 cades *corpychoun*[204]
    Adam[205] de Nyweton: 3 lasts 4 M
    John de Fenton: 2 lasts
    Nicholas de Lydeford: 2½ lasts
    Robert de Lydeford: ½ last
    Thomas Golde: 1 last 1 M
    Richard Baret: 6 lasts 10 M
    Ives Byrch: 2 lasts
    John Treydevers: 4 lasts
    Philip Lovecok: 2 lasts
    Richard Dyrkyn: 1 last
    John Pachecote: 1 M (customed)
    Thomas Codelep: 1 cade
    Thomas Jacop: 3 cades
    Thomas Jacop: 7 dickers[206]
    Thomas Codelep [and] Robert de Lydeford: 22 dickers hides

[203] *Ex* (probably meant to be Exmouth) written in first but crossed through.
[204] A type of herring; see p 50, n. 13 above.
[205] *Richard Baret* crossed through and *Adam* written next.
[206] 7 *dickers* crossed through.

Thomas Codelep: 1 barrel pitch
John le Perour: 1 barrel pitch, (...)
Thomas Codelep: 1 barrel alum, 1 barrel copperas [*coperos*]
Philip Lovecok: 4 barrels pitch, 40 salt-cellars [*iixx seler'*]
Thomas Golde: 3 barrels alum
Ives Byrch: 1 fother lead
John Treydevers: 1 fother lead
Thomas le Furbour [and] John Whytebrother: 4 M iron
John Whytebrother [and] Nicholas Waleys: 2 C copper [*coper*]
Robert de Lydeford: 3 C copper
Ives Byrch: ½ C iron
Adam de Nyweton: ½ C iron
John Treydevers: 1 M iron
Ives Byrch: 2 dozens of cloth
John Treydevers: 1 bale alum
Adam Osebern: ½ last 1 cade [herring]
Thomas Cadefelde: 5 cades [herring]
Thomas Baril: 1 cade [herring]
Adam Osebern: 3 quarters wheat
Custom: 1d in the pyx

Ship called *cog Johan* of Teignmouth
Master: Elias Prucz
Docked: 29 December 1319
Cargo: 100 tuns 15 pipes wine of which:
Gilbert de Cumbe: 25 tuns
The same Gilbert and John de Bovy: 9 pipes
The same John: 21 tuns
Richard le Cok: 8 tuns 4 pipes
John de la Mare: 1 tun (customed, paid)
Michael de Bovy: 4 tuns (customed, paid)
Martin le Cok: 2 pipes
Thomas le Forbour: 10 tuns
Thomas le Barbour: 6 tuns
William Austyn: 3 tuns
Thomas Gervays: 1 tun (customed, paid)
Walter Prodomme: 4 tuns (customed)
Walter de Swengtille: 4 tuns
Cecilia de Smalecumb: 4 tuns
Ives Byrch: 4 tuns
And 5 tuns for portage
And 1 bale almonds
Custom: 2s [which] the Receiver received

Ship called *nau' Sancti Martini* of Exmouth
Master: Pelegrinus de la Roche
Docked: 29 December 1319
Cargo: 100 pipes wine
Arnulph de Viele: all (customed)
Custom: Richard le Seler is responsible for the custom; 2½ marks
[which] the Receiver received

Ship called *le Michel* of Exmouth
Master: Richard Harvest
Docked: 4 January 1320
Cargo: Philip Lovecok and Robert de Cridyton carpenter: 250 (quarters) wheat

Ship called *la Grace Dieu* of Abbeville
Master: Marcus de Sotervyle
Docked: 6 January 1320
Cargo: 114 quarters wheat of which:
   William de Chaggeford: 82 quarters wheat
   Elias Slegh: 10 quarters
   Nicholas Lovecok: 14 quarters
   (Robert de Criditone carpenter): 6 tuns 1 pipe woad
   And 12 stones weld for portage
Custom: woad, 7s

Ship called *la Rode cog* of Lyme
Master: Robert Sampson
Docked: 12 January 1320
Cargo: Adam le Hangard: 10 tuns [woad], 200 quarters wheat
   William de Lym: 100 quarters wheat
   The shipmaster and his fellows: 200 quarters wheat
Custom: woad, 10s [which] the Receiver received

Ship called *le Bryaunt* of Wissant [*Whytsond*]
Master: William Seyne
Docked: 3 February 1320
Cargo: John le Poter: 10 tuns woad, 14 barrels potash, 5 stones weld, 110 quarters corn
   William Seyne: 10 M herring, 16 quarters corn
Custom: 10s [which] the Receiver received

Ship called *le neof Seynt Esperit* of St Valéry
Master: William Bryaunt
Docked: 9 February 1320
Cargo: Peter le Moner: 13 tuns woad, 53 *coketz* potash, 220 quarters wheat
   Guyot: 42 garbs weld
   Also 60 M onions for portage
   The shipmaster: 14 quarters wheat
Custom: 13s {paid}

Ship called *le Sauve* of Yarmouth
Master: John Catfeld
Docked: 13 February 1320
Cargo: Thomas Furbour, Thomas de Codelep, John Beauforest: 200 quarters wheat

Ship called *la Margarete* of Exmouth
Master: John Averey
Docked: 15 February 1320
Cargo: John le Yung, Walter de Hugheton, John Dollyng: 400 quarters wheat

Ship called *le cog Notre Dame* of Teignmouth
Master: Richard Mugge
Docked: 15 February 1320
Cargo: Gilbert de Cumbe, Henry de Rocombe, Richard Mugge, John
Ylberd: 300 quarters wheat

Ship called *la Rode cog* of Lutton [*Leuton*]
Master: Alexander le Bule
Docked: 16 February 1320
Cargo: Alexander le Bule: 60 quarters salt

Ship called *la Sauve* of Lymington
Master: Roger le Gyst
Docked: 23 February 1320
Cargo: Roger le Gyst shipmaster: 62 quarters salt

Ship called *le Michel* of Exmouth
Master: Richard Harvest
Docked: 25 February 1320
Cargo: Robert de Cridytone, Richard Harvest, Peter Golloc, Adam
Slegh: 300 quarters corn and 6 pipes potash woad

Ship called *le Welyfare* of Lyme[207]
Master: Richard le Rydere
Docked: 23 August 1320
Cargo: Peter le Moner: 300 quarters corn

(m. 13d) [**1319/20** merchandise account continued]

Ship called *le Langbord*[208]
Master: Robert Stanbrigg
Docked: 25 February 1320
Cargo: 400 quarters wheat [of which]:
  Philip Lovecok: 85 quarters
  William de Chaggeford: 120 quarters
  William de Christnestowe: 40 quarters
  Robert de Stanbrigg: 90 quarters
  And 40 quarters for portage
  Thomas Petyt: 2 tuns woad
  Henry de Hugheton: 25 quarters
Custom: woad, 2s

Ship called *le Nicholas* of Teignmouth
Master: Walter William of Teignmouth
Docked: 25 February 1320
Cargo: Ralph de Thornbury, John de Nyweton, and Walter Peres:
  240 quarters wheat
  John Cok: 1 seam garlic

---

[207] There is an X in the left-hand margin next to this entry; see above, pp 42–3.
[208] Idem.

Ship called *la Annote* of Lymington
Master: Nicholas Graunger
Docked: 26 February 1320
Cargo: 10 quarters wheat, 34 quarters beans, 10 quarters vetches, 10 quarters barley

Ship called *le Michel* of Teignmouth
Master: Walter Tolle
Docked: 14 March 1320
Cargo: Richard Tolle: 3 tuns wine of which 1 for portage and 1 customed
 Richard de Tavistok: 370 quarters corn
Custom: 4d in the pyx

Ship called *la Johanette* of Teignmouth
Master: G. Whetepayn
Docked: 5[209] April 1320
Cargo: Gilbert in the Combe, Gilbert Whetepayn, Wymond de Wyght: 120 quarters wheat

Ship called *la Rose* of Exmouth
Master: Harlewin Bolt
Docked: 1 April 1320
Cargo: Walter de Hugheton: 140 quarters corn

Ship called *le Blyze* of Hook [*Hamelehok*]
Master: Robert Gilbe
Docked: 5 April 1320
Cargo: John de Hareforde of Wales: 60 quarters corn, wheat, rye and barley, 2 stones weld

Ship called *la Welyfare* of Lyme[210]
Master: Richard Rydere
Docked: 8 April 1320
Cargo: Peter le Moner: 12 tuns woad, 200 quarters corn
 And 42 quarters corn for portage
Custom: woad custom, 12s {paid}

Ship called *la Rode cog* of Lyme
Master: Robert Sampson
Docked: 8 April 1320
Cargo: 22 tuns woad of which:
 Adam Hangard: 12 tuns, 4 barrels potash
 Michael le Poter: 10 tuns [woad]
 The same Adam, Michael and the shipmaster: 400 quarters corn
Custom: woad, 22s

Ship called *la Michel* of Exmouth
Docked: 10 April 1320
Cargo: 241 quarters wheat [of which]:

[209] *The same* crossed through and *5* written in.
[210] There is an X in the left-hand margin next to this entry; see above, pp 42–3.

Philip Lovecok: 20 quarters
Peter Golloc: 70 quarters
Robert de Cridyton: 70 quarters
Henry Hugheton: 60 quarters
Adam Slegh: 20 quarters
Richard Harvest: 20 quarters
Adam Slegh: 2 quintals iron
Henry de Hugheton: 3 pieces cloth
Adam Slegh: 3 pieces cloth
Richard Havest: 1 M onions
Custom: iron, 1d in the pyx

Ship called *le Nicholas* of Teignmouth
Master: Walter Willame
Docked: 10 April 1320
Cargo: Thomas le Furbour, John Skuther, Robert Boterel: 250 quarters wheat

Ship called *le neof Seynt John* of Teignmouth
Master: Roger Payn
Docked: 10 April 1320
Cargo: Ives Byrch: 140 quarters corn, 1 barrel oil

Ship called *le Annoce* of (Keyhaven)[211]
Master: Nicholas Graunger
Docked: 10 April 1320
Cargo: 140 quarters corn [of which]:
  Philip Lovecok: 75 quarters
  Nicholas Lovecok: 20 quarters
  Nicholas Graunger shipmaster: the rest

Ship called *la Rousse* of Port-en-Bessein in Normandy [*du Port en Normandie*]
Master: John Sules
Docked: 10 April 1320
Cargo: Michael de Bassewych of Caen: 100 quarters corn, 2 C canvas
Custom: canvas, 1d

Ship called *la Sauve* of Yarmouth
Master: John Catfeld
Docked: 14 April 1320
Cargo: John Skuter, Thomas Furbour, John Toillero, Ralph de Nyweton mercer: 350 [quarters] corn
  Ralph de Nyweton: 1 fardel canvas

Ship called *le Plente* of Hook [*Hamelehok*]
Master: Richard le Walshe
Docked: 15 April 1320
Cargo: John Petyt: 160 quarters corn

---

[211] *Teignmouth* crossed through and *Keyhaven* written above.

Ship called *le Rode cog* of Teignmouth[212]
Master: Luverych in the Combe
Docked: 23 April 1320
Cargo: Peter le Moner: 8 tuns woad
  Luverych in the Combe: 2 tuns 1 pipe wine
  Also 300 quarters wheat and rye mixed
  The crew [*nautorum navis*]: 40 quarters corn
Custom: woad, 8s; wine, 12d; {paid}

Ship called *la Deu la Garde* of[213] Jersey [*Geresy*]
Master: Osbert Alysaundre
Docked: 24 April 1320
Cargo: Osbert Alysaundre shipmaster: 20 quarters barley, 10 quarters
  wheat, 3 quarters beans, 8 quarters oats, 18 bacons, 500 eggs

Ship called *la Johanette* of Guernsey
Master: Robert Egenas
Docked: 30 April 1320
Cargo: Thomas le Taillour: 400 quarters corn viz., wheat [and] rye
  mixed, 4 quarters beans, 6 bacons
  The shipmaster: 3 pieces linen cloth, 1 C onions [*leygnes*]

Ship called *le cog de Touz Seyntz*
Master: Robert Deveneys
Docked: 4 May 1320
Cargo: Robert Poute: 50 quarters salt

Ship called *la Rose* of Exmouth
Master: Herlewin Bolt
Docked: 9 May 1320
Cargo: 120 quarters corn of which:
  Walter de Hugheton: 98 quarters corn
  William de Chaggeford: 10 quarters
  And the rest for portage

Ship called *la Margaret* of Hook [*Hamelehok*]
Master: Roger Toctere
Docked: 9 May 1320
Cargo: Vincent de Benavenel: 120 quarters wheat, 20 stones weld

Ship called *le Deugard* of Guernsey
Master: Geoffrey de Maners
Docked: 12 May 1320
Cargo: Osbert Alysaundre: 45 quarters rye, ½ quarter beans

Ship called *la Plente* of Hook [*Hamelehok*]
Master: Richard le Walshe
Docked: 16 May 1320
Cargo: Adam de Nyweton and John de Hereford: 150 quarters corn

---

[212] There is an X in the left-hand margin next to this entry; see above, pp 92–3.
[213] *Ierne* (for Yarmouth or possibly Guernsey) is crossed through.

Ship called *le Annoyse* of Keyhaven
Master: Nicholas Graunger
Docked: 16 May 1320
Cargo: Philip Lovecok and Nicholas Graunger the shipmaster: 160
    quarters corn

Ship called *la Mariole* of London
Master: John Brewere
Docked: 23 May 1320
Cargo: Peter de Burdeaux: 600 quarters rye

Ship called *le Nicholas* of Teignmouth
Master: Walter Willam
Docked: 8 June 1320
Cargo: Philip Lovecok: 240 quarters corn
    And 30 quarters corn for portage

Ship called *le Blyze* of Hook [*Hamelehok*]
Master: Robert Gilbe
Docked: 8 June 1320
Cargo: Thomas Jacop and John de Nyweton: 1000 [*x^c*] iron spurs, 2
    fardels drapery, and chair, lantern and coffer of Rouen [*cathedr'*
    lat'ne & coffr' Rotomag']
    The shipmaster: 100 [*C*] spurs for portage
Custom: ...

Ship called *la Margarete* of Exmouth[214]
Master: John Averey
Docked: 9 June 1320
Cargo: Peter le Moner and the crew [*sociorum navis*]: 500 quarters corn

Ship called *la Deu Gard* of Guernsey
Master: Geoffrey de Maners
Docked: 9 June 1320
Cargo: Osbert Alysaundre: 6 pieces canvas containing [ ]
Custom: ...

1320/21 (m. 12) ROLL OF CUSTOMS OF WINE LANDED AT
       THE PORT OF EXMOUTH FROM THE FEAST OF ST
       MICHAEL IN THE 14TH YEAR OF KING EDWARD [II]
       UNTIL ETC.,

Ship called *la Langbord*
Master: Robert Stanbrigge
Docked: 20 October 1320
Cargo: 34 tuns (2 pipes) wine [of which]:
    Philip Lovecok: 5 tuns
    Walter de Hugheton and Nicholas Busse: 8 tuns
    Henry de Hugheton: 11 tuns
    Robert de Stanbrigg: 7 tuns
    Also 3 tuns for portage

[214] There is an X placed in the left-hand margin of this entry; see above, pp 192–3.

Ship called *le Peter* of Sidmouth
Master: Roger Sangere of Sidmouth
Docked: 29 October 1320
Cargo: 45 tuns 8 pipes wine of which:
  John de Bayone: 35 tuns 5 pipes
  Philip Lovecok: 2 pipes for his drink [*potu suo*]
  William le Barbour: 3 tuns, customed
  The shipmaster: 1 tun 1 pipe for portage
  John Pyttyng: 1 tun for portage, 8 quintals iron
  Ralph atte Mulle: 1 tun wine (portage)
  Philip Lovecok: 2 tons[215] iron
  The shipmaster: 21 quintals iron
  John de Bayone: 4 C iron
  All the mariners: 8 C iron
Custom: wine, 12d; iron, 14d; all in the pyx

Ship called *la Welyfare* of Lyme
Master: Richard Rydere
Docked: 20 October 1320
Cargo: 63 tuns 6 pipes [wine] of which:
  Richard Forst': 20 tuns (customed)
  Adam Vode: 15 tuns 6 pipes (free)
  Nicholas le Baker: 12 tuns (free)
  Walter Prodhomme: 11 tuns 1 pipe (free)
  Also 4 tuns for portage
  Nicholas le Carpend': 100 pounds pitch
  Nicholas le Baker: 1 dozen budge skins [*de Boge*], 1 bale almonds
Custom: ½ mark

Ship called *le Nicholas* of Teignmouth
Master: Philip Sperk
Docked: 20 0ctober 1320
Cargo: Bernard Lengouie: 18 tuns 1 pipe wine
Custom: Richard Plegh for the custom; 6s 4d {paid to the Receiver}

Ship called *le Godyer* of Teignmouth
Master: Julian Bolt
Docked: 20 October 1320
Cargo: 63 tuns (5)[216] pipes wine of which:
  Thomas le Forbour: 16 tuns 2 pipes
  John Beauforest: 6 tuns
  Thomas le Barbour: 8 tuns
  William Austyn: 4 tuns (1 pipe)
  William Chaggeford: 3 tuns
  Roger Leyz taillor: 2 tuns
  Gilbert[217] in the Combe: 16 tuns 1 pipe in his custody (of which 2
    [tuns] customed)

[215] *Wine* crossed through.
[216] *4* crossed through and *5* written above.
[217] *Le P* crossed through.

The shipmaster: 3 tuns of which 1 tun customed and 2 for portage
William Torre: 1 tun for portage
Robert de Torre: 1 tun for portage
John Row: 2 tuns of which 1 tun customed
Richard atte Bourne: 1 tun for portage
Michael de Bovy: 1 pipe (customed)
Custom: 20d of which 12d in the pyx; {afterwards all in the pyx}

Ship called *le Michel* of Hook [*Hamelehok*]
Master: Henry Warine
Docked: 20 October 1320
Cargo: Philip Lovecok: 12 tuns 1 pipe [wine]
    John le Queynte of Amiens [*Amyas*]: 3 tuns woad, 4 pipes potash
Custom: woad, 3s in the pyx

Ship called *le cog Nostre Dame* of Exmouth
Master: Walter Edmound
Docked: 20 October 1320
Cargo: 115 tuns 8 pipes [wine] of which:
    Thomas de Tetteburne: 22 tuns 4 pipes
    William Ralle: 35 tuns
    John le Perour: 25 tuns 2 pipes
    Thomas Thoraud: 25 tuns 2 pipes wine
    Thomas Thoraud and Michael Thoraud: 1 bale almonds
    Henry de Hugheton: 2 tuns
    The shipmaster: 2 tuns for portage
    Walter Prouz: 1 tun for portage
    Richard Davy: 1 tun for portage
    Robert Jan: 1 tun for portage
    Richeman de Wynchelese: 1 tun for portage
Custom: no custom because all are in the freedom

Ship called *le Gaynge Ben* of Teignmouth
Master: Thomas Payn
Docked: 31 October 1320
Cargo: ... tuns 7 pipes [wine] of which:
    Gilbert in the Combe: 21 tuns 1 pipe
    Richard le Keu of Bridford: 19 tuns
    John de la Mare: 2 tuns (customed)
    John de Bovy: 5 tuns
    Thomas de Cornwaylle: 5 tuns (customed)
    Thomas ... : 8 tuns
    Roger Leyz tailor: 7 tuns
    Thomas le Barbour: 4 tuns
    William de Chaggeford: ... ...
    Henry de Hugheton: 8 tuns
    William Ralle: 3 tuns
    Nicholas de Godescote: 4 tuns (customed)
    ... ... : ... ...
    Richard de Tavistok: 1 tun (customed)
    Thomas Colepol: 14 tuns 2 pipes (customed)
    Geoffrey ...: ... ...

... ... : ... tuns (1 tun for portage)
William Grygge: 1 tun (portage)
The shipmaster: 1 tun for portage
Thomas Cole... : ... ...
Custom: ...

Ship called ...*ile* of Sidmouth
Master: Ralph le Sangere
Docked: 20 October 1320
Cargo: 97 tuns 13 [pipes wine of which]:
    ... ...e : 25 tuns 2 pipes
    Michael de Bovy: 3 tuns (customed, paid)
    Richard le Keu of Bridford: ... ...
    ... ...y : 23 tuns 3 pipes
    Thomas de Cornwaille: 5[218] tuns (customed, paid)
    Martin Cocus: ... ...
    John de la Mare: 2 tuns
    John Bateman: 5 tuns
    The shipmaster: 2 tuns for portage and ...
    ... Todewille: 1 tun for portage
    William Sangere: 1 tun (portage)
    William Burel: 1 tun (customed)
    Richard Rubeis: ... ...
    Robert Slegh: 1 tun (customed)
    Edward Peytevyn: 1 tun (customed)
    John Vele: 1 tun (portage)
    Adam ... : ... ...
    ... Vynterhak: 1 tun (portage)
    Ralph le Sangere: 10 quintals iron, 2 bales ...
    ... ... : ... ...
Custom: ...

... ...*n* of Bordeaux
Master: Gyrard Deyrn
Docked: 4 November 1320
Cargo: 72 tuns ... [wine of which]:
    ... ... : ... tuns 1 pipe
    Michael de Bovy: 2 tuns
    Thomas Lythenard: 1 tun and the rest ...
    Robert de Cr... : ... tuns
    John le Yung: 4 tuns
    Walter de Hugheton: ...
    ... ...odewill: 1 tun
    Thomas Codelip: 9 tuns
Custom: ... for the rest

...[219]
Docked: 14 November 1320

---

[218] *4* crossed through and *5* written above.
[219] A large portion of the left-hand side of this membrane and the entire bottom half have been torn away.

1320/1 (m. 11) ROLL OF CUSTOMS OF WOAD AND OTHER
MERCHANDISE LANDED AT THE PORT OF EXMOUTH
FROM THE FEAST OF ST MICHAEL IN THE FOUR-
TEENTH YEAR OF KING EDWARD [II] UNTIL ETC...

Ship called *le Nicholas* of Hook [*Hamelehok*]
Master: Robert Scotlere
Docked: 18 October 1320
Cargo: Peter le Moner: 13 tuns woad, 30 barrels potash, 300 stones
    weld, 9 seams onions
    And 15 bushels corn, 40 M onions for portage
Custom: woad, 13s; onions, 4½d; all received

Ship called *le Godyer* of Ottermouth
Master: Nicholas Hok
Docked: 19 October 1320
Cargo: William le Breuwer and (Adam)[220] de Nyweton mercer: 80
    quarters corn
    John le Poter: 8 tuns woad
    John Petyt: 6 tuns 1 pipe [woad] (paid to Receiver)
    William Bruwere: 1 fardel canvas
    Adam de Nyweton: 1 fardel canvas
    William Bruwere: 2 barrels oil
    Adam de Nyweton: 5 barrels canvas [*baril' canabi*], 1 sack [*sacul'*] cumin
    William Bruwer: 5 seams onions
    And 1 seam onions for portage and 1 seam garlic for portage
Custom: William Bruwer and Adam de Nyweton for the custom; 15s;
    7s paid to the Receiver

Ship called *la neof Seynt Johan* of St Valéry
Master: John le Gros
Docked: 19 October 1320
Cargo: John de Hangard: 6 tuns woad, 300 stones weld
    And 7 seams onions for portage
    The shipmaster: 20 seams onions
Custom: R. for the custom; woad, 6s; onions, 10d; [which] {Martin received}

Ship called *la neof Seynte Marie* of Santander [*Seynt Andet*]
Master: Godsales Peres
Docked: 16 November 1320
Cargo: Philip Lovecok and John de Bayone: 300 quarters salt
    Richard Lovecok: 6 tuns 2 pipes (wine)

Ship called *la cog Seynt Martyn* of Jersey
Master: William de Mount
Docked: 20 November 1320
Cargo: Robert Jacop: 4 C onions, 3 seams garlic
    Ralph atte Putte: 400 yards canvas
Custom: 7d in the pyx

----

[220] *Ralph* crossed through and *Adam* written above.

Ship called *le Langbord*
Master: Geoffrey atte Wille
Docked: 23 November 1320
Cargo: Philip Lovecok, Walter de Hughetone and Robert de Stanbrigg: 400 quarters salt

Ship called *le neof Seynt Marie* of Sluis [*Estclus*]
Master: Quentin Rever
Docked: 24 November 1320
Cargo: John Lyverlace: 3 frails onions, 66 barrels potash, 18 barrels pitch, 8 barrels tar, 4 C copper, 2 tuns seam [*saym*], 7 pieces wax
Custom: no custom because in the freedom of Taunton

Boat called *le Rode cog* of Poole
Master: Richard Moune
Docked: 13 December 1320
Cargo: Richard Moune shipmaster: 10 quarters salt

Ship called *le Godyer* of Ottermouth
Master: Nicholas Hok
Docked: 16 December 1320
Cargo: William le Bruwer: 100 quarters corn, 2 barrels potash, 40 stones weld, 20 M onions, 1 bale alum
    Also 1 seam onions
Custom: ½d in the pyx
Pavage: 3¼d

Ship called *le Rode cog* of Exmouth
Master: William Elys
Docked: 19 December 1320
Cargo: 31½ lasts 1 M [herring] of which:
    John Whytebrother: 3 lasts 4 M
    Geoffrey le Degher: 1 last
    John de Fenton: 1 last
    Thomas le Furbour: 3 lasts 4 M
    John Treydevers: 3½ lasts 3 M
    Ralph de Thornbury: 1 last 9 M
    Ives Byrch: 1 last
    John le Perour: 2 lasts
    Nicholas Waleys: 5 lasts
    Nicholas de Lydeford: 3 lasts
    Robert de Silferton: 3 lasts
    Thomas le Barbour: 1 last
    John de Pachecote: 5 M (customed)
    Matthew, servant of Ralph de Thornbury: 1 M (customed)
    Thomas le Spicere: 1 last
    Thomas Furbour, John Whytebrother, John Beauforest: 300 M iron [*CCC^m ferri*]
    Also 8 C copper, 1 pipe blades? [*de verges*], 3 barrels potash
    Thomas Slyvere: 4 copes figs (customed)
    Geoffrey Degher: 1 cope figs
    Thomas Slyvere: 2(½) C canvas [*canaz*] (customed)
Custom: John Beauforest for the custom; 20½d; {all in the pyx}

Ship called *le Johannette* of Dartmouth
Master: John le Baker of Dartmouth
Docked: 23 December 1320
Cargo: John de Nyweton: 60 quarters salt

Ship called *le Peter* of Exmouth
Master: John[221] de Wyke
Docked: 30 December 1320
Cargo: 14 lasts herring, ½ last scorpions [*scorpoun*] of which:
    Philip Lovecok: 3 lasts
    Thomas Jacop: 4½ lasts
    Gilbert in the Combe: 2 lasts
    John de Nyweton: 3 lasts
    William Beauforest: ½ last
    William Ralle: 1 last
    John Stevene: 1 M [herring], 1 barrel pitch
    The shipmaster: 4 barrels pitch
Pavage: 3d

Ship called *le cog Notre Dame* of Weymouth
Master: Edward Bachil'
Docked: 18 January 1321
Cargo: Girald de Caprespynes: 160 quarters rye, 2 bales almonds
Custom: 3d
Pavage: 6s 8d [which] the Receiver received

Ship called *le neof Seynt Jake* of Abbeville
Master: Counteys de Kervye
Docked: 23 January 1321
Cargo: Peter Blaunchard and John de la Consture: 4 frails onions
    The crew [*nautorum navis*]: 4 frails onions, 6 quarters wheat, 46 M
    onions
Custom: ½ mark [which] {the Receiver received}
Pavage: 8s 1½d [which] {the Receiver received}

Ship called *la Juliane* of Audresselles [*Otresale*]
Master: Thomas le Counte
Docked: 7 March 1321
Cargo: 21 tuns woad of which:
    Peter[222] le Moner: 5 tuns
    John le Queynte: 6 tuns
    Michael Poter: 10 tuns
    The same Peter: 25 *coketz* potash
    Michael Poter: 160 stones weld
Custom: 21s [which] {the Receiver received except for 6s}
Pavage: woad, 21s; potash, 6d

---

[221] *Adam* crossed through and *John* written in.
[222] *Philip* crossed through and *Peter* written in.

Ship called *l'Emmengard* of Waban [*Whoban*]
Master: Peter Rynet
Docked: 7 March 1321
Cargo: John Poter: 10 tuns woad, 30 *coketz* potash, 160 [stones] weld,
80 M onions
Also 41 M onions for portage
Custom: [woad], 10s; {onions, 10d}; [which] {the Receiver received}
Pavage: {woad, 10s; potash, 7½d; onions, 6d}

Ship called *la Rose* of Exmouth
Master: Harlewin Bolt
Docked: 10 March 1321
Cargo: 140 quarters corn of which:
Adam de Nyweton and Thomas Golde: 111 quarters
The shipmaster: 21 quarters corn
John Jullen: 4 quarters
The said Adam and Golde: 2 barrels oil, 2 pieces cloth
John Jullon: 5 stones weld
Pavage: 12½d

Ship called *la Johanette* of Audresselles [*Oterleseyle*]
Master: William Favel
Docked: 10 March 1321
Cargo: John Body: 13 tuns woad, 96 quarters corn
Custom: 13s [which] {the Receiver received}
Pavage: [woad], 13s; {corn}, 4s

Ship called *la cog Seynt Johan* of Bordeaux
Master: Girald Drew
Docked: 11 March 1321
Cargo: Girald Renaud: 428 quarters corn
Pavage: [ ]

Ship called *la Margarete* of Yarmouth
Master: John Abraham
Docked: 12 March 1321
Cargo: 8 tuns wine of which:
Walter Launde of Winchelsea: 3 tuns
John de Arondel: 5 tuns
(The same Walter): 200 quarters wheat, 100 quarters rye
Robert de Silferton: 1 bale almonds
Custom: {Robert Lideford for the custom}; 20d
Pavage: 10d; from the ship, 3d [*De Nau'*]

Ship called *la Johanette* of Teignmouth
Master: Gilbert Whetepayn
Docked: 15 March 1321
Cargo: 10 tuns 1 pipe wine of which:
Gilbert in the Combe: 6 tuns 1 pipe
The shipmaster: 4 tuns of which 2 tuns for portage
Gilbert in the Combe: 16 quintals iron
The shipmaster: 40 quintals iron

Wymond Tolle: 16 quintals iron
Thomas atte Bourne: 8 quintals iron
The shipmaster: 3 quintals iron
Michael de Bovy: 25 quintals iron
Custom: wine, 8d; iron, 2s 9½d [which] {the Receiver received for
　iron}
Pavage: 22d with the ship;[223] also 5d of pavage

Ship called *le Johanette* of Winchelsea
Master: Robert de Brocdon of Winchelsea
Docked: 16 March 1321
Cargo: Peter le Moner: 10 tuns woad, 180 quarters corn, 200 stones
　weld
　And 30 M onions for portage
　The shipmaster: 30 quarters corn
Custom: 10s [which] {the Receiver received}
Pavage: 17s 8d

Ship called *le Nicholas* of Yarmouth
Master: Henry Lacy
Docked: 16 March 1321
Cargo: Richard Dyrkyn: 200 quarters salt

Ship called *la Johanette* of Dartmouth
Master: Gregory Hurt
Docked: 16 March 1321
Cargo: Walter de Hugheton: 4 tuns 6 pipes wine, 5 M iron, 2 copes
　figs, 1 bale almonds
　The shipmaster Gregory Hurt: 20 yards linen cloth

Ship called *la Grace Deu* of Yarmouth
Master: Thomas Rodelond
Docked: 16 March 1321
Cargo: Gerald Payn and Char [*et Char*]: 430 quarters corn
　And 2 tuns wine for portage
Pavage: 17s 11d

Ship called *la neof Seynt Michel* of Bayonne
Master: Bydaud de Coyntes
Docked: 16 March 1321
Cargo: Gerald de Vyrers: 475[224] quarters corn
　One of the mariners: 1 pipe wine
Pavage: 20s 2d

Ship called *le Juvenette* of[225] Lymington
Master: Roger Hake
Docked: 20 March 1321
Cargo: Stephen Perryn: 220 quarters rye, 30 quarters beans, 13 tuns
　3 pipes wine

---

[223] *Also the ship, 3d* crossed through.
[224] *Tuns* crossed through.
[225] *Ply* crossed through.

And 4 bales almonds (containing 8 C), 200 pounds archil
Custom: wine, 5s 4d {paid to the Receiver}; almonds, 2s
Pavage: 8s 5½d

Ship called *la Margarete* of Exmouth
Master: Richard Edmound
Docked: 22 March 1321
Cargo: 444 quarters corn of which:
   Walter de Hugheton: 150 quarters
   John Busse: 28 quarters
   Lawrence le Yung: 10 quarters
   John Averey: 14 quarters
   Walter Kerdewill: 10 quarters
   Nicholas de Godescote: 20 quarters
   Roger le Whyte: 20 quarters
   Robert de Stanbrigg: 19 quarters
   Walter Slegh: 19 quarters
   Walter Cok: 3 quarters
   John de Bayone: 107 quarters, 2 copes fruit
   The shipmaster and mariners: 44 quarters corn for portage
   Roger Serle: 2 M onions
   The shipmaster: 1 M onions
   Walter Cok: 4 M onions
Pavage: John de Bayone and Walter Kerdewill for the pavage; 6s 4d

Ship called *le Michel* of Exmouth
Master: Peter Golloc
Docked: 7 April 1321
Cargo: canvas of which:
   Ives Byrch and John de Nyweton: 7 seams canvas
   John Toillero: 1 seam canvas
   Adam Slegh: 6 C canvas
   Alexander de Shyrborne: 9 cloths
   Robert de Criditon: 12 C canvas
Custom: 8d in the pyx
Pavage: 2s 0½d of which 16d paid

Ship called *le Godyer* of Ottermouth
Master: Nicholas Holt
Docked: 12 April 1321
Cargo: William le Bruwer: 87 quarters corn, 50 stones weld
Pavage: 3d

Ship called *le Godyer* of Sidmouth
Master: Robert Vyneter
Docked: 13 April 1321
Cargo: John de Nyweton, William de Christnestouwe, John Cok: 260
   quarters corn
   Richard Whyot: 9 quarters corn
   The same William: 40 gallons grease [*uncti*], 4 tuns teasels [*cardoun'*]

With all together? [*Universis*][226]

(m. 11d) [**1320/1** merchandise account continued]

Ship called *la neof Seynt Johan* of Looe
Master: Geoffrey Gladwyne
Docked: 16 April 1321
Cargo: 250 quarters salt [*CC quart' salis et di' C*] of which:
   Richard Dyrkyn and Richard Lovecok: 205 quarters
   The shipmaster: (70 quarters salt)[227]
   And 16 tuns 6 pipes wine of which:
      Richard Dyrkyn: 6 tuns
      Richard Lovecok: 7 tuns 2 pipes
      Thomas Huchoun: 1 tun for portage
      John Nyel: 1 tun for portage
      Thomas Coraunt: 1 tun for portage
      William Greye: 1 pipe[228] for portage
      Geoffrey Gladwyn: 1 pipe for portage
      Roger Taillour: 1 pipe for portage
      Adam Lukeys: 1 pipe for portage
Pavage: sum, 22½d; from the ship, 3d

Ship called *la Mariote* of Hook [*Hamelehok*]
Master: William Pipere
Docked: 17 April 1321
Cargo: Thomas Codelep, Ralph de Nyweton and Roger Leyz tailor:
   50 quarters corn
   And 1 *rundlet* archil

Ship called *la Allowe* of Waban [*Woban*]
Master: John del Trenke
Docked: 18 April 1321
Cargo: Jakyn de Puyuz and Baldwin Yvoyt: 90 quarters corn
Pavage: 4s of which 2s 1d paid

Ship called *le cog Seynt Andreu*
Master: Roger Payn
Docked: 23 April 1321
Cargo: 4 tuns 3 pipes wine of which:
   John de Nyweton: 2 tuns 1 pipe
   William Muchele: 2 tuns 2 pipes
   John de Nyweton: 2 tons iron
   Thomas le Blake soaper [*sopere*]: (16)[229] quintals iron
   The shipmaster: 4 quintals iron
Custom: wine, 16d in the pyx; iron, 8d in the pyx
Pavage: iron, 4d

---

[226] Probably a scribal scribble, written in large, neat letters at the very bottom of the tail of the membrane.
[227] *45 quarters* crossed through and *70 quarters salt* written above.
[228] *Tun* crossed through and *pipe* written next.
[229] *20* crossed through and *16* written above.

Ship called *le Gabriel* of Lyme
Master: William Barry of Lyme
Docked: 26 April 1321
Cargo: William Barry of Lyme: 140 quarters salt

Ship called *le Peter* of Exmouth
Master: Elias Dollyng
Docked: 27 April 1321
Cargo: Philip Lovecok: 300 quarters salt
  Philip Lovecok and William Ralle: 17 M iron
  Alexander de Clist: 21 quintals iron
  The shipmaster: 2 quintals iron
  Walter Pruz: 10 quintals iron
Custom: 11½d
Pavage: 5½d [and] ¼d

Ship called *le Langbord*
Master: Geoffrey atte Wille
Docked: 3 May 1321
Cargo: 340 quarters salt of which:
  Philip Lovecok and Walter de Hugheton: 240 quarters
  Robert de Stanbrigg and the crew [*nautorum navis*]: all the rest

Ship called *le Blyze* of Hook [*Hamelehok*]
Master: Robert Gilbe
Docked: 6 May 1321
Cargo: 7 tuns 1 pipe woad of which:
  William Blakeman of Melcombe: 4 tuns
  Robert de Crokhorne: 3 tuns 1 pipe
  Robert Gilbe shipmaster: 3 garbs weld
Custom: 8s

Ship called *le Michel* of Lostwithiel
Master: John Oty
Docked: 10 May 1321
Cargo: Raymond de Vylers: 100 quarters salt

Ship called *la Johanette* of Cherbourg [*Shyrdebourgh*]
Master: Richard de la Tour
Docked: 20 May 1321
Cargo: William Fratre of London: 2 M canvas
Custom: no custom because of the freedom of London

Ship called *le Michel* of Teignmouth
Master: Wymond de Wyght
Docked: 26 May 1321
Cargo: Stephen Perryn: 300 quarters corn, 2 rundlets archil, 4 bales
  almonds
  Reginald Tolouse: 6 tuns woad (paid custom and pavage)
Custom: woad, 6s; [and] 18d
Pavage: 22s 9d

Ship called *le Peter* of Sidmouth
Master: Roger Sangere
Docked: 1 June 1321
Cargo: 28 tuns 1 pipe woad of which:
    Peter le Moner: 12 tuns
    Michael Poter: 9 tuns 1 pipe
    John le Poter: 7 tuns
    Peter le Moner: 10 *coket* potash assessed as 1 tun
    Michael le Poter: 10 *coket* [potash assessed] as 1 tun
    John le Poter: 10 *coketz* [potash] assessed as 1 tun
Custom: 29s
Pavage: 18s 10½d; from the ship, 3d

Ship called *la Margarete* of Ottermouth
Master: Stephen Crabbe
Docked: 1 June 1321
Cargo: Hugh Sampson: 100 quarters wheat, 1 pipe woad

Ship called *le Alyzotte* of Poole
Master: John le Blower
Cargo: 7 pipes wine of which:
    Raymond de Vyleres: 6 pipes
    The shipmaster: 1 pipe
    The same (Raymond) Vyleres: 300 quarters corn
Custom: 2s [which] {the Receiver received}
Pavage: Richard Plegh for the pavage; 12s 10½d; from the ship, 3d

Ship called *le cok Seynt Juliane*
Master: Thomas le Lange
Docked: 8 June 1321
Cargo: Richard de Oxneford: 6 tuns 1 pipe woad, 1 tun vinegar, 2½
    seams dyes? [*Dygoun*]
Custom: 7s 4d; Richard de Tavistok for the custom and pavage
Pavage: 7s

Ship called *la Rose* of Lymington
Master: Roger Calwe
Docked: 20 June 1321
Cargo: 60 barrels potash of which:
    Stephen atte Wode: 27 barrels potash, 7 barrels pitch
    Also 25 quarters rye
    Also 2 trendles wax, 1 fardel cloth
    Richard Makepes: (20)[230] barrels potash, 12 quarters rye
    Robert Cane: 20 barrels potash, 3 pieces cloth
    Also 2 tuns teasels [*cardouns*]
Pavage: Stephen de Bosco for the pavage; 6s 7d

---

[230] 7 crossed through and *20* written above.

Ship called *la cog Seynt Michel* of Le Vivier
Master: Lawrence Hughe of Le Vivier
Docked: 29 June 1321
Cargo: Hervicus le Jeoune: 60 quarters corn, 2 pieces linen cloth
Custom: 2d in the pyx
Pavage: Walter de Sweygnthulle and Elias Horloc for the pavage; 2s
    7d

Ship called *le Michel* of Exmouth
Master: Peter Golloc
Docked: 30 June 1321
Cargo: 200 quarters salt of which:
    Robert de Stanbrigg: 50 quarters
    Adam Slegh: 50 quarters salt
    Men of Kenton: the rest
    Adam Slegh: 2 quintals iron
    The shipmaster: 2 quintals iron
Pavage: [ ]

Ship called *le holoc Seynt Johan* of Guernsey
Master: Peter le Cornaill
Docked: 11 July 1321
Cargo: Peter le Cornaill: 19 oxen [*bobus*]
Custom: Thomas Golde for the custom and pavage; cattle [*aver'*], 9½d
    [which] {the Receiver received}
Pavage: 9½d

Ship called *la Rose* of Guernsey
Master: Peter Pylet
Docked: Peter Pylet: (13)[231] oxen, 40 quarters corn
Custom: Thomas Golde for the custom and pavage; cattle, 6½d
Pavage: 2s 2½d; from the ship, 3d

Ship called *la cog Seynt Katerine* of Jersey
Master: John Pycard
Docked: 13 August 1321
Cargo: John Pycard shipmaster: 26 seams garlic (then paid at the
    port for 19 seams), 12 seams onions, also 1½ C linen cloth
Custom: 2s 9d [which] the Receiver received

Ship called *la Blyze* of Hook [*Hamelehok*]
Master: Robert Gilbe
Docked: 24 August 1321
Cargo: 12 tuns woad of which:
    Thomas Thoraud: 8 tuns[232] (free)
    Richard Whyot: 4 tuns
    Also 40 stones weld
Custom: woad, 4s

---

[231] 7 crossed through, then *20* written above and crossed through, and then *13* written in.
[232] *4 tuns* crossed through.

Ship called *le cog Nostre Dame* of Hook [*Hoke*]
Master: Richard Godale
Docked: 25 August 1321
Cargo: 32 tuns woad of which:
  Peter le Moner: 8 tuns
  John le Poter: 14 tuns
  Michael le Poter: 10 tuns
  Michael Poter and John le Poter: 120 stones weld
Custom: woad, 32s
Pavage: 32s

Ship called *la neof Seynt Savour* of Barfleur
Master: Simon Bacon
Docked: 26 August 1321
Cargo: John Pyket: 18 tuns woad
  Also 4 *coketz* potash (portage)
  Also 6 seams garlic for portage
Custom: woad, 18s {paid all}
Pavage: 18s {paid 10s}

Ship called *la Johanette* of Guernsey
Master: Robert Ageneys
Docked: 28 August 1321
Cargo: John de Bayone and William Fratre of London: 55 quarters
  corn, 14 *coketz* potash, 112 [*Cxii*] fish, 2 frails onions, 3 M iron, 26
  garbs weld
Custom: ...

Ship called *la Johanette* of *Otevyle* [Hauteville-sur-Mer?]
Master: Totzt est le Roy
Docked: 28 August 1321
Cargo: Peter le Moner: 28 *coketz* potash
  John le Poter: 16 *coketz* potash
  The same John and Michael: 200 stones weld
  The crew [*nautorum navis*]: 80 cords garlic and 18 M onions for
    portage
  6 *coket'* allowed to them for 1 (tun) [*alloc' eis vi coket' pro 1 (dol')*][233]
Pavage: 5s 6d

Ship called *le hollouw* of St Malo [*Seynt Malloc*]
Master: Guillaume Jencoun
Docked: 19 August 1321
Cargo: Walter Michel of Plymouth: 26 seams garlic
Custom: 2s 2d {paid into the pyx}

---

[233] The last line of the entry reads *Et est magr' Totzt est le Roy alloc' eis vi coket pro i (dol)*.
Since the *a* of *alloc'* is quite large, it seems to indicate that a new phrase begins here; the
phrase notes that 6 cokets of potash are assessed as if they were one tun.

Ship called *le Vert Boys* of Le Vivier
Master: John Beuman(?)
Docked: 5 September 1321
Cargo: Stephen Gauter: 26 seams (garlic)
   Aleyn Molend': 26 seams [garlic]
   John Doo: 28 seams garlic and 2 C for portage
Custom: 5s(?) {[which] the Receiver received}

Ship called *le batel de St Michel* in Guernsey
Master: Nicholas Perryn
Docked: 18 September 1321
Cargo: Nicholas Perryn: 3 frails onions which contain 60 seams, 100
   yards linen cloth
Custom: ...

APPENDIX 1:

TRANSCRIPT OF THE ACCOUNT FOR 1310–11

The following account was chosen to illustrate the original text because it is the first surviving account to separate imports of wine and other merchandise into different sections and because it is preserved in excellent condition. In the following transcription, abbreviations have been extended but suspensions left as they occur, except for those following forenames and surnames. As in the translated text, editorial insertions are enclosed in square brackets, interlineated words or phrases are placed in round brackets, and additions clearly made after the original entry was written are enclosed in curly brackets.

PCA Roll 1, m. 24: [**1310/11**]

Vina applicantia ad portum de Exemuth post festum Sancti Michaelis Anno Edwardi Regis filii Regis Edwardi quarto

Vendag'

Navis que vocatur le Godyer de Exemuth applic' ad portum de Exemuth cum xlv dol' vini unde Ricardus le Keu xi dol' Willelmus le Keu viii dol' Martinus le Keu viii dol' Willelmus Buffet ii dol' Adam Broun ii dol' Thomas Toraud ii dol' Johannes Horn i dol' Nicholaus de Bradecrofte ii dol' cust' Gilbertus de Cumb vi dol' Walterus de Porte iii dol' et est magister Johannes Morkyn

Margin: Vinum
        ii dol' cust' viiid
        in pix'

Navis que vocatur la Margarete de Exemuth applic' ad portum de Exemuth cum L dol' iiii pip' vini unde Philippus Lovecok xxx dol' iii pip' Walterus de Hugheton i dol' Johannes de Bayona i dol' Robertus de Irlond x dol' i pip' et viii dol' de portag'

Margin: Vinum
        null' cust'

Navis que vocatur Godyer de Exemuth applic' ad portum de Exm' cum cxxxiii dol' vini vii pip' unde Johannes de Smalecomb habet xxi dol' & i pip' Walterus de Pourte vi dol' (i pip') Hugo le Garscoyng iiii dol' Robertus Gosce i dol' Adam de Smalecombe[1] Robertus Belechere

---

[1] *Adam de Smalecombe* crossed through.

iii dol' Willelmus le Ku de Brid' v dol' i pip' Martinus le Ku vii dol' i
pip' Johannes de Dodescomb i dol' Gilbertus de Cumb iii dol'
Nicholaus de Bradecrofte (custum' viiid) i dol' i pip' Johannes de
Somery (custum' iiiis) xii dol' Gilbertus Pycard (custum' iis) v dol' i
pip' Adam Peror x dol' Willelmus Boffet ii dol' Thomas Forbur ii dol'
Thomas Toraud vii dol' i pip' Michaelis Toraud ii dol' Magister
Hamond (custum' iiiid) i dol' Willelmus de Okampton iii dol'
Robertus de Okampton ix dol' Johannes Horn iii dol' Nicholaus
Busse iii dol' Ricardus Harvest (portag') i dol' Ricardus Golde
(portag') i dol' Johannes de Wreyford (custum' iis iiiid)² vii dol'
Egidius Bolt (custum' iiiis) xii dol'³ et est magister navis Ricardus
Harvest.

Margin: custuma xis
in pixidie

Navis que vocatur la Sauve de Exemuth applic' cum iiii^{xx}vi dol' et x
pip' vini unde Ricardus le Keu xvi dol' i pip' Willelmus Buffet v⁴ (iiii)
dol' Gilbertus de Cumb iii dol' Robertus de Okampton ii dol'
Johannes le Perour i dol' Willelmus le Keu i dol' Nicholaus de
Bradecrofte ii dol' cust' in pix' Matillis de Trickote et Johannes de
Trickote viii dol' di' Thomas Tregony le Baker x dol' (iii pip')
Walterus de Langeden i dol' Michaelis de Oxton i dol' Ricardus de
Gatepath i dol' Robertus de Criditon i dol' ($^\wedge$ di')⁵ cust' Thomas le
Furbur i dol' et di' Willelmus de Criditon quondam serviens Episcopi
i dol' cust' Galfridus atte Boghe xi dol' iii pip' Henricus Lovecok i dol'
Willelmus Arcedekne i dol' Willelmus Jobbe habet in custod' sua
quinque dol' i pip' unde Aluredus Aylward i pip' Johannes David i
dol'⁶ Ricardus Engelond v dol' cust' Robertus de Irlond iii dol'
Henricus le Megr' ii dol de beverag' P. Walterus Edmund i dol' i pip'
Henricus le Carpunter i dol' de port' Luverych ii dol' i pip' unde i
dol'⁷ de port'. Et est magister Walterus Edmund.

Margin: ix dol' di' cust' unde
Willelmus le Keu r' iiis et pos' in pix'

Navis que vocatur la Grace Deu de Dertemuth applic' ad portum de
Exemuth cum iiii^{xx}vii dol' i pip' vini unde Philippus Lovecok xlviii
dol' i pip' Walterus de Hugheton vi dol' Johannes de Bayona iii dol'
Nicholaus Page vii dol' Thomas le Baker ii dol' Gilbertus de Ridmor i
dol' Willelmus Austyn ii dol' Ricardus de Spaxton vii dol' Ricardus

---

² *Custum' iis iiiid* crossed through.
³ The rest of the line is left blank; *et est magister navis Ricardus Harvest* appears at the
beginning of the following line.
⁴ The *v* crossed through and *iiii* written above.
⁵ *Di'* written below the line.
⁶ The remainder of the line is left blank; *Ricardus Engelond* starts on the following line.
⁷ The phrase *unde i dol'* is underlined.
⁸ The phrase *i dol'* crossed through.

Dyrkyn ii dol' et i dol (iiiid in p.) cust' Robertus Gosce iii dol'
Willelmus Mounteyn ii dol' cust'. Et ii dol' de port'. Et est magister
Nicholaus Swyft. Item i dol' cust' iiiid in p. Et pro cust' Willelmi
Mounteyn Robertus Gosce.

Margin: vii dol' cust'
              in pix'

Navis que vocatur la Croys de Dertemuth applic' ad portum de
Exem' cum xxiiii dol' vini unde Johannes Stiward viii dol' Johannes
Bataille xvi dol' burgens' de Wynchelse. Et est magister Rogerus le
Pyper.

Margin: vinum null' cust'

Navis Sancti Martini de Sancto Walroy applic' ad portum de Exem'
cum x dol' Wayd Johanni Mouset CLx petr' Wolde eiusdem—Et est
magister eiusdem navis Willelmus Blogoy.

Margin: Wayd & Wold
              cust' xs W. le Keu r' xs

Rek   Rek   Rek   Rek   Rek

Navis que vocatur la Sauvee de Exemuth applic' cum sale Roberti de
Irlond Galfridi de la Boghe Thome de Tetteburn et aliorum. Et cum
viii dol' vini unde Robertus de Irlond i dol' Walterus Edmund i dol[8] ii
dol' Luverych ii dol' Willelmus Jobbe ii dol' Gascoyng i dol' de port'.
Et est magister Parisius Edmund.

Margin: Nulla custuma

Navis que vocatur la Seinte Marie Cog de Exemuth applic' cum
iiii^{xx}xiii dol' xix pip' vini unde Walterus de Porte viii dol' v pip'
Ricardus de Gadepath iiii dol' iii pip' Willelmus de Gadepath iii dol' i
pip' Johannes le Perour iii dol' Adam le Perour iii dol' Thomas le
Furbur iii dol' Robertus de Criditon ii dol' (viiid in p.) cust' Thomas
de Tetteburne & Johannes de Trickote xv dol' (ii)[9] pip' Galfridus le
Degher vii dol' (iis iiiid in p.) cust' Michaelis Toraud ii dol' Johannes
Girard ii dol' Petrus Godlok i dol' Paye Gosse i dol' de port' Leticia de
Ridmor i dol' Philippus Lovecok xxvi dol' v pip' Walterus Lovecok iii
dol' Johannes Lovecok ii dol' i pip' (viiid in p.) cust' Walterus de
Hugheton iiii dol' i pip' Johannes de Bayona iii dol' Willelmus Ralle i
pip' (iiid in p.). Et est magister Petrus Godlok. [10] ii dol' ii pip' cust' pro
quibus Philippus Lovecok r'.

[9] The *i* crossed through and *ii* inserted above.
[10] The following phrase is scribbled at the lower left end of the entry.
[11] *Robertus* crossed through.

Margin: Vina

Navis que vocatur la Margarete de Exem' applic' cum Lxi dol' v pip' vini unde Philippus Lovecok xxiii dol' v pip' Walterus Lovecok iii dol' Walterus de Hugheton ii dol' Johannes de Bayona ii dol' Robertus de Irlond vi dol' Johannes Gayllard de Plymmouth (calumpn') xi dol' cust' Robertus[11] Vincentius Tak vii dol' Adam Slegh iii dol' unde (iiiid in p.) duo de port' Nicholaus de Lideford iii dol' Rogerus Serle i dol' de port'. Et iiii quint' (id in p.) ferr' Ade Slegh Johannes Vyssh' (id in p.) ii quint' ferr'. Et est magister idem Adam.

Navis que vocatur le bonan de Exemuth applic' ad portum de Toppesham cum Lxi doleis & xii pipis vini unde Willelmus le Keu de Brydef' v dol' & i pip'—Martinus le Keu de Brydef' x dol' &[12] ii pip'—Ricardus (^ le Keu) de Brydef' ii dol'—Willelmus de Gatpbath ii dol' —Gilbertus Pykard (viiid) ii dol'[13]—Willelmus Dyne x dol' (iiiis viiid) & iiii pip'[14]—Ricardus de Tavystok (iiiid) i dol'[15]—Willelmus le Bruere i dol'—Johannes le Ercediakene iiii dol'—Johanne David iii dol' & i pip'—Nicholaus de Ryouns (iiiid)[16] i pip'—Robertus de Irlond i pip'—Ricardus de Gatepath ii pip'—Johannes de Smalecomb xiii dol'—Robertus de Ochampton iiii dol'—Robertus Belechere iii dolea—Willelmus le Skynnere i dol'—Sunt in eadem iii bal' de amigdal'—unde i Johannis de Smalecomb—i Willelmi de Skynnere & i Willelmi le Bruere—Et i Bal' de corduwan Ade Broun et i Bala de arguil Ricardi de Brydef'[17] Stavystok & Ade Broun—Et est magister navis Ricardus Harvest.

Margin: Vinum
       Custum' vis
       ut patet super cap'
       quos Willelmus le Keu
       recepit

Navis que vocatur la Hynde de Yepiswych applic' ad portum de Exem' cum iiii[xx] dol' iiii pip' vini—unde Adam le Perour iiii dol'—Thomas Le Foubour iiii dol'—Gilis Boolt x dol (^ i pip')—Johannes Leverich vii dol'—Johannes de Bovy x dol' & ii pip'—Henricus de Covyntre vii dol'—Gilbertus in the Comb xii dol' i pip'—Walterus de Porte vi dolea—Stephanus Wyldlere viii dol'—Et ad portag' xii dol'—Et est magister Pyk.

[12] *i p* crossed through.
[13] A curving line is drawn over the top of the entry from *Gilbertus* to here.
[14] A curving line is drawn over the top of the entry from *Willelmus* to here.
[15] A curving line is drawn over the top of the entry from *Tavystok* to here.
[16] A curving line is drawn over the top of the entry from *Nicholaus* to here.
[17] *Brydef'* crossed through.
[18] *Allec'* is expunged.

Margin: Custum' vini
              unde xix dol' & ii pip'
              custumat' & est
              cust' viis quos
              W. le Keu recep'

Summa custume vini - xxxiiis viiid - unde domino H. de Curtenay - xis iid ob.

[m. 24d]

Navis que vocatur Godyer de Tengem' applic' ad portum de Exem' xxviii die Novembr' cum v dol' de Wayde que sunt Thome Golde & Stephani le Bruere et vi pip' cinerum que sunt eorumdem et vii quar' ordei et iii quar' fab' que sunt eorumdem et vi pip' cinerum que sunt Walteri de Morchard et iiii quar' fab' eiusdem et vi quar' ordei eiusdem. Et est magister navis Willelmus Chaste.

Navis que vocatur Seint Lowy de Abevill applic' ad portum de Exem' die veneris post festum Sancti Andree cum xxiiii dol' Wayde Petri le Monyer. Et cum xv m^l de oygn' de port'. Et est magister Hugo Gyllard.

Margin: xxiiiis
         quos Willelmus le
         Keu recepit

Navis que vocatur Godyer de Oterymouth applic' ad portum de Exem' xiiii die December cum c iiii^{xx} quart' frumenti Nicholai Busse et aliorum videlicet Egidii de Tignemuth et aliorum nautarum. Et v^c sepi predicti Egidii cust'. Et est magister Ricardus Dollyng.

Margin: Blad'

Navis que vocatur la Margarete de Gernemuth applic' cum xl last' allec'[18] x^{ml} allec' unde Philippus Lovecok v last' di' Walterus Lovecok v last' iii^{ml} Willelmus de Smalecoumbe vi last' di' Nicholaus le Skynner iii last' x^{ml} Matthaeus le Skynner i last' ii^{ml} Willelmus de Okampton i last' Johannes Whytebrother iii last' ii cad' Robertus de Okampton i last' Wydo Maynard di' last' Thomas Farth' di' last' Thomas le Furbur i last' Ricardus Gaudethon i last' Thomas de Molton ii last' di' Jordanus de Venella i last' di' Semannus atte Sonde burg' de Gernemuth vi last' iii^{ml} Nicholaus le Skynnere iii^{ml}. Et est magister Robertus le Corteler.

Margin: Nullam cust'

Navis que vocatur Benvenue de Seint Walry applic' cum iiii^{or} fraell' de

---

[19] *Ipsius* crossed through.

oignouns et Wald que omnia sunt Willelmi le Brewer et Walteri le War' et est magister Johannes de Goseford.

Margin: Cust' nullam

Navis que vocatur la Katerine de Gernesye applic' cum xxx quart' ordei i quart' fabarum ii quart' di' pisarum iiii quart' aven' xl miliar' oygn' (vd in pix') vi ragad' friscis Roberti de Genes et xx quart' frumenti Johannis de Sancto Nicholo. Et est magister predictus Robertus.

Margin: Oign'
        Blad'

Navis que vocatur la Margaret de Romeneye applic' ad port' de Exem' cum CLx qr' fab' & pis' unde null' proven' custum'. Et est magister eiusdem Johannes Laurenz.

Margin: Cust' null'

Navis que vocatur Godale de Gosport applic etc... cum L quart' mixtilium et c petr' Wold' de Willelmi le Brewer et est magister Stephanus de Dagevill.

Margin: cust' null'

Navis que vocatur la Margarete de Caleys applic' cum xxx quart' fr' mixtilium W. de Porte & Stephani de Smalecumb et est magister Copyn Harpe.

Margin: Cust' null'

Navis vocatur Seynt Johanas Cog applic' ad portum de Toppesham cum xx quar' frumenti Petri La Cornayll xl quar' ordei ipsius Petri ii qr' pis' & fab' - eiusdem Petri - i qr' aven' eiusdem - m^l makerell' sals' ipsius[19] eiusdem Petri et (est) magister navis idem Petrus.

Margin: Cust'
        pl' de custum' J. de
        Sancto Nicholo. id ob in p'

Navis que vocatur la Floryete de Salune? [Salvin?] applic' cum viii dol' Wayde Johannes de Kent et est magister Ricardus le Coverour.

Margin   Wayd' cust' xs Willelmus le Keu r'

Navis que vocatur la Lowys de Abevile applic' cum xvi dol' Wayde et c

---

[20] *Katerine* crossed through.

petr' Walde que omnia sunt Petri le Monyer. Et est magister Hugo Gyllard - Willelmus le Keu rec' xvis.

Margin: Wayd'
         Cust' xvis

Navis que vocatur la Holoc de Seynt Lowis applic' ad portum de Exem' cum iiii^{xx} petr' Wolde Pagani le Bruere & Stephani de Ellecombe - iiii Bal' alym eorumdem - xxxvi capell' eorumdem - C cultell' eorumdem - xx Lantarne eorumdem - ii petr' molares parvi eiusdem Pagani - ii Bal' alym Walteri de Morchard - xii capell' & L cultell' eiusdem Walteri - Et est magister Navis Johannes Rydel.

Margin: Custum'

Navis que vocatur la Nichol' de Calcheshorde applic' iii die Jul' cum iiii dol' Wayde Radulphi Burgeys et xv^c baterie Laur' le Potyer et est magister Robertus Toppe. Et pro custuma Johannes Mozet solvend infra xv dies proxima sequentes - {Willelmus le Keu r'}.

Margin: Wayd'
         Bater'
         summa vis vid

Navis que vocatur la Nostr' Dame de Loveris applic' ad portum de Exem' eodem die cum xii dol' Wayde que sunt Ricardi Mounteyn cc petr' de cain xx^{ml} cardon' ii (pec') pann' sarg' de cain i dol' plen' tuall' & mapp' eorumdem cum ii pec' linee tele et est magister Johannus Adam. Et sunt pro cust' Willelmus le Degher et Gilbertus de Nymet solv' infra viii dies proxima sequent' - {Willelmus le Keu r' xiis}.

Margin: Summa xiis

Navis que vocatur la Osanne de Cabowe applic' cum xxx quart' frumenti et xx quart' ordei et i petra molari et xii^c (iid ob in p') makerel' Ricardi Osanne et est magister idem Ricardus.

Margin: Blad'

Navis que vocatur la Floryete de Cabowe applic' cum xxxvi quart' ord' et xii quart' frumenti i duod' calig' et di' cent canobii Willelmi Cokerel et est magister Petrus de Geneyes.

Margin: Blad'

Navis que vocatur la Holhop de Seint Lowys applic' cum xxviii quart' frumenti Nicholai le Graunt et est magister Johannes (Rydel).

Margin: Blad'

Navis vocatur la Seinte Katerine[20] Margarete de Exem' applic' cum cc sal' Philippi Lovecok Roberti de Irlond et est magister [ ][21]

Margin: Sal'

Navis que vocatur la cog Seint Lowys de Maullo applic' cum Lv quart' frumenti & ordei Thome Lukeys. Et est magister Philippus Peytevyn.

Margin: Blad'

Navis que vocatur Seint Nicholas de Vivers applic' cum ii[ml] & di' trac' allee et ii sum' oygn' Roberti Russel et est magister Laur' Hughe. Et est pro cust' Johannes de Sancto Nicholo - {Willelmus le Keu r'}.

Margin: Allea Oign'
vs iiiid ob
W. le Keu r'

Navis que vocatur la Joanette de Gernesye applic' cum xxx sum' de oygn' Ricardi Geneys & soc' suorum et est magister idem Ricardi et xx virg' linee tele.

Margin: Oygn'
xvd in p.

Navis que vocatur la Cocke Seint Johan de Vyver applic' cum ii[ml] di' trac' allee et xl virg' linee tele Ivonis le Britum et v oll' butiri eiusdem Ivonis et est magister Gylyot Pycherel. Et pro cust' Johannes de Sancto Nicholo Aluredus Aylward.

Margin: Summa vs vd
W. le Keu r'

Vina custum' anno Regis Edwardi quarto[22]

---

[21] Blank space left for shipmaster.
[22] Written in large letters at the bottom of the membrane.

APPENDIX 2:

MAYORS, STEWARDS, AND RECEIVERS
IN EXETER, 1266–1321

The following list names the chief municipal officers of Exeter in those years for which local port customs accounts are printed in this volume. Civic elections took place annually on the Monday after Michaelmas and the results were usually enrolled on the dorse of the first membrane of the new court roll, along with the names of the electors.[1] The most important city officials chosen at these elections were the mayor and the four stewards, one of whom eventually became known as the "receiver" and as such was responsible for receiving the town customs, rents, and other financial dues.[2] Although a receiver was not specifically named in the civic election returns until 1311/12, the emergence of the office can be traced in the city's port customs accounts several decades earlier.

In the late thirteenth century, references to the collection or supervision of port customs in the local accounts show how one or two of the stewards regularly stepped forward to take on more responsibility for the town's financial affairs. In the account of 1287/8, one of the stewards for that year, Richard Aleyn, supervised the deposit of custom on one cargo into the town pyx (cash box). Aleyn had previously served as city clerk, so he was probably better educated than most of the stewards and therefore more equipped to take on the burdens associated with the emerging office of receiver.[3] Ten years later in 1297/8, custom from another cargo was paid to Nicholas Page per William Buffet. Both were stewards that year but Page was probably acting as receiver since the money was paid to him. In the following year, customs payments were made once to the steward Nicholas Page and once to the steward William de Carswell. A similar situation occurred in 1299/1300 when

---

[1] The mayor's court rolls (MCR) survive for 1264–66, 1271, 1285–92, and for all years from 1295 to 1459 except one. For the method of election and political structure in Exeter, see B. Wilkinson, *The Mediaeval Council of Exeter*, Manchester, 1931, particularly the "Introduction", by R. C. Easterling, pp xiii–xxxiv; and Maryanne Kowaleski, 'The Commercial Dominance of a Medieval Provincial Oligarchy: Exeter in the Late Fourteenth Century,' *Mediaeval Studies*, xlvi (1984), pp 355–84.

[2] The office of mayor in Exeter dates from about 1205 while the four stewards (usually called *senescalli*, but also *prepositi* and sometimes *baillivi*) who aided the mayor first appeared about 1224; see R. C. Easterling, 'List of Civic Officials of Exeter in the 12th and 13th Centuries, c. 1100–1300', *TDA*, lxx (1938), pp 455–94. For a recent summary of the office of receiver, see Margery M. Rowe and John M. Draisy, 'Introduction', *The Receivers' Accounts of the City of Exeter 1304-1353*, DCRS, new series, xxxii (1989), pp viii–xi.

[3] Easterling, 'List', p 487; *Exeter Freemen 1266–1967*, ed. Margery M. Rowe and Andrew M. Jackson, DCRS, extra series, i (1973), p 3.

payments were handed over to Roger Beyvin and Robert de Newton, both of whom served as stewards that year.[4]

From 1302/3 (the year of the first surviving customs account), one steward began to be singled out more regularly to receive customs or place customs monies into the pyx; in that year, Walter de Porte was mentioned four times in this capacity. The office of "receiver" was itself noted for the first time in the account of 1303/4; the steward Henry de Triccote probably filled the office since he appears receiving port customs five times. In the account of 1304/5, Robert de Newton was specifically named receiver and was linked to customs collection in the account nineteen times; his name, moreover, appears at the bottom of one of the account's membranes. The first extant receivers' account also survives from this year; Robert de Newton's name appears at the head of that account and the one following as well, although he was termed only "steward", not "receiver" in these early accounts.[5] Nonetheless, it is clear that by 1302 one of the stewards was recognized as the chief financial officer, and two years later this steward began to be called the receiver, even though he was not officially designated as such in the annual elections until 1311.

Although one of the four stewards began to take on the duties associated with the office of receiver during this period, others involved in town government also helped with the collection of port customs. Two mayors, Robert Beyvin and Philip Lovecok, occasionally witnessed the placement of customs monies into the town pyx.[6] Some of the other stewards also supervised such deposits, or funnelled custom monies to the receiver or town pyx themselves.[7] All of these "helpers" had themselves served as receivers in previous years or were long-time stewards whose position of trust allowed them to exercise such responsibilities on behalf of the city. Significantly, the participation of these officials declined as time went on and the receiver emerged as the acknowledged financial officer. After 1311, officials other than the receiver were rarely mentioned in connection with the collection of port customs.

Besides the mayor and stewards, the only other individual regularly linked to the collection of port customs was Philip Denebaud; once in 1304/5 and five times in 1305/6 he either received custom or chan-

---

[4] In MCR 1299/1300, m. 38d (p 65, above), the phrasing seems to imply that John Pycard received customs (or was the receiver of customs) that were then paid to Robert de Newton. While Pycard may have owned property in Exeter (see DRO, ECA ED/M/297), there is no record of his entry to the freedom or election to civic office. He may have been employed by Newton to help collect custom; wealthy and busy oligarchs often employed such agents or sub-collectors to help them fulfill some of their official duties.

[5] DRO, ECA CRA 1304/5, 1305/6; printed in *The Receivers' Accounts of the City of Exeter*, pp 1–3.

[6] Beyvin did so once in 1303/4, three times in 1304/5, and four times in 1305/6. Lovecok witnessed such payments twice in 1316/17.

[7] William de Carswill did so twice in 1304/5; Walter de Porte, five times in 1304/5, and once in 1305/6 (when he was not a steward); Walter de Langden twice in 1305/6; Henry de Tricote once in 1305/6; Philip Lovecok once in 1310/11; John Davy once in 1316/17; and Martin le Keu of Bridford once in 1318/19 and once in 1320/1.

nelled it into the pyx. Denebaud served as town clerk and chief bailiff
for many years so his involvement in the collection of town custom is
not surprising.[8] His interest may also have been personal since part of
his annual stipend in 1305/6 was paid out of amounts collected for
custom.[9] In 1303/4, another town clerk, Alured Aylward, also
received customs monies, but he promptly handed the sum over to
the receiver.[10] The only person without an offical role in town government to collect port customs was Thomas Thoraud who in May 1317
received custom from three importers of wine on the *cog Notre Dame*
of Exmouth. Thomas was, however, the son of Michael Thoraud, the
receiver that year, and was probably filling in for him temporarily.[11]
Thomas himself served as a steward several years later.[12]

In several instances, it seems that the receiver's interest in the collection of customs extended to the compilation of the written account
itself. Two of the receivers, Robert de Newton and Michael Thoraud,
may have personally supervised these accounts since during their
tenures the accounts contain many annotations about their receipt of
custom in a very rough, non-clerical hand.[13] These annotations, written in large, clumsily-formed letters, are very brief and usually make
simple statements such as "R. de Neweton received", "all paid", or
"Michael received". They are distinctly different from the more usual
scribal additions which are composed in hands similar to those that
wrote the main entries.

A comparison of the importers' names and those on the following
list of officeholders also shows the pervasive mercantile interests of
the city's political hierarchy. All of the receivers and most of the other
town officers frequently appeared as importers in the accounts printed here. Together with the common council of twelve (which was not
a regular feature of town government until the 1340s), the mayor
and stewards formed the political elite of medieval Exeter. These
men represented but a tiny fraction of the urban population and
most served in high public office many times. Entry into the upper
echelons of the city hierarchy demanded substantial wealth which, as
these customs accounts illustrate, may often have come from invest-
ment in maritime trade. It appears that even by the late thirteenth

---

[8] He served as city clerk or chief bailiff from 1303/4 to at least 1314/15; see Easterling,
'List', p 490; and DRO, ED/M/197, 199, 202–4, 220, 224; ECL D&C 21, 61-4.

[9] See above, pp 107, 111.

[10] Unlike Denebaud, he probably never served as chief bailiff; see *Exeter Freemen*,
pp 9, 10, 13.

[11] Above, p 144. *Exeter Freemen*, p 10.

[12] MCR 1325/6, m. 1d (under the name of Thomas de Oxton; both Michael and
Thomas were sometimes known under the surname "de Oxton" rather than
"Thoraud").

[13] These are enclosed in curly brackets in the text although no effort has been made
to distinguish these annotations from other later additions by scribes. In the 1304/5
account, there are about eleven such annotations, in 1305/6, about nine, and in
1316/17, also nine. Newton served as receiver in the first two years and Thoraud in the
last year.

century, Exeter was ruled by a small merchant oligarchy that con-trolled the bulk of both trade and government in the town.[14]

Unless noted otherwise, the election results given below may be found on m. 1d of the mayor's court roll for the year stated in the left-hand column. The names of receivers who were not specifically named as such in the election results (but who performed duties com-mensurate with the office of receiver) are enclosed in square brackets. Those men who were commonly known by more than one name have their alias also listed, separated from their other surname by a slash.

Year	Mayor	Receiver	Stewards
1265/6[15]	Walter de Okeston		Nicholas de Ilchester
			Thomas de Langdene
			Martin Durling
			John de Fenton
1285/6[16]	Alured de Porta		Walter de Langedene
	David le Taylur		Stephen de London
			Henry de Esse
			John Horn
1287/8	John Soth	[Richard Aleyn]	Richard Aleyn
			Richard Mounteyn
			William de Carswille
			John Wele
1288/9	John Soth		Walter de Langeden
			William de Gatepath
			William Buffet
			Jordan de la Venella
1290/1	John Soth		Henry de Coldecote
			John Wele
			William de Gatepath
			Richard Mounteyn
1295/6	John Soth		Walter de Langeden
			William de Carswille
			William Boffet
			Roger le Wetene/ Beyvyn[17]
1296/7	Walter Tauntefer		Walter de Langeden
			William de Carswill
			Robert de Newaton
			Roger Beyvyn/le Wetene

[14] See Kowaleski, 'Provincial Oligarchy', for a longer discussion of this group in the late fourteenth century.

[15] Officers identified from deeds as in Easterling, 'List', p 481.

[16] The first mayor, Alured de Porta, served until December 1285 when he was exe-cuted for his role in the murder of the Precentor of the Cathedral. The seneschals who served with him cannot be identified (Easterling, 'List', p 486). The next election (at which David le Taylur and the stewards named here were elected) took place on 28 February 1286 (MCR Roll 1, m. 26d), the date of the earliest court for the incomplete MCR that survives for that year.

[17] Roger le Wetene (also Whetene, Hwetene) and Roger Beyvyn (also Beyvin) were the same person; see MCR 1288/9, m. 6d (p 49, above). Easterling, 'List', mistakenly treats them as two different people.

1297/8[18]	Walter Tauntifer	[Nicholas Page]	William Buffet
			William de Karswille
			Roger le Wetene/Beyvyn
			Nicholas Page
1298/9[19]	Walter Tauntefer	[Nicholas Page or William de Carswell]	William de Carswell
			Nicolas Page
			Roger le Hwetene/Beyvyn
			Robert de Nyweton
1299/ 1300[20]	John Horn	[Roger Beyvin or Robert de Neweton]	Nicholas Page
			Roger Beyvin/le Wetene
			Robert de Neweton
			Stephen de Bommani/ Munteyn
1300/1[21]	William de Gatepath		Jordan de Venella
			William de Kerswell
			Robert de Nyweton
			John le Perour
1301/2[22]	Walter Tauntefer		Walter de Langeden
			William de Carswill
			Roger Beyvyn/le Wetene
			John Gerveys
1302/3[23]	Roger Beyvyn/ le Whetene	[Walter de Porte]	Walter de Langeden
			William de Carswill
			Robert de Nyweton
			Walter de Porte
1303/4	Roger le Whetene/ Beyvyn	[Henry de Triccote]	Walter de Langeden
			William de Carswill
			William Boffet
			Henry de Triccote

[18] MCR 1297/8, m. 1d contains only the heading for the election, not the results. Officers have been identified from deeds (DRO ED/M/180; DRO 51/1/1/5–6); see also Easterling, 'List', p 489 (although note that Easterling treats Roger Beyvyn and Roger le Wetene as two different people).

[19] MCR 1298/9, m. 1d contains no election results although a later hand (probably that of the sixteenth-century chamberlain, John Hooker) wrote in *Tempore Walteri Tauntifer maioris*. Officers have been identified from a deed in DRO, ECA Book 53A, f. 22; see also Easterling, 'List', p 489 (although she mistranscribed Hweten as Nwetene). Page and Carswell each appear once receiving port customs.

[20] The election results on MCR 1299/1300, m. 1d list the last steward as Stephen de Bommani but two deeds of that year give his name as Stephen Munteyn; in other deeds he appears as Stephen de Bodmani. They all refer to the same person; see DRO ED/M/183, 186–188; ECL D&C 61–63. Beyvin and Newton each appeared once this year associated with collection of port customs.

[21] Only the heading and names of fourteen electors are given on MCR 1300/1, m. 1d although a later (probably sixteenth-century) hand has written in William Gathpath as the mayor. Officers identified from a fine on DRO, ECA Misc. Roll 2, no. 1 as in Easterling, 'List', p 489.

[22] MCR 1301/2, m. 1d omits the names of the stewards so they have been supplied from deeds of that year (DRO ED/M/191; ECL D&C 168, 543); see also Easterling, 'List', p 489.

[23] MCR 1302/3, m. 1d lists only four electors. The names of the officers have been supplied from a deed of that year (DRO ED/M/195); see also Easterling, 'List', p 490.

1304/5	Roger le Whetene/ Beyvyn	[Robert de Nyweton]	Walter de Langeden William de Carswille Robert de Nyweton Walter de Porte
1305/6	Roger le Whetene/ Beyvyn	[Robert de Nyweton]	Walter de Langeden William de Carswill Robert de Nyweton Henry de Tricote
1310/11[24]	Walter Tauntefer	[William le Keu of Bridford]	Walter de Langeden Peter Soth Philip Lovecok William le Keu of Bridford
1312/13	William de Gatepathe	John de Smalecombe	Philip Lovecok William de Carswill Thomas Fartheyn John de Smalecombe
1315/16	Philip Lovecok	[Matthew Pelliparius]	Thomas Farthein Richard le Seler Ralph Tinctor Matthew Pelliparius
1316/17[25]	Philip Lovecok	Michael Thoraud	Michael Thoraud John Treydeners
1316/17[25]	Philip Lovecok	Michael Thoraud	Michael Thoraud John Busse John Davy
1317/18	Roger Beyvyn/ le Wetene	Martin le Keu of Bridford	William de Carswille Thomas Fartheyn Martin le Keu of Bridford Matthew Pellipar'
1318/19	Philip Lovecok	John Treideners	Martin le Keu of Bridford John Treideners skinner Thomas le Espicer Robert de Wottone
1319/20	Roger Beyvyn/ le Wetene	Robert de Wotton	William de Carswill John Davy Robert de Wotton Thomas le Spicer
1320/1	Philip Lovecok	Thomas le Furbour	Martin le Keu of Bridford Thomas le Furbour Walter de Sweyngthulle Thomas Fartheyn

[24] William le Keu was noted receiving custom amounts ten times in the acounts while Philip Lovecok appeared once in this capacity.

[25] No receiver was designated in the election returns in MCR 1316/17, m. 1d, but further down the membrane Michael Thoraud was specifically termed the *receptor* of the payment for the farm of the ferry at Pratteshide. Thoraud was also frequently noted receiving port customs this year.

APPENDIX 3:

GLOSSARY OF WEIGHTS AND MEASURES

The following list provides brief definitions of the weights and measures employed in the Exeter accounts printed in this volume. The most common spelling of these weights and measures (usually written in Latin but occasionally in English or French), are given here in italics, within square brackets. Weights and measures for which there is no known English equivalent have been left in italics.

The local port customs accounts of Exeter also provide unusually early equivalents for some weights and measures, although it is not clear whether they were meant to offer standard equivalents used at Exeter or to mark deviations from the norm. Those recorded in the Exeter accounts during the fourteenth century are noted here and referenced by the date of the port customs account (PCA) in which they occurred. The Latin wording is given for those not included in the accounts translated above. Otherwise only the most common and oldest known equivalents have been listed here since many such references date from the fifteenth century or later, several hundred years after these accounts were compiled.[1]

astr'   indeterminate measure used for pitch.

bale   [*bala, bale*]; a measure of quantity or capacity which varied by commodity. It usually denoted a large bundle that was wrapped in canvas and tightly bound. At Exeter, 1 bale of wool yarn weighed 1.5 C (MCR 1298/9, m. 28d, above, p 61), and 1 bale of madder and alum contained 2.5 C (PCA 1360/1: *3 bales madder unde quibus ii C di'; 3 bales alum unde quibus bale ii C di'*). Four bales of almonds contained 8 C (PCA 1320/1, p 195 above).

barrel   [*barrellus, baril*]; a measure of capacity, generally a cylindrical wooden vessel. For herring, the barrel contained about 30 gallons. At Exeter, 1 barrel of oil could contain 7 gallons (PCA 1397/8: *ii baril' que continent' xiv gal' olei*) or 13 gallons (PCA 1398/9: *ii bar' que cont' xxvi galon' olei*). One entry (PCA 1315/16, p 139 above) implies that a barrel of woad was equivalent to one quarter.

---

[1] The following sources were particularly useful in identifying weights and measures: R. E. Zupko, *A Dictionary of Weights and Measures for the British Isles: the Middle Ages to the Twentieth Century*, Philadelphia, 1985; R. E. Zupko, *French Weights and Measures before the Revolution*, Bloomington IN, 1979; Henri Touchard, 'Les douanes municipales d'Exeter (Devon). Publication des rôles de 1381 à 1433', thèse complémentaire pour le Doctorat ès Lettres, Université de Paris, 1967; H. Hall and F. J. Nichols, eds., 'Select Tracts and Table Books relating to English Weights and Measures', *Camden Miscellany XV*, Camden 3rd series, xli (1929); Charles Du Fresne Du Cange, *Glossarium mediae et infimae latinitatis*, 10 vols in 11, Paris, new edition, 1937–38.

bushel [*bussellus*]; measure of capacity used for grain and other dry products. The local markets at Exeter employed a heaped bushel of 10 gallons for grain rather than the standard Winchester bushel of 8 gallons.[2]

C [*C, centum, cent*]; equivalent to a hundred by tale or a hundredweight depending on the commodity. Boards, canvas, fish, garlic, linen cloth, onions, and skins were counted by tale but varied from the short hundred (100) to the long hundred (120 or more). At Exeter, the short hundred seems to have been used for herring, and for cloth (where it contained 100 ells), but the long hundred was used for many northern French goods.[3] The hundredweight used for copper, iron, grease, salt, spices, wax and other goods also varied, from 100 to 112 pounds. At Exeter, 1.5 cwt of iron made up 8 quintals (PCA 1318/19, p 170, above), and 1.5 C of herring equalled 1 seam (PCA 1335/6, merchandise account: *i di' C allec qui fac' i summe*). See also **bale** (for almonds, alum, madder, and wool yarn), **charge** (for salt), **fardel** (for canvas and cloth), **quintal** (for iron), **seam** (for fish), and **trendle** (for wax).

cade [*cadus, cade*]; a small barrel, often used for herring. Equivalent to a mease; 20 cades made up 1 last.

cark [*carch, cark*]; weight used for spices and alum; equal to 3-4 cwt.

charge [*charge*]; variable measure of capacity for salt. At Exeter it equalled 11.5 quarters (PCA 1303/4, p 80, above), or 10 cwt (PCA 1394/5: *xl charge salis (est cccc)*), or just under 9.17 quarters (PCA 1396/7: *xviii (clxv quart') charges salis*); in the late fourteenth and fifteenth centuries, it was normally 8 quarters although it varied from 4.3 to 8.5 quarters at times.[4] In most ports, the charge equalled 5 quarters.

chest [*cista*]; variable measure of capacity.

coffin [*cofyn*]; measure of capacity similar to a chest; used for rosin.

coket [*coket, coketz*]; measure of capacity, perhaps derived from *concha, conqua*, a bowl or basin which may have been equal to about 54 pounds.[5] At Exeter, 10 *cokets* of potash were assessed as 1 tun (PCA 1320/1, p 198, above); and, in the same year, 6 *cokets* were allowed for 1 tun (PCA 1320/1, p 200, above) for customs purposes.

cope [*cope, copula*]; variable measure of capacity used for fruit.

---

[2] William H. Beveridge, 'A Statistical Crime of the Seventeenth Century', *Journal of Economic and Business History*, i (1929), pp 503–33.

[3] Touchard, 'Les douanes municipales', p xxiv.

[4] Touchard, 'Les douanes municipales', p xx–xxi.

[5] Du Cange, ii, p 447.

cord [*corde*]; variable measure of quantity originally based on the length of a cord or rope. For garlic, the cord was probably the same as a tress which contained 15–25 heads. At Exeter, there were about 4.9 cords in each seam (PCA 1335/6, merchandise account: *xxvi^c cord alleii qui fac liii summis*).

dicker [*dacrum, dyker*]; measure of quantity equal to 10; commonly used for hides, where 10 dickers equals 1 last.

dozen [*duodena*]; measure of quantity equal to 12; used for cordwain where 12 hides were probably meant.

ell [*ulna*]; measure of length for cloth, usually 45 inches. See also **piece**.

fardel [*fardel, fardell*]; measure of capacity used for cloth and other merchandise. At Exeter, 1 fardel of canvas contained 4 C (PCA 1304/5, above, p 97), or 300 yards (PCA 1356/7: *i fardel canobi cont' ccc virg'*), or 7 fardels contained 30 C (PCA 1360/1: *xxx centum canobi in vii fardel'*). For cloth at Exeter, 1 fardel contained 64 cloths (PCA 1322/3 merchandise account: *i fardell cont' lxiiii panni*).

fother [*fother*]; weight for lead, usually of 2100 pounds.

frail [*fraellus, frail, frayl*]; measure of capacity of uncertain size. At Exeter, 1 frail of raisins contained 100 pounds (PCA 1322/3: *1 frael reysouns cont' C li'*); 1 frail of onions contained 20 seams (PCA 1320/1, p 201, above).

gallons [*galona*]; liquid measure and measure of capacity which was not standardized in this period, but usually contained 4 quarts or 8 pints. See also **barrel** (for oil).

garb [*garba*]; weight of uncertain poundage; used for weld.

graner' a bale of uncertain sized used to measure woad.

hundred and **hundredweight; see C**

jar [*jar, jarre*]; variable measure of capacity; used for oil.

last [*lestum, lastum, last*]; measure of capacity which varied according to commodity. Equal to 20 dickers of hides. Normally, 1 last herring equalled 10 seams or 10 M, but in one entry at Exeter, 3 lasts of herring contained 32 M (PCA 1316/17, p 149, above).

M [*mell', mil, mill, m'*]; a thousand by tale or the thousandweight; equivalent to 10 hundreds or hundredweights and thus varied according to commodity. See also **last** (for herring) and **seam** (for garlic).

mease [*mis*]; measure of quantity for herring; there were 20 mease to 1 last.

pack [*paccum, pack, pak*]; a bundle used as a measure for items such as cloth. The number of cloths or pieces in each pack varied widely although it often included 10 in the later middle ages. At Exeter, however, one pack contained 43 cloths (PCA 1322/3 merchandise account: *pacca panni cont' xliii pannos*).

piece [*pecia*]; measure that varied according to commodity; often used for cloth. At Exeter, 1 piece of canvas contained 30 yards (PCA 1315/16, above, p 137; and 1394/5: *1 pecia canabi continent' xxx virg'*); 1 piece linen cloth contained 60 ells (PCA 1316/17, p 151, above), although Breton linen cloth could vary from 36 to 100 ells per piece.[6] Also at Exeter, 2 pieces cloth of Rouen may have contained 41 ells (PCA 1317/18, p 162, above).

pipe [*pipa, pipe*]; measure of capacity for liquids and dry products that varied according to commodity; equal to 0.5 tun or ton, or about 126 gallons.

pot [*pott*]; measure of capacity of about 14 gallons; used for butter and grease.

pound [*libra*]; a weight that varied according to the measuring system used (e.g., mercantile, troy or tower weights). See also **frail** (for raisins).

quarter [*quarterium, quarter*]; measure of weight (0.25 cwt) or capacity; equivalent to a seam. Used for coal, grain, salt, and woad. At Exeter, each quarter of grain contained 8 bushels, and there were 3 quarters in each ton (PCA 1383/4: *x dol' ord que continent xxx quart', ix dol' fab' que cont' xxvii quart', iii dol' frumentum que cont' ix quart'*). See also **charge** (for salt) and **barrel** and **tun** (for woad).

quintal [*quintal*]; usually equivalent to a hundredweight but varied according to commodity. At Exeter, 1.5 C of iron contained 8 quintals (PCA 1318/19, p 170, above).

roll [*rolia, rote*]; a cylindrical bundle of varying size, often used for cloth. At Exeter, one roll contained 26½ cloths (PCA 1322/3 merchandise account: *xxvi pannos di' panni pro una Rolia*).

rundlet [*rondelet*]; measure of capacity often used for wine but here used for archil; a small cask equivalent to 0.5 barrel (roughly equal to 16-18 gallons or 13 pounds).

sack [*sacca, sacula*]; measure of capacity that varied by commodity; for wool, equal to 26-28 stone.

seam [*summa*]; measure of capacity and weight, equal to the quarter for dry products. At Exeter, 1 seam fish imported by a Cornishman equalled 0.25 C (PCA 1398/9: *CC vidz. viii sum piscis*). For garlic at Exeter, 24 tresses [of garlic] equalled one horseload [*summa equi*] (PCA 1303/4, p 82, above) and 25 sums were in 1 M garlic (PCA 1304/5, p 92, above). See also **C** (for herring), **cord** (for garlic), and **frail** (for onions).

---

[6] Touchard, 'Les douanes municipales', p xxviii.

stone [*petra*]; weight normally equal to 8–14 pounds although it could vary from 5 to 32 pounds depending on the commodity.

thousand and

thousandweight; see M

ton [*dolea, dolium*]; weight equal to 20 cwt. The ton by weight is difficult to distinguish from the tun by capacity since the same Latin word was used for both. Items like iron, for example, are here noted in tons, but could also be measured in tuns. See also **quarter** (for grain) and **tun**.

trendle [*trendel*]; uncertain measure of capacity (a round oval or tub) used for wax. At Exeter, it weighed 1 C (PCA 1316/17, p 220, above).

tress [*tracis*]; measure of quantity for garlic and onions; usually included 15–25 heads or tops braided together. See also **seam**.

tun [*dolea, dolium*]; measure of capacity for liquids and some dry products; usually 252 gallons but could be smaller. It was difficult to distinguish from the ton since *dolium* was used for both terms, although the tun of capacity was sometimes written as *dolium plen' de* (above, p 49 for teasels, and p 124 for iron). At Exeter, 1 tun woad contained c. 4.11 quarters (PCA 1395/6: *ix dol' waide cont. xxxvii quart'*), but normally 1 tun was reckoned at 6 quarters elsewhere and at Exeter in the late fourteenth and fifteenth centuries.[7] See also **coket** (for potash), and **ton**.

yard [*virga*]; measure of length; usually 36-37 inches for cloth; see also **fardel** (for canvas) and **piece** (for canvas and cloth).

---

[7] E. M. Carus-Wilson, 'La guède française en Angleterre: un grand commerce du moyen age', *Revue du nord*, 35 (1953), p 98.

INDEX

Surnames, forenames, and ship names are alphabetized in their standardized form (usually the most common spelling of the name); spelling variations have been placed in round brackets after the standardized names and cross-referenced if sufficiently different from the standardized form. The counties of English locations and départements of those in France are given in round brackets; other places and regions are identified by country. A * denotes Exeter residents. References to wine and common measures in the body of the text have not usually been indexed.

THE DEVON AND CORNWALL RECORD SOCIETY

(Founded 1904)

President
The Rt Revd Geoffrey Hewlett Thompson, MA,
Lord Bishop of Exeter

Hon. Secretary:
J.D. Brunton, LLB, BA, c/o Devon and Exeter Institution,
7 Cathedral Close, Exeter EX1 1EZ.

Hon. Treasurer:
D.M. Hay, Esqr., c/o Devon and Exeter Institution,
7 Cathedral Close, Exeter EX1 1EZ.

Hon. Editors:
Professor N. I. Orme, MA, DPhil, DLitt, FSA, FRHistS.
Mrs Margery M. Rowe, BA, DAA.

The Devon and Cornwall Record Society (founded 1904) promotes the study of history in the South West of England through publishing and transcribing original records. In return for the annual subscription (£9; libraries £12), members receive the volumes as published (normally annually) and the use of the Society's library, housed in the West Country Studies Library, Exeter. This includes transcripts of parish registers relating to Devon and Cornwall as well as genealogical works.

Applications to join the Society or to purchase volumes should be sent to the Assistant Secretary, Devon and Cornwall Record Society, c/o Devon and Exeter Institution, 7 Cathedral Close, Exeter EX1 1EZ. New series volumes 7, 10, 13, 16 and 18, however, should be obtained from the Treasurer of the Canterbury and York Society, St Anthony's Hall, York YO1 2PW.

PUBLISHED VOLUMES, NEW SERIES
(Volumes starred are available only in complete sets)

6. *The Exeter Assembly: The Minutes of the Assemblies of the United Brethren of Devon and Cornwall, 1691–1717, as Transcribed by the Reverend Isaac Gilling*, edited by Allan Brockett (1963).

7. *The Register of Edmund Lacy, Bishop of Exeter, 1420–1455: Registrum Commune*, Vol. I, edited by G.R. Dunstan (1963).

*8. *The Cartulary of Canonsleigh Abbey*, calendared and edited by Vera C.M. London (1965).

*9. *Benjamin Donn's Map of Devon, 1765*, with an introduction by W.L.D. Ravenhill (1965).

10. *The Register of Edmund Lacy, Bishop of Exeter, 1420–1455: Registrum Commune*, Vol. II, edited by G.R. Dunstan (1966).

*11. *Devon Inventories of the Sixteenth and Seventeenth Centuries*, edited by Margaret Cash (1966).

*12. *Plymouth Building Accounts of the Sixteenth and Seventeenth Centuries*, edited by Edwin Welch (1967).

13. *The Register of Edmund Lacy, Bishop of Exeter, 1420–1455: Registrum Commune*, Vol. III, edited by G.R. Dunstan (1968).

14. *The Devonshire Lay Subsidy of 1332*, edited by Audrey M. Erskine (1969).

15. *Churchwardens' Accounts of Ashburton, 1479–1580*, edited by Alison Hanham (1970).

16. *The Register of Edmund Lacy, Bishop of Exeter, 1420–1455: Registrum Commune*, Vol. IV, edited by G.R. Dunstan (1971).

17. *The Caption of Seisin of the Duchy of Cornwall (1337)*, edited by P.L. Hull (1971).

18. *The Register of Edmund Lacy, Bishop of Exeter, 1420–1455: Registrum Commune*, Vol. V, edited by G.R. Dunstan (1972).

19. *Cornish Glebe Terriers, 1673–1735, a calendar*, edited by Richard Potts (1974).

20. *John Lydford's Book*, edited by Dorothy M. Owen (1975).

21. *A Calendar of Early Chancery Proceedings Relating to West Country Shipping, 1388–1493*, edited by Dorothy A. Gardiner (1976).

22. *Tudor Exeter: Tax Assessments 1489–1595, including the Military Survey, 1522*, edited by Margery M. Rowe (1977).

23. *The Devon Cloth Industry in the Eighteenth Century: Sun Fire Office Inventories, 1726–1770*, edited by Stanley D. Chapman (1978).

24. *The Accounts of the Fabric of Exeter Cathedral, 1279–1353, Part 1: 1279–1326*, edited by Audrey M. Erskine (1981).

25. *The Parliamentary Survey of the Duchy of Cornwall, Part 1: (Austell Prior-Saltash)*, edited by Norman J.G. Pounds (1982).

26. *The Accounts of the Fabric of Exeter Cathedral, 1279–1363, Part II: 1328–53*, edited by Audrey M. Erskine (1983).

27. *The Parliamentary Survey of the Duchy of Cornwall, Part II (Isles of Scilly-West Antony and Manors in Devon)*, edited by Norman J.G. Pounds (1984).

28. *Crown Pleas of the Devon Eyre of 1238*, edited by Henry Summerson (1985).

29. *Georgian Tiverton: the Political Memoranda of Beavis Wood, 1768–98*, edited by John Bourne (1986).

30. *The Cartulary of Launceston Priory*, edited by P.L. Hull (1987).

31. *Shipbuilding on the Exe: the Memoranda Book of Daniel Bishop Davy (1799–1874)*, edited by Clive N. Ponsford (1988).
32. *The Receivers' Accounts of the City of Exeter, 1305–53*, edited by Margery M. Rowe and John M. Draisey (1989).
33. *Early-Stuart Mariners and Shipping: the Maritime Surveys of Devon and Cornwall 1619–1635*, edited by Todd Gray (1990).
34. *Joel Gascoyne's Map of Cornwall, 1699*, with an introduction by W.L.D. Ravenhill and Oliver Padel (1991).
35. *Nicholas Roscarrock's Lives of the Saints: Cornwall and Devon*, edited by Nicholas Orme (1992).
36. *The Local Customs Accounts of the Port of Exeter, 1266–1321*, edited by Maryanne Kowaleski (1993).
37. *Charters of the Redvers Family and the Earldom of Devon in the Twelfth Century*, edited by Robert Bearman (1994, forthcoming).

EXTRA SERIES

I. *Exeter Freemen, 1266–1967*, edited by Margery M. Rowe and Andrew M. Jackson (1973).
II *Guide to the Parish and Non-Parochial Registers of Devon and Cornwall, 1538–1837*, compiled by Hugh Peskett (1979).